ARKANSAS

LOUISIANA

MISSISSIPPI

TEXAS

Gulf of Mexico

MARTIN

Martinville

New Iberia

ERIA

ST. MARTIN

Franklin

ST. MARY

ACADIANA TABLE

To Roxanne, for joining me on the journey.

Inspiring | Educating | Creating | Entertaining

Brimming with creative inspiration, how-to projects, and useful information to enrich your everyday life, Quarto Knows is a favorite destination for those pursuing their interests and passions. Visit our site and dig deeper with our books into your area of interest: Quarto Creates, Quarto Cooks, Quarto Homes, Quarto Lives, Quarto Drives, Quarto Explores, Quarto Gifts, or Quarto Kids.

First published in the United States of America in 2016 by
The Harvard Common Press, an imprint of The Quarto Group,
100 Cummings Center, Suite 265-D, Beverly, MA 01915, USA.
T (978) 282-9590 F (978) 283-2742 QuartoKnows.com

The Harvard Common Press titles are also available at discount for retail, wholesale, promotional, and bulk purchase. For details, contact the Special Sales Manager by email at specialsales@quarto.com or by mail at The Quarto Group, Attn: Special Sales Manager, 100 Cummings Center, Suite 265-D, Beverly, MA 01915, USA.

21   7

ISBN: 978-1-55832-863-1

Digital edition published in 2016
eISBN: 978-1-55832-869-3

Library of Congress Cataloging-in-Publication Data available

Design: Sakar Design Studio
Cover Image: George Graham
Page Layout: Megan Jones Design
Photography: George Graham except as follows: Roxanne Graham, page 14; Graham Family, page 104; Carlos Lerma, page 313 and back cover insert photo.

Printed in China

ACADIANA TABLE

CAJUN AND CREOLE
★★★ HOME COOKING ★★★
FROM THE
HEART OF LOUISIANA

GEORGE GRAHAM

HARVARD
COMMON
PRESS

CONTENTS

INTRODUCTION:
WELCOME TO MY ACADIANA TABLE

S YOU THUMB THROUGH THIS BOOK, I AM ASSUMING YOU ARE EITHER A FULL-FLEDGED FAN OF LOUISIANA COOKING OR JUST INTRIGUED BY FOOD THAT IS FOREIGN TO YOUR CULINARY COMFORT ZONE. IF YOU'RE IN THE FIRST CAMP, THEN THIS BOOK WILL CHALLENGE YOUR CONVENTIONAL WAY OF THINKING ABOUT CAJUN AND CREOLE CULTURE AND WILL REINFORCE YOUR LOVE OF IT WITH A DEEPER DIVE. BUT, IF YOU'RE JUST WINDOW SHOPPING FOR A QUICK GLIMPSE BEHIND THE CURTAIN, HOLD ON TO YOUR WOODEN SPOON, CINCH UP YOUR APRON, AND GET READY FOR A CULINARY "TALE SPIN" THROUGH THE SMOKY, SPICY, SMOTHERED, SEARED, AND SIZZLING HOT WORLD OF SOUTH LOUISIANA ROOTS COOKING AND THE PEOPLE WHO PRACTICE IT EVERY DAY.

THE ROOTS OF SOUTH LOUISIANA COOKING

Jambalaya, crawfish pie, filé gumbo—these iconic dishes are all that most know about the food culture of Louisiana. But there's so much more. A few years ago, I embarked on a journey to peel back the layers of history and culinary mystery to reveal the cultural mystique of Cajun and Creole cooking and make it accessible for all. This is not a book about quick-and-easy, no-fuss shortcuts to a meal in minutes. On the contrary, it is an exploration of the cultural significance and time-honored techniques of one of America's most unique food cultures. Learning to cook Cajun and Creole comes down to this: history, techniques, ingredients, methods, and a willingness to explore the culture of these colorful foodways.

From a food perspective, Acadiana is a unique region of America—the culture is laid back and casual, but people take their cooking seriously and with an adventurous spirit. The old methods and traditional recipes are held in reverence, but changing tastes and innovative techniques are readily accepted. Multicultural influences have always blended with Cajun and Creole foodways, but never more than today.

This is food that folks hunger for. This isn't the branded and packaged, menu-tested and marketed, touristy trappings of a travel-weary visitor longing for a taste of authentic Louisiana food. No, it's real food—roots food—cooked by real cooks connected to traditional food traditions fed by a pipeline of culinary artisans with skills that defy conventional cooking methods. It is taste, texture, and terroir. It is culinary artistry. It is my Acadiana.

MY CULINARY JOURNEY

For more years than I'd like to count, I've been immersed in the colorful Cajun and Creole food scene of my Acadiana. I've been exploring the region's restaurants and honky-tonks, lunchrooms and dives, steam tables and smokehouses. Along the way, I've been devouring its panéed, fricasséed, and étoufféed best; its fried, smothered, stuffed, grilled, and smoked delicacies; its cracklin's, crawfish, and crabs; and its po'boys, pig, and potent potions.

I drive the back roads—paths to culinary enlightenment, I call them—curiously searching for new tastes, new delights, new delicious discoveries. And I'm never disappointed. Every trip, every stop, every chance meeting is a story to be told, a lesson to be learned. I live to eat. I love to cook. And I enjoy writing about it all. I've owned a restaurant. I've cooked on television, on the Food Network. And still, I am just as curious about food as when I had that first taste of a deep dark gumbo. This book is not an end to my journey, but rather a beginning of my exploration of what perfumes my world and adds spice to my life—Cajun and Creole cooking.

And this book reflects my love of the culture of Louisiana, the colorful eccentricity of its people, the joie de vivre of its many celebrations, and the uniqueness of its foodways. I am writing this book without any preconceived notion of whether you are a fan of Cajun and Creole cooking—but my mission is that, once you've read it, you will be.

BORN AND FED IN LOUISIANA

I was raised on a roux. My seasoned sense of taste, shaped at an early age by a black Creole cook who worked in my father's restaurant, is responsible for my adventurous style of cooking. Long before I attained proper stovetop height, I stood on a wooden orange crate beside the commercial range near the back door of the busy kitchen in the Acme Café and helped to stir the roux cooking on the stovetop. I recall times wearing a woolen mitten on my right hand to keep the explosive hot lava–like roux from splattering on me—a cautionary measure I learned the hard way. (I still have the scar to prove it.) With a schoolboy's curiosity, I soaked up, breathed in, and consumed every morsel of knowledge I could scrape from the bottom of that pot. Those experiences stirred my soul and fanned the flames of a culinary passion high enough to last a lifetime. I loved it so.

And there were other influences. My brother, Jackie, was a passionate cook; his Creole shrimp dip made the holidays extra special and extra spicy. My older sister, Marie, was the adventurous gourmet cook who left small-town Louisiana and cooked her way across America. My mother, Peggy, was a nurturing cook who understood that the kitchen is the heart of the home. Her fried chicken is the one I measure all others by. And my father, George, Sr., was a natural cook who took patient steps to share his knowledge with me. My recipes for ribs and my dad's famous Chic Steak Sandwich are just a couple I learned at his hand, in his kitchen.

And these days, my wife, Roxanne, shares her passion for Cajun cooking and her treasure trove of knowledge passed down from generations of good cooks. My daughter, Lauren, continually challenges my adventurous side with her youthful approach

to food with a focus on freshness. In our family of cooks, there is constant experimentation and no room for culinary complacency.

I am inspired by the talent of the many celebrated chefs of Louisiana: John Folse, Emeril Lagasse, John Besh, Donald Link, and Paul Prudhomme, among others. I admire their love of Louisiana and their passion for preserving and promoting its foodways. From Chef Prudhomme, I learned the importance of layering flavors: want to add water, stop, add stock instead; time to add dried rosemary, think again, add fresh; reaching for a store-bought roux, forget it, make your own. Remember, there are no shortcuts in the quest for excellence.

THIS COOKBOOK

Truth be told, I never made a conscious decision to write a cookbook, but looking back, I can now see it was destined. My culinary path was lined with signposts, and what began with a love of eating, and then cooking, quickly turned into recipe development, writing, photography, and blogging—all with a focus on food. The cookbook was inevitable.

When you browse the table of contents, you will see an eclectic array of recipes, but when you look at the collective body of work, I believe you will begin to understand the depth and breadth of Acadiana's vast culinary culture. There are lessons to be learned here: not just cooking, but also a deep understanding of the culture that has preserved these recipes and methods for generations.

But don't be intimidated. There's much to explore in this book, and if you're not exactly excited about cooking with turtle or crawfish heads, there's still plenty to like. There's everyday farm-to-table fare, simple salads, soups, sandwiches, sides, and from along the coast, fresh seafood with a light touch. These are mostly easily home-prepared recipes that require only an investment in good-quality ingredients and a bit of time.

Reading the recipe tips, ingredient explanations, headnotes, and stories accompanying the recipes will serve you well. They are written to be a treasure map of sorts: a guide to the faces and places, the methods and madness, the sources and shared secrets of my beloved Cajun and Creole culture. Mine them for insight and inside information and then plan your culinary trek—your appetizing adventure—by following the recipe directions.

MY STYLE OF COOKING

As a whole, cookbook writers tend to be methodical, meticulous, and downright obsessive in the way they approach a recipe. But cooks like me are prone to freewheeling improvisation that defies conventional recipe techniques. My job (one I take most seriously) is to provide cultural context for a decidedly balanced interplay between instruction and inspiration. I can assure you that it won't be your typical bland and boring recipe-laden package tour. Let's have fun, aspire to be better cooks, learn something, and most important, eat some delicious South Louisiana food.

Curiosity drives me, and when it comes to a subject that I've come to feel passionately connected to, I want to know everything I can about it. Call it a journey of discovery and a lifelong quest to sop up every last bit of culinary history I can. Somewhere along the way I connected with the people of Acadiana, all of whom have a story to tell. And these are proud people with a rich sense of their heritage and a clear understanding of the importance of preserving it.

I subscribe to a particular culinary theory: that the best cooks are the ones who ask questions, the ones who push past the how, the ones that probe into the who, what, why, and where of cooking. This is the kind of book *Acadiana Table* is. You are reading my words because you are interested in the cuisine of South Louisiana, but my goal (a sneaky one, at that) is to alter the way you think about cooking. After spending some time with this book, it is my hope—no, my clear goal—for you to begin exploring the food culture of your own home turf. You see, no matter where you live, there is a magical world of growers, cooks, artisans, and culinary enthusiasts who make your region unique.

LET'S COOK

There's nothing fussy about this cookbook—no pretense or snobbery. It's just shameless down-home cooking in an unabashed way to achieve spectacular results. My aim is to be mindful of culinary tradition and respectful of the rich heritage of cooks who came before me. That said, I want to turn Cajun cooking on its ear and push the limits beyond tried-and-true to new-and-nuanced interpretations of classics. There is a certain level of risk in cooking if you aspire to elevate your game. Playing it safe is not an option if you want to discover flavors and tastes that astound, amaze, and enliven your palate. That's what this book is all about.

I use bold ingredients—hog lard, pork liver, cayenne pepper, and chicken feet, to name a few—and take pride in them. We'll make the basics: roux, boudin, cracklin's, and gumbo. We'll also make jambalaya (the Creole way), smoked ponce (the Cajun way), and crawfish étouffée (the only way). I'll give you my riff on red beans that puts the cream in the beans and even share my momma's fried chicken recipe for crackling crisp skin. And you'll learn a technique for sweet potatoes that will bring thanks to your Thanksgiving table.

Sourcing some of these ingredients may take some extra effort. While I do offer substitutions whenever possible, it's simply impossible, for example, to make a Cajun turtle sauce piquante with anything but snapping turtle. But it's surprising how many of these ingredients are readily available with just a little exploration. And isn't that exploration part of the fun of discovering new cuisines? For your convenience, I offer product information and online mail-order options in the Sources section on page 314. Rest assured, follow my lead and nothing should stand in your way to creating delicious Cajun and Creole dishes.

In these pages, you'll find a mash-up of recipes that defies trends or tradition. If you don't like rural nose-to-tail cooking, you'll love my Cajun contemporary take on a blackened Brussels sprouts salad. And if slow-smoked sausages are not your thing, then try a fresh-out-of-the-water grilled redfish recipe. If sweet desserts aren't to your liking, bite into my savory sweet-and-hot carrots. The table is set: Just pull up a chair and take a seat, and I guarantee you'll find something delicious on my Acadiana table.

FIRST YOU MAKE

CHAPTER

ONE

A ROUX

★ ★ ★ ★

ONCE I WAS TELLING A FRIEND THAT I HAD PLANS TO MAKE A GUMBO FOR THE WEEKEND. WITHOUT HESITATION, SHE ASKED, "CAJUN GUMBO OR CREOLE GUMBO?" WELL, AFTER A TWENTY-MINUTE EXPLANATION OF THE DIFFERENCES BETWEEN THE TWO, AND OF MY PARTICULAR PHILOSOPHY REGARDING WHERE WE ARE IN THE EVOLUTION OF LOUISIANA COOKING, I COULD SEE THAT MY FRIEND REGRETTED EVEN ASKING THE QUESTION. BUT, IT IS A DIFFICULT SUBJECT AND ONE THAT HAS ENGAGED THE HIGHEST LEVEL OF SCHOLARLY STUDY.

So what is the difference between Cajun and Creole cuisine? For a Louisiana food writer chronicling the regional cooking of my home state, that's akin to asking, "What's in a gumbo?" There is no clear answer, and that is the beauty of the culture and the cuisine. At the risk of becoming embroiled in culinary controversy, let me shed some light on this long and sometimes heated debate.

The difference between the two is best explained by looking at the history of the two cultures and their geography. First of all, it is essential to know that New Orleans and the Acadiana region of southwest Louisiana are separated by more than 100 miles (161 km). The Mississippi River and the Atchafalaya Basin—a vast wetland refuge—divide the two. And even more dramatic, these two regions are separated by the timing of history and cultural circumstance.

In the early 1700s, Europeans of wealth and stature settled in the city of New Orleans and brought with them a palate for more gentrified cuisine reminiscent of their French, Spanish, or English roots. Over time, slaves, servants, and cooks of African descent learned these sophisticated techniques and blended them with their peppery, herb-infused cooking. Before long, tastes mingled into a soulful mix that became the defining taste of Creole. Cooking with tomatoes, cream, butter, cheeses, and other more refined ingredients led to the rich cuisine

for which New Orleans has become famous. French sauce techniques helped define aristocratic standouts such as shrimp rémoulade, trout meunière, oysters Bienville, crabmeat Ravigote, and so many other great Creole specialties. And those European classics were joined by more rustic Creole foods such as gumbo z'herbes, smoky red beans and rice, and stew pots thickened with okra, as well as a tomato-infused version of jambalaya.

Meanwhile, in the marshes of southwest Louisiana a different sort of culinary evolution was taking place. In 1755, the expulsion of the French Acadians from Nova Scotia by the British resulted in the migration of thousands of destitute families to the wetlands of southern Louisiana. All along the Gulf Coast and northward into the prairie region of Acadiana, these settlers put down roots. These were not people of wealth, but simple farming families. To survive, they trapped, fished, and hunted for food and applied their basic rural French culinary skills to simple fare that fit their palate. Settlers along the coastal parishes made their livelihood by shrimping, crabbing, and harvesting oysters. Farther inland, farming the flatlands with sugarcane and rice as predominant crops led to favorites for the table using all of these indigenous ingredients. The Atchafalaya Basin was a wild source for crawfish, and eventually the rice fields were flooded after the harvest for farming crawfish in a controlled aquaculture environment. Over time, the Germans settled in the region north of Lafayette and brought with them sausage-making and smokehouse skills that blended beautifully into the gumbo of flavors we now know as Cajun.

Community plays an important part in Cajun foodways. Even today, celebrations erupt whenever families come together to cook a whole hog. The boucherie and the cochon de lait are French traditions that are important to the Cajun way of life. Even crawfish boils are family celebrations that bring people together over food. Food is a key ingredient of the joie de vivre of living in South Louisiana.

I've heard Cajun food described as a basic and unrefined method of rustic, rural farm cooking. I disagree. To me, that description shortchanges the talent and taste of the culinary art of the French Acadians. I believe the evolution of this original cuisine is based on artisanal techniques handed down for generations and preserved as a cultural treasure. Pride and passion for Cajun foodways are as much

defining elements of the people as the music, dance, and language. Deep, dark gumbos, tangy tasso, rich crawfish étouffée, and black-iron-pot rice and gravy are original dishes steeped in historical reverence for a culture that endures.

But the explanation doesn't end there. I contend that, over many generations, Cajun and Creole cuisines have converged into a unique, cross-cultural cuisine that is represented throughout Louisiana. The holy trinity of spices—onions, bell pepper, and celery—is the divine starting point of both cuisines. Okra often appears in gumbos on both sides of the Atchafalaya Basin, and a bowl of creamy red beans with smoked andouille is a link that tastefully bridges the two cultures. The beauty of eating in Louisiana is the blending of flavors in unexpected and unique directions.

Let the debate end. What's the true Louisiana cuisine? Who cares? The blurring of the lines of distinction between these two cultures has resulted in an original American cuisine.

CAJUN SEASONING BLEND

This dry seasoning blend delivers a mix of distinct, yet perfectly balanced, spice components—all working in combination to deliver a wallop of Cajun flavor. And it's multipurpose: It infuses a deep, savory spiciness when added to the pot, it penetrates with a peppery punch when used as a rub, and it adds a zing when sprinkled on a finished dish.

Add all of the ingredients to a food processor and blend. Pour into an airtight container and store at room temperature for up to 6 months.

MAKES 1¼ CUPS (ABOUT 190 G)

¼ cup (72 g) salt

¼ cup (36 g) granulated garlic

¼ cup (24 g) finely ground black pepper

2 tablespoons (14 g) sweet paprika

2 tablespoons (14 g) onion powder

2 tablespoons (12 g) finely ground white pepper

1 tablespoon (12 g) celery salt

1 tablespoon (5 g) cayenne pepper

TABLE TIP

This blend forgoes the dried herbs (oregano, thyme, basil, and so forth), which allows you to control those flavors in your dish individually. The heat level is moderate, so feel free to add more cayenne, red pepper flakes, or hot sauce to your finished dish. This home-prepared blend does not contain the anti-caking compounds found in many commercial spice blends, so store it in a dry place.

ROX'S ROUX (DARK CAJUN ROUX)

It all starts with a roux. So what's the logical starting point for making a roux? Three simple elements: oil, flour, and a heavy cast-iron pot. I like the neutral taste and high smoke point of canola oil; simple all-purpose flour is standard; and a black pot is a must. Cast iron retains heat and makes for slow and steady cooking, ideal for a roux. Along with a wooden spoon, a controllable heat source, and an hour of your life, you're good to go.

But making a dark Cajun roux from scratch is a dying art. Not too many years ago, there wasn't a Cajun or Creole household in South Louisiana that didn't have the unmistakably intense aroma of a dark roux—pungent and nutty, like roasting coffee beans—wafting through the kitchen. Home cooks were taught basic roux-making skills early on, and it was a rite of passage to pass it on to the next generation.

Times have changed.

With the proliferation of jarred and powdered roux products, as well as packaged gumbo mixes, the art of roux making is dying off. Don't get me wrong, some prepared roux products are very good, and I use them sometimes myself. But there is no substitute for a scratch-made roux, and I believe it is the obligation—no, responsibility—of roux makers to hand down this timeless artisanal skill to their children. I know my wife has.

Rox can make a roux—as deep and dark as blackstrap molasses and just as rich.

My wife, Roxanne, doesn't cook every night, nor does she profess to be a culinary artisan, but she is one of the best natural cooks I know. For her roux, she follows a strict set of guidelines handed down by generations of good Cajun cooks before her. She was born and raised in the little southwest Louisiana town of Jennings, and I sometimes tease her that her grandmother's black iron pot and well-worn wooden gumbo spoon were her dowry. Truth be told, to her they are more valuable than anything money could buy.

On a cold January day, she can work magic in that pot with a roux-infused chicken and sausage gumbo like none other I've tasted.

A roux is the foundation on which gumbo is based. Rox's roux is nursed and nourished with a serious attention to detail that defies logic. It's as if my wife goes into a semi-lucid state of consciousness that is mesmerizing. She stirs and stirs and focuses on color, texture, and smell. For an hour, she stirs—no phone calls, no conversations, no distractions whatsoever. It goes from white, cream, beige, tan, and brown, to mahogany and beyond.

There is an instinctive point of departure—a point of no return that she pushes beyond. A less brave or sure-handed cook would stop short. She has the confidence and courage to pursue that hauntingly dark depth of a rich chocolate-colored roux. Hershey bar chocolate is the terminus, and anything more is burnt and destined for the disposal.

With her wooden spoon scepter in her right hand, my gumbo queen rules the kitchen.

Place the flour and oil in a large cast-iron pot over medium heat. With a long-handled wooden spoon, stir. Constant stirring and moving the flour around the bottom of the pot is the key to browning the flour evenly to prevent burning. This early stage goes slowly as you begin to see the white flour take on first a beige and then a tan color.

MAKES 3 CUPS (700 ML)

3 cups (375 g) unbleached all-purpose flour

3 cups (700 ml) canola oil or vegetable oil

Continue stirring slowly and evenly, scraping the bottom and the circular crevices of the pot to move the flour around in the hot oil. In about 30 minutes, you should begin to see a brown color developing and smell the first hints of toasted flour. This is when the stirring becomes even more crucial.

At this point, the least bit of inattention could result in burnt flecks of flour appearing—a sure sign you've ruined the roux. Watch your heat and lower it if the roux is cooking too fast. Constant stirring to keep the flour from staying in one place too long prevents burning. You will begin to smell an even nuttier aroma as you see the color turn darker mahogany. Most stop here, but you want to keep going until you achieve a deeper, darker chocolate-like color and the roux has the consistency of melted chocolate.

Forget time at this point. You are now cooking by instinct, sight, and smell. The utmost attention to your stirring is needed, and when you see that Hershey chocolate darkness, you will know you have arrived.

Welcome to Rox's roux. Turn off the heat, but continue stirring until it begins to cool down and quits cooking. Spoon the roux into a bowl immediately.

CHICKEN AND SMOKED SAUSAGE GUMBO

I suspect you've never had a spoonful of gumbo like the chicken and sausage gumbo my wife makes—dark and smoky, with a velvet-like thickness enveloping tender browned chicken spiced with hickory-infused andouille. While most opt for rice only, Roxanne's bowl of gumbo is crowned with a scoop of creamy, mustard-stained potato salad and a hard-boiled egg—a South Louisiana tradition. Oh, and a generous sprinkle of filé powder is a given.

Heat the oil in a large skillet over medium heat. Once sizzling hot, add the chicken pieces skin-side down. Brown the chicken on one side and then turn to brown the other side. Remove the chicken from the skillet and put in a large gumbo pot with a lid.

In the same skillet over medium-high heat, add the onions, bell pepper, and celery. Sauté until the onions turn translucent, about 5 minutes. Add the garlic and parsley and stir until combined. Add the smoked sausage and sauté just until it begins to brown. Add 1 cup (235 ml) of the chicken stock to the skillet and scrape the bottom to loosen the brown bits of flavor and then add the contents of the skillet to the large gumbo pot.

At this point, add enough chicken stock to the gumbo pot to cover all the chicken and vegetables. Season with the cayenne and stir to combine. Add the roux and stir. Bring the pot to a boil and then lower the heat to a simmer. Cover the pot and let it cook for 1 hour.

Remove the chicken pieces. Skim the surface of any excess oil. Taste the gumbo. If you prefer your gumbo thinner, add more stock. If you prefer your gumbo thicker, add more roux. Season with salt and pepper to taste. Cover the pot and simmer for 30 minutes longer.

Uncover the pot and skim the surface again of any excess oil. At this point, you can leave the chicken on the bone or remove the bones and skin from each of the pieces. Add the chicken back to the pot to reheat, along with the whole peeled eggs. Cover and simmer for 20 minutes longer.

Sample the finished gumbo and season with hot sauce to taste. Ladle the gumbo into large bowls over a mound of rice. Garnish with diced green onions and add a bit of filé powder, if you like.

SERVES 6 TO 8

¼ cup (60 ml) canola oil

4 whole chicken thighs, bone-in and skin-on (about 1½ pounds, or 680 g)

2 whole chicken breasts, bone-in and skin-on (about 2½ pounds, or 1.1 kg)

2 cups (320 g) diced yellow onion

2 cups (300 g) diced green bell pepper

2 cups (240 g) diced celery

2 tablespoons (20 g) minced garlic

½ cup (30 g) chopped fresh flat-leaf parsley

2 cups (450 g) smoked pork sausage sliced into bite-size pieces

12 cups (2.8 L) Dark Chicken Stock, plus more if needed (page 215)

1 teaspoon cayenne pepper

1 cup (235 ml) dark roux, plus more if needed (page 14)

Kosher salt and freshly ground black pepper

6 to 8 large eggs, hard-boiled and peeled

Dash of hot sauce

8 cups (1.3 kg) cooked long-grain white rice

1 cup (100 g) diced green onion tops

Filé powder

TABLE TIP

Eat gumbo like a Cajun: In addition to rice, most Cajun folks serve cold-and-creamy, mustardy, potato salad with their dark chicken and sausage gumbo. A spoonful along the rim of the bowl provides a cool contrast to the hot gumbo. And the tradition of a few peeled hard-boiled eggs added at the final stage of cooking is still seen in many gumbo pots. Ice-cold beer and hot French bread are a given.

What's That?

Filé (*fee-LAY*) is a Cajun/Creole powdered seasoning made from dried and ground sassafras leaves (not the root, as many believe). Preston Nunez is a third generation filé maker from Creole, Louisiana, and he uses leaves grown in Oak Grove, Louisiana. Preston grinds them fresh and sells his artisanal filé in mason jars. Filé is used almost exclusively in gumbo and provides an earthy, umami taste. Earlier in culinary history, filé was used as a thickener instead of okra or roux. These days the ground leaves are used most often for enhancing flavor. Filé is found on most any Louisiana grocery shelf. Buy it in small quantities; like most spices, filé powder loses its punch over time.

SUNRISE IN

CHAPTER

TWO

ACADIANA

BREAKFAST IN SOUTH LOUISIANA IS A CELEBRATION OF FARM-TO-TABLE GOODNESS. THE FARM-ING TRADITIONS OF THE REGION ARE ROOTED IN A STRONG WORK ETHIC THAT IS HANDED DOWN THROUGH GENERATIONS OF FRENCH ACADIAN FAMILIES THAT HARVEST SUGARCANE, RICE, SWEET POTATOES, SOYBEANS, AND OTHER SIGNIFICANT CROPS. EARLY TO BED AND EARLY TO RISE IS THE ROUTINE OF CAJUN AND CREOLE FARMERS.

Acadiana is rice culture. This is home to rice growers who farm the flat, flooded fields and then bring their grain to the many rice mills of the area. In the 1950s and 1960s, my wife's grandfather, Clodius Fontenot, was a farmer in northern Jeff Davis Parish between Jennings and Hathaway. As was prevalent at the time, he lived on and farmed a piece of land owned by another family in a mutually beneficial exchange.

His typical day started an hour before daylight sipping a cup of deep, dark Louisiana coffee as he headed off to the fields. Long about 8 a.m., he returned to the house with his farmhands to sit down to a hearty Cajun breakfast prepared by loving hands. My wife's grandmother, Mo Mo Eve, mixed up biscuits and sweet dough breakfast pies from scratch, and she fried up fresh sausages and farm-raised eggs to feed the crew. And there was always a pot of couche couche on the stove. It was a major production, yet a daily ritual that the hungry men depended on.

Not to be confused with Mediterranean couscous, couche couche is very rural Cajun breakfast food made from cornmeal and usually combined with milk and sugarcane molasses. French Acadian farm families love their couche couche much like grits are favored throughout the Deep South. It is rarely seen in restaurants, but go to any Louisiana high school football game and you'll hear a familiar cheer, "Hot Boo Dan, Cold Coosh Coosh, Come on Cajuns, Poosh, Poosh, Poosh."

Early life in South Louisiana was a matter of survival and making the most of what you had. Those French culinary traditions live on, and over the years breakfast remains an important and culturally significant meal in Acadiana.

DUCK EGG AND SQUASH BLOSSOM TART

At the farmers' market, I'm always on the lookout for edible treasures that send my culinary senses soaring. And I was delighted when I found these two little gems: duck eggs and squash blossoms. Instantly, I began to think about a most memorable *petit déjeuner* I once had in the French countryside town of Arles. A brilliant combination, it was a quiche-like tart that featured a variety of field-fresh vegetables with farmhouse eggs and briny shrimp. Those, I believe, were hens' eggs, so my take on this Provençal classic—using local duck eggs from Belle Écorce Farms in St. Martin Parish—is just that much more luxurious. I like to serve this tart with mixed greens, slices of tomato, and cold watermelon. Pair it all with a champagne-laced mimosa and this could be a brunch to remember.

Preheat the oven to 350°F (180°C, or gas mark 4).

Spray a 12-inch (30 cm) round tart pan with nonstick spray.

Open the can of crescent rolls and position the dough on a cutting board. Carefully unroll the 8 dough triangles and spread out on the surface of the board. Match up the triangles to form 4 large rectangles. Move the first rectangle to the tart pan and drape the edge of the dough along the rim with the rest of the dough inside, covering the bottom. Do this for each section of remaining dough until you have the rim and the bottom of the pan covered.

With a fork, puncture holes in the bottom of the dough and the edges along the inside rim. Before blind baking, protect the outer edges of the dough from overbrowning by covering with aluminum foil. Take long strips of foil and place on top of the outer rim of the dish where the dough extends upward.

Place the pan on a baking sheet and bake until the bottom of the dough is golden brown, about 15 minutes. Take out of the oven and remove the aluminum foil from around the rim. Leave the pan on the baking sheet.

Meanwhile, make the custard by whisking the eggs and milk in a medium bowl. Add the salt and thyme; then add the yellow and green onions. Whisk and set aside.

Prepare the squash by cutting off the flower ends and reserving. Slice the squash into very thin rounds and place in a microwaveable container. Cut the tips of the asparagus off the stalks and place the tips into the container. Add 1 tablespoon (15 ml) water, cover the container, and microwave on high for 1 minute. Remove from the microwave and dry the par-cooked vegetables with a paper towel.

Place the shrimp on the cutting board and with a sharp knife carefully cut each in half horizontally along the length of the back of the shrimp. You should now have 8 pieces of shrimp.

Pour the egg custard into the tart crust until it reaches just below the rim. Position the squash blossoms decoratively in sections of the custard, along with the asparagus tips and slices of squash.

SERVES 4

1 can (8 ounces, or 225 g) crescent dinner roll dough, such as Pillsbury

3 duck eggs or 5 large chicken eggs

½ cup (120 ml) whole milk

1 teaspoon kosher salt

1 teaspoon chopped fresh thyme

½ cup (80 g) finely diced yellow onion

2 tablespoons (12 g) finely diced green onion tops

6 small squash with flower blossoms

8 green asparagus spears

4 jumbo (16/20 count) shrimp, peeled and deveined

½ cup (75 g) fresh goat cheese

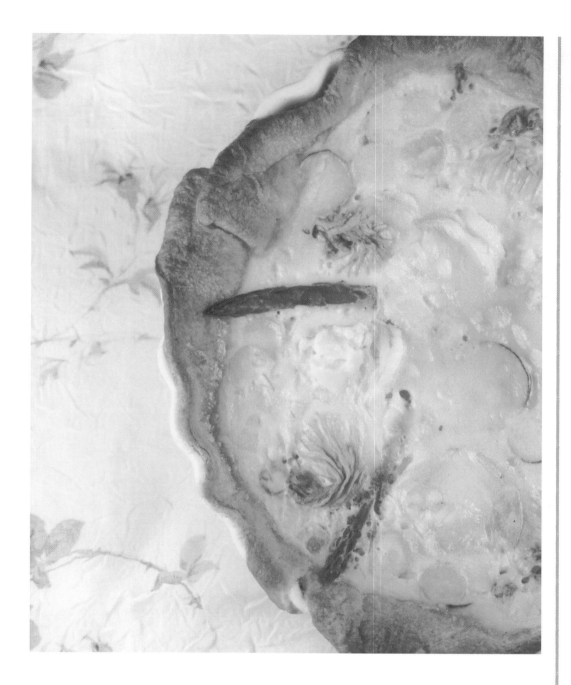

Place the outer side of each of the shrimp halves into the custard so that the ends appear above the surface. Distribute several small bite-size pieces of the goat cheese among the vegetables and shrimp.

Bake until the custard is fully set, about 20 minutes. Watch carefully and do not let the tart overcook and the exposed dough edge begin to burn. Remove immediately and let the tart rest for 5 minutes before slicing into wedges.

This tart is great served warm, at room temperature, or even cold the next day.

LEMON-PECAN PANCAKES WITH SOUTHERN COMFORT MOLASSES

Stacked high and oozing with the slow drizzle of dark and smoky Southern Comfort molasses, these tart lemon pancakes strike a counterbalance of flavors. The crunchy toasted pecans, along with a cascade of confectioners' sugar, royally crown this elegant breakfast dish.

SOUTHERN COMFORT MOLASSES

Put the sugar and ¼ cup (60 ml) of the water in a heavy saucepan over medium-high heat. Bring to a boil and then lower the heat to medium. While shaking the pan from side to side, continue slowly boiling until the sugar dissolves and a dark caramel forms.

Immediately add the remaining ¼ cup (60 ml) of water to stop the cooking. Add the Southern Comfort and bring back to a low boil. Add the molasses, butter, and salt. Cook down until thickened, about 5 minutes. Remove from the heat and keep warm for serving.

LEMON-PECAN PANCAKES

Put the flour, baking powder, salt, and cinnamon in a large mixing bowl. Whisk to combine.

In another large bowl, put the eggs, lemon zest, lemon juice, and buttermilk. Whisk to combine. Add the dry ingredients to the wet ingredients and whisk to combine. The mixture should be a pourable pancake batter consistency. If not, add more buttermilk. Add the chopped pecans and stir to combine.

Heat a large nonstick pan coated with nonstick spray over medium heat. Ladle a portion of batter and cook until done on both sides, about 3 to 5 minutes total. Move the pancakes to a platter and keep warm until ready to serve.

For serving, stack the pancakes on individual plates and add toasted pecan halves between the layers and along the edges. Drizzle with the Southern Comfort Molasses. Dust with confectioners' sugar and garnish with lemon slices.

TABLE TIP

I love the Deep South flavor of Southern Comfort, but any good bourbon will work as well. If this sauce hardens, simply reheat before serving.

SERVES 4

SOUTHERN COMFORT MOLASSES (MAKES ABOUT 1½ CUPS, OR 355 ML)

1½ cups (300 g) granulated sugar

½ cup (120 ml) water

¼ cup (60 ml) Southern Comfort liqueur or bourbon

6 tablespoons (120 g) sugarcane molasses

2 tablespoons (28 g) unsalted butter

½ teaspoon salt

LEMON-PECAN PANCAKES

3 cups (375 g) unbleached all-purpose flour

1 tablespoon (14 g) baking powder

1 teaspoon salt

1 teaspoon ground cinnamon

2 large eggs, beaten

2 tablespoons (12 g) lemon zest

¼ cup (60 ml) freshly squeezed lemon juice

1½ cups (355 ml) buttermilk, plus more if needed

1 cup (110 g) finely chopped pecans

1 cup (100 g) toasted pecan halves

Confectioners' sugar

Thin lemon slices

GATOR GRILLADES AND GRITS

For more than a generation, grillades and grits has been a mainstay dish of Creole cooking. Sautéed veal in a dark gravy with plain grits has been on restaurant menus for years. Tourists eat it up and locals order it for its nostalgic value. Once a stalwart entrée, it has lately grown stale—well, until this version. Creamy grits cooked slowly, infused with butter and fresh goat cheese, float on the platter anchored by a rich infusion of Creole tomatoes cooked down with pan-sautéed alligator. Yes, alligator. Served with hot biscuits, this is one breakfast entrée you can sink your teeth into.

GRITS

In a medium pot over high heat, bring the water to a boil. Reduce to a simmer and add the grits and 1 cup (235 ml) of the cream to the pot. Stir the pot every few minutes and cook on low until creamy, about 20 to 30 minutes.

Add the butter to bring a depth of flavor and an even creamier consistency. Stir continuously and vigorously and add the remaining 1 cup (235 ml) of cream once you detect the mixture is becoming dry. Stir more with rapid beats and add a splash more of the cream, if needed. Season the grits with salt and pepper.

Once you have achieved a creamy texture and consistency without any lumps, begin adding the goat cheese in small spoonfuls, whisking until fully incorporated and achieving a rich creaminess. Take off the heat and let rest in a warm place.

GRILLADES

Cut the alligator into bite-size pieces and coat in the flour. Heat the olive oil in a cast-iron pot over medium-high heat and sauté the alligator meat until browned, about 8 minutes. Transfer the meat to a platter and set aside.

In the same pot, sauté the celery, bell pepper, and onions until browned, about 8 minutes. Add the garlic, tomatoes, tomato purée, and sugar. Lower the heat to a simmer and cook for 2 minutes or until combined. Stir in the basil, thyme, oregano, Worcestershire, and red wine.

Add the alligator meat, cover, and continue cooking over low heat until the wine has evaporated, the meat is tender, and the tomato gravy has thickened, about 30 to 40 minutes. Just before serving, add the green onions and parsley. Season with salt and pepper to taste.

Plate a mound of grits in the center of each plate and the gator grillades on the side.

SERVES 4

GRITS

2 cups (475 ml) water

2 cups (280 g) coarse stone-ground yellow grits

2 cups (475 ml) heavy cream, plus more as needed

8 tablespoons (1 stick, or 112 g) unsalted butter

Kosher salt and freshly ground black pepper

1 cup (150 g) fresh goat cheese

GRILLADES

1 pound (455 g) boneless, skinless Louisiana alligator fillet

1 cup (125 g) unbleached all-purpose flour

2 tablespoons (28 ml) olive oil

1 cup (100 g) chopped celery

1 green bell pepper, diced

2 cups (320 g) chopped onions

2 tablespoons (20 g) minced garlic

1 cup (180 g) diced tomato

2 tablespoons (32 g) tomato purée

1 teaspoon granulated sugar

1 tablespoon (3 g) chopped fresh basil

1 tablespoon (2 g) chopped fresh thyme

1 tablespoon (4 g) chopped fresh oregano

1 tablespoon (15 g) Worcestershire sauce

1 cup (235 ml) dry red wine

1 cup (100 g) diced green onion tops

1 cup (60 g) chopped flat-leaf parsley

Sea salt and freshly ground black pepper

PÊCHE PECAN PAIN PERDU

This pain perdu combines fresh peaches with a white peach liqueur–infused sauce, elevating this everyday breakfast into an elegant brunch standout. The bite of toasted pecans introduces a textural crunch that builds complexity. The rich custard of the soaked bread doused with the peach compote creates a bright contrast, and it all comes together splendidly when topped with velvety chantilly cream.

PAIN PERDU

Preheat the oven to 200°F (93°C).

Slice the bread loaf into 2-inch (5 cm) thick slices. You'll need 4 slices for this recipe. Save any leftover French bread to make toasted croutons.

In a large bowl, crack the eggs. Add the sugar and salt. With a wire whisk, beat the eggs until thoroughly mixed. Add the milk, cream, and buttermilk powder and whisk until combined. Add the peach liqueur (if using), molasses, vanilla, and cinnamon. Whisk until combined. Add the 4 pieces of French bread to the custard mixture and let soak on one side for 5 minutes. Turn and let soak for 5 minutes more. Keep turning as needed until the bread slices are soaked through.

Set a large skillet over medium heat and spray with nonstick spray. Add the soaked French bread slices and cook until browned on one side, about 5 minutes. Turn and brown on the other side. Move to a baking sheet and warm in the oven for 10 minutes. If longer holding time is needed, turn the oven off and let them stay in the still-warm oven.

PEACH COMPOTE

Put the pecan halves in a large skillet over medium heat and stir until toasted on each side, about 5 minutes. Add the cinnamon and nutmeg and let toast for an additional 1 minute. Add the butter and let melt. Add the granulated sugar, brown sugar, and salt. Bring to a bubbly simmer and add the peaches. Stir until the peaches release their juices and begin to soften, about 5 minutes.

Turn the burner to high and bring to a rapid sizzle. Add the peach liqueur (if using). If you like, light the pan and flambé the peaches until the flames burn off, about 1 minute. Lower the heat to low and cook for about 5 minutes longer. (Note: While dramatic, flaming the mixture is not necessary. The liquor mostly burns off during the added cooking time.) Turn the heat off and keep warm until serving.

WHIPPED CREAM

Put the cream, confectioners' sugar, peach liqueur (if using), and vanilla in a metal bowl. With an immersion blender, blend on high speed until the consistency of whipped cream with stiff peaks.

For serving, place a French toast piece on each plate. Cover each with the peach compote, evenly distributing the peach slices and pecans. Spoon a liberal topping of cream over the top. Garnish with a dusting of confectioners' sugar, the pecans, and mint. Serve with warm maple syrup on the side.

SERVES 4

PAIN PERDU

1 loaf day-old French bread

10 large eggs

2 tablespoons (26 g) granulated sugar

1 teaspoon salt

1½ cups (355 ml) whole milk

½ cup (120 ml) heavy cream

1 tablespoon (8 g) buttermilk powder

2 tablespoons (28 ml) peach liqueur (optional), such as DeKuyper Pêche white peach

1 tablespoon (20 g) sugarcane molasses

1 tablespoon (15 ml) vanilla extract

2 tablespoons (14 g) ground cinnamon

PEACH COMPOTE

1 cup (100 g) pecan halves

1 tablespoon (7 g) ground cinnamon

1 teaspoon ground nutmeg

8 tablespoons (1 stick, or 112 g) unsalted butter

2 tablespoons (26 g) granulated sugar

2 tablespoons (30 g) light brown sugar

1 teaspoon kosher salt

4 cups (680 g) peeled and sliced fresh peaches

½ cup (120 ml) peach liqueur (optional)

WHIPPED CREAM

4 cups (946 ml) heavy cream, chilled

½ cup (60 g) confectioners' sugar, plus more for garnish

2 tablespoons (28 ml) peach liqueur (optional)

1 teaspoon vanilla extract

FOR SERVING

½ cup (55 g) finely chopped pecans

4 fresh mint sprigs

1 cup (320 g) maple syrup, warmed

TABLE TIPS

★ Use a full-size French bread loaf, not a thin baguette. Ask the baker for day-old (not stale) or buy it fresh and let it sit out overnight.

★ Use firm, not overly ripe peaches. Frozen peach slices work as well, but never use canned. As always, the liquor is optional, but the white peach liqueur I use adds an elegant, yet under-stated, touch of flavor to this dish.

What's That?

Pain perdu (*pan pare-DEW*) is French for "lost bread"—the Louisiana version of French toast. And this foodway favorite is steeped in historical meaning and cul-tural significance for the Acadiana table. For early French-speaking Cajun settlers living off the land in the farmland of South Louisiana, baking bread was a way of life. Those who excelled at the art took pride in it, and soon bakeries flourished, with artisan-made loaves of French bread always the specialty of the house. No one wasted a thing in those days, and day-old French loaves became the building blocks of savory stuffing, custardy bread pudding, and most unique of all, pain perdu.

SUNFLOWER BUTTER MUFFINS

Sunflowers spring to life in South Louisiana as they follow the arc of the sun throughout the summer months. You'll be a follower, too, once you've tried these muffins. Sunflower butter has the texture of its peanut cousin, but with a floral taste that complements the nut-like flavor. The whole-wheat flour gives the muffins a bread-like texture. With the crunch of sunflower seeds and a hit of Louisiana sugarcane molasses, these sweet ingredients bake up into a muffin masterpiece. They are not overly sweet, so feel free to drizzle with honey or more molasses when serving.

Preheat the oven to 375°F (190°C, or gas mark 5). Spray 9 cups of a standard muffin pan with nonstick spray.

In a large bowl, combine both flours, both sugars, the baking powder, and salt.

In another large bowl, combine the sunflower butter, milk, eggs, molasses, and softened butter.

Add the dry ingredients to the bowl containing the wet ingredients. Stir to combine thoroughly. Fill each of the sprayed muffin compartments with the mixture. Sprinkle the tops of the batter with the sunflower seeds.

Bake until golden, about 20 minutes. Test for doneness by inserting a wooden skewer into the center of a muffin and checking to see that it comes out clean. Serve hot with fresh butter.

TABLE TIP

I find sunflower butter at my local natural food store.

MAKES 9 MUFFINS

1 cup (125 g) unbleached all-purpose flour

1 cup (120 g) whole-wheat flour

¼ cup (50 g) granulated sugar

2 tablespoons (30 g) dark brown sugar

2 teaspoons (9 g) baking powder

½ teaspoon salt

½ cup (130 g) sunflower butter

1 cup (235 ml) whole milk

2 large eggs, beaten

1 tablespoon (20 g) sugarcane molasses

3 tablespoons (42 g) unsalted butter, softened

½ cup (73 g) shelled sunflower seeds

What's That?

Sugarcane molasses may sound like a specialty product, but it's not. In Southern cuisine, the use of sorghum molasses is also prevalent, which is why I specify sugarcane molasses in my recipes. Steen's is the South Louisiana brand most used, and Grandma's is a national brand of sugarcane molasses, but there are many other brands as well.

PEPPER POT EGG SKILLET

This savory black-iron breakfast pan launches a pepper punch on top of a smooth, custardy foundation. It forgoes the usual piecrust to cut the carbs, and it has the added advantage of being microwaveable. Fresh eggs are plentiful on rural farms in Acadiana, as are seasonal peppers, greens, and herbs. Fresh chaurice sausage—a fiery pork sausage—adds a unique peppery flavor, which builds another layer of complexity in this zesty one-skillet breakfast casserole. Hot biscuits with honey go great with this spicy dish.

Preheat the oven to 450°F (230°C, or gas mark 8).

Heat 1 tablespoon (15 ml) of the oil in a 10-inch (25 cm) cast-iron skillet over medium-high heat. Add all of the peppers and onions and cook until they just begin to soften, about 5 minutes. Add the kale and cook until it begins to wilt, about 5 minutes. Add the garlic, parsley, and rosemary and continue cooking to combine, about 3 minutes. Transfer to a bowl.

In the same skillet, heat the remaining 1 tablespoon (15 ml) oil. Add the chaurice and cook until browned, about 8 minutes. Turn off the heat and add the vegetable mixture back to the skillet.

In a large bowl, whisk together the eggs, buttermilk, and cheddar cheese. Continue whisking the mixture, adding the Worcestershire, a dash of hot sauce, the Cajun Seasoning Blend, a sprinkle of salt, and a few grindings of pepper.

Add the egg mixture to the skillet and stir into the meat and vegetables. Place the skillet in the oven and bake uncovered until the eggs are fully set, about 25 minutes. Let rest for 10 minutes before serving.

Serve family-style in the center of the table and cut slices for each guest.

SERVES 4 TO 6

2 tablespoons (28 ml) canola oil, divided

2 cups (184 g) sliced mini sweet peppers (red and yellow)

1 red bell pepper, sliced

1 yellow bell pepper, sliced

1 cup (115 g) thickly sliced red onion

1 cup (67 g) tightly packed kale, stemmed

1 teaspoon minced garlic

1 tablespoon (4 g) chopped flat-leaf parsley

1 tablespoon (2 g) chopped fresh rosemary

1 pound (455 g) fresh (raw) chaurice or breakfast sausage

7 large eggs, beaten

½ cup (120 ml) buttermilk

½ cup (58 g) shredded Cheddar cheese

1 teaspoon Worcestershire sauce

Dash of hot sauce

1 teaspoon Cajun Seasoning Blend (page 13)

Kosher salt and freshly ground black pepper

What's That?

Chaurice (*sha-REESE*) is a spicy South Louisiana pork sausage often used in gumbo and other highly seasoned foods calling for a depth of flavor and heat. Some say it is akin to Spanish chorizo, but other than the name, they are quite different. I've seen it available both smoked and raw. It can be found in many rural markets and smokehouses throughout Acadiana.

BUTTERNUT SQUASH BREAD WITH FIG BUTTER

This bread conjures up sweet memories of my childhood on Montgomery Street. The smell, the texture, and the taste are like flashbulbs firing synapses to my brain that lead me home again. A slather of softened fig butter cloaking this hot-out-of-the-oven ginger and brown sugar–infused butternut squash bread adds just enough velvety sweetness to crave a return to those comfort-filled days. It's as wonderful in the evening as in the morning, too: A cold glass of milk . . . a warm goodnight . . . sweet dreams.

BUTTERNUT SQUASH BREAD

Preheat the oven to 375°F (190°C, or gas mark 5). Grease a 4 x 9-inch (10 x 23 cm) loaf pan with softened butter.

In a large bowl, sift both flours, the baking powder, and baking soda. Stir in the allspice, ginger, cinnamon, and salt.

In another large bowl, whisk the eggs, oil, butter, yogurt, vanilla, and milk until thoroughly combined. Add the brown sugar, squash, apples, and 2 tablespoons (15 g) of the pecans. Stir until combined and evenly distributed.

Add the dry ingredients to the wet ingredients and stir until combined. Pour into the loaf pan and spread the mixture evenly; sprinkle the remaining 2 tablespoons (15 g) of pecans over the batter.

Bake until golden brown, about 45 minutes to 1 hour. The bread is done when a wooden skewer inserted in the center comes out clean. Let cool for 10 minutes on a wire rack.

FIG BUTTER

Chop the figs into very small chunks and combine them with the softened butter in a small bowl. Add the canning syrup and salt and stir to combine. Cover and refrigerate until ready to serve.

Remove the bread by running a sharp paring knife around the edges of the pan. Invert and remove the loaf and place on a platter. Serve with the fig butter on the side.

SERVES 8

BUTTERNUT SQUASH BREAD

1½ cups (180 g) whole-wheat flour

1½ cups (188 g) unbleached all-purpose flour

1 teaspoon baking powder

1 teaspoon baking soda

1 teaspoon ground allspice

1 teaspoon ground ginger

1 teaspoon ground cinnamon

½ teaspoon salt

3 large eggs

⅓ cup (80 ml) canola oil

1 tablespoon (14 g) unsalted butter, melted

¾ cup (150 g) plain Greek yogurt

2 teaspoons (10 ml) vanilla extract

⅓ cup (80 ml) whole milk

½ cup (115 g) firmly packed dark brown sugar

2½ cups (613 g) mashed cooked butternut squash (from a 2½-pound [1.1 kg] squash)

2 tart apples, peeled and grated, such as Granny Smith

4 tablespoons (28 g) chopped pecans, divided

FIG BUTTER

4 whole canned figs, plus 1 tablespoon (15 ml) canning syrup

8 tablespoons (1 stick, or 112 g) unsalted butter, softened

Pinch of kosher salt

BLACKBERRY SWEET DOUGH PIES

In the coming years, as the crumbs accumulate in the crease of the fold and the blackberry-stained page gets darker with use, this recipe will continually remind you of how spellbinding a Cajun sweet dough pie can be.

Preserves, jellies, and cobblers are the typical Southern treatment for blackberries, but in South Louisiana, sweet dough pie is the ultimate prize. Acadiana has a sweet dough heritage. Mo Mo Eve, my wife's grandmother, God rest her soul, was renowned for her sweet dough—the best in Jeff Davis Parish, they say. Rox says her secret was flaky dough and a light hand with the sugar. And I think this simple breakfast pie does her proud.

Combine the dry ingredients by sifting the flour, baking powder, and salt into a large bowl. In another bowl, whisk together the softened butter, ½ cup (100 g) of the sugar, and the vanilla until thoroughly combined. Add two eggs and milk to the butter mixture and stir to combine. Add the dry ingredients to the wet ingredients and mix until combined. On a cutting board sprinkled with flour, dump out the mixture and form into a dough ball. Cover with plastic wrap and refrigerate until it is chilled.

Put 2 cups (290 g) of the blackberries and the remaining ½ cup (100 g) sugar in a heavy pot over medium heat. Stir the mixture until the berries cook down, the sugar begins to melt, and the filling just begins to thicken, about 5 minutes. Remove from the stovetop and pour into a bowl. Let the filling cool to room temperature.

Meanwhile, preheat the oven to 400°F (200°C, or gas mark 6).

Remove the dough from the refrigerator. On a surface sprinkled lightly with flour, roll out the dough to approximately ¼ inch (6 mm) thick. Using a 5-inch (13 cm) round plate as a guide, cut out 4 dough circles. Spoon 3 to 4 tablespoons (45 to 55 g) of blackberry filling into the center of each dough round. Leave 1 inch (2.5 cm) of dough exposed around the edges. Fold the exposed part of each dough circle just over the edge of the filling and overlap it in a rustic pattern. Neatness doesn't count here. Try to give it a rough, handmade look.

From the remaining 1 cup (145 g) of blackberries, top the exposed fruit filling by placing in whole berries. Beat the remaining egg in a small bowl and whisk with the water to make an egg wash. With a brush, coat the pastry edges with the egg wash. Place the pies on a silicone baking mat or a parchment paper–lined baking sheet and bake until golden brown, about 15 to 20 minutes.

Transfer the pies to a platter and serve either piping hot or at room temperature, preferably with a cup of dark-roast Louisiana coffee.

MAKES 4 INDIVIDUAL PIES

5 cups (625 g) unbleached all-purpose flour

3 teaspoons (14 g) baking powder

2 teaspoons (12 g) salt

8 tablespoons (1 stick, or 112 g) unsalted butter, softened

1 cup (200 g) granulated sugar, divided

1 tablespoon (15 ml) vanilla extract

3 large eggs, divided

⅔ cup (160 ml) whole milk

3 cups (435 g) fresh blackberries, divided

1 tablespoon (15 ml) water

TABLE TIP

These pies are not the typical turnover style, sealed at the edges, half-moon pies, but rather round, rustic individual pies with the berries shining through, like mini galettes. When dealing with anything sweet, my approach is that less is more. These little pies are best when the pastry is the canvas for painting on the sweetness of the fruit filling, balancing taste and texture into a true work of art.

SHRIMP OMELETTE

At breakfast, lunch, or dinner, a classic French omelette is perfection on a plate. But an omelette made without regard for French technique is nothing more than folded scrambled eggs. Seems that the French—and French Acadians, as well—take their omelette making seriously. My egg-filled combination is an artful interpretation featuring Gulf shrimp, fresh tomatoes, green onions, bacon, tasso, Brie cheese, and Cajun spices. Whether it's cracking just one simple egg or 5,000, it is worth learning the basics of this time-honored technique.

SAUCE

In a small bowl, whisk the mayonnaise, sour cream, lemon juice, and hot sauce to combine thoroughly. Refrigerate until ready to use.

SHRIMP OMELETTE

Inspect the shrimp to make sure the vein is removed and cleaned thoroughly. Sprinkle with Cajun Seasoning Blend on both sides. Heat the olive oil in a small nonstick skillet over medium heat. Add the shrimp and sauté until done, about 5 minutes. Transfer to a plate and keep warm. Wipe out the skillet.

Crack the eggs into a medium bowl and whisk until beaten. Add the half-and-half and season lightly with the hot sauce, salt, and pepper. In the same nonstick skillet over medium heat, melt the butter. Swirl the pan to cover the bottom and sides with the butter. Add the egg mixture and with a rubber spatula, stir the eggs. Continue stirring just until the eggs begin to set and then smooth them out to cover the bottom of the pan. Add the Brie evenly along one half of the eggs and distribute the bacon and tasso on top of that. Add the shrimp to the same side of the egg mixture.

With the spatula in hand, move the pan over a serving plate and ease the egg onto it. Flip over the plain half to seal the omelette. Let sit for 1 minute as the hot egg melts the cheese. Top with a spoonful of sauce and the diced tomatoes. Garnish with the green onion stalk and a generous sprinkle of green onion tops. Serve immediately with extra hot sauce on the side.

SERVES 1

SAUCE

2 tablespoons (28 g) mayonnaise

2 tablespoons (30 g) sour cream

½ teaspoon freshly squeezed lemon juice

1 tablespoon (15 ml) hot sauce

SHRIMP OMELETTE

4 jumbo (16/20 count) shrimp, peeled and deveined

1 teaspoon Cajun Seasoning Blend (page 13)

1 tablespoon (15 ml) olive oil

3 large eggs, at room temperature

1 tablespoon (15 ml) half-and-half

Dash of hot sauce

Kosher salt and freshly ground black pepper

2 tablespoons (28 g) unsalted butter

2 tablespoons (18 g) Brie cheese, rind removed and thinly sliced

2 tablespoons (10 g) crumbled crispy cooked bacon, at room temperature

2 tablespoons (19 g) finely diced tasso (preferably) or smoked ham, at room temperature

1 tablespoon (11 g) diced red tomato

1 tablespoon (11 g) diced yellow tomato

1 green onion

2 tablespoons (12 g) diced green onion tops

THE 5,000-EGG OMELETTE

I'm obsessed with the art of omelette making. And when the first Sunday in November rolls around, I'm standing at attention in Magdaline Square in historic downtown Abbeville, Louisiana. On this one day, Abbeville morphs into a rural French village circa the 1700s, with townspeople reveling in an epicurean tradition that defines who they are. The Confrerie D' Abbeville hosts the 5,000-Egg Giant Omelette Celebration and, as the ceremonious occasion begins, legions of chefs proudly wearing their tall toque blanche and white chef's coats parade the streets with baskets of farm-fresh eggs in hand. A 12-foot (3.7 m) diameter stainless-steel skillet over a wooden bonfire is at the end of the procession, and it's then that things get cracking. Folks line up for blocks for a taste of history and a generous sampling of their French heritage dating back to Emperor Napoleon.

SWEET POTATO WAFFLES WITH ALMOND CANE SYRUP

My homegrown Evangeline sweet potatoes deliver a depth of Louisiana flavor to these waffles every time. Laced with cinnamon and molasses, the waffles have a perfect balance of earthiness and sweetness. And when topped with warm almond sugarcane syrup, it's a sweet way to start your day.

★ ★ ★ ★ ★

WAFFLES

Whisk together the flour, baking powder, salt, brown sugar, and cinnamon in a large bowl.

Put the egg whites, milk, molasses, butter, and lemon juice in another mixing bowl and whisk to combine. Add the dry ingredients to the wet ingredients and whisk to combine.

Add the sweet potato mash and stir to combine. The batter should be thick, but pourable. If too thick, add a bit more milk.

Preheat a waffle iron and spray with nonstick spray. Add the batter according to the manufacturer's instructions and cook until done, about 5 to 8 minutes.

ALMOND CANE SYRUP

Heat a nonstick pan over medium heat and add the almonds. Watch carefully as the almonds begin to toast and you begin to smell their nutty aroma. Turn off the heat and add the sugarcane syrup, constantly stirring until it cools down a bit. Pour into a pitcher and keep warm for serving.

Move the waffles to a large platter and top with the warm Almond Cane Syrup. Serve on individual plates with a dollop of whipped cream and garnished with mint.

SERVES 4

WAFFLES

2 cups (250 g) unbleached all-purpose flour

1 tablespoon (14 g) baking powder

1 teaspoon salt

¼ cup (60 g) firmly packed light brown sugar

1 teaspoon ground cinnamon

6 egg whites

1 cup (235 ml) whole milk, plus more if needed

1 tablespoon (20 g) sugarcane molasses

4 tablespoons (½ stick, or 55 g) unsalted butter, melted

1 teaspoon freshly squeezed lemon juice

1½ cups (338 g) mashed sweet potato

ALMOND CANE SYRUP

1 cup (92 g) sliced almonds

1½ cups (355 ml) sugarcane syrup

1 cup (60 g) whipped cream or prepared whipped topping

Small fresh mint sprigs

What's That?

Sugarcane syrup is a basic staple of every household in Acadiana. While the rest of the world happily drizzles maple syrup, Cajun families swear by their cane syrup, and no breakfast table would be complete without a bright yellow can of Steen's. Based in Abbeville, Louisiana, the C. S. Steen's syrup mill has been turning out their sweet elixir for more than 100 years, and it is a key ingredient replacing corn syrup in many culturally significant dishes of the region. There are other Louisiana brands available, but Steen's is the one you'll find most often on supermarket shelves.

SIMMERING

BLACK POTS

CHAPTER

THREE

ONG BEFORE THE HERALDED CHEF PAUL PRUDHOMME BLACKENED HIS REDFISH, OLD-TIME CAJUN COOKS HAD ALREADY EMBRACED THE BLACK ARTS—COOKING ARTS, THAT IS. SEARING ON HOT IRON UNTIL AN ASH-LADEN CRUST FORMS IS A FUNDAMENTAL FOUNDATION OF FARMHOUSE COOKING. I UNDERSTOOD THIS LONG AGO FROM STUDYING FRENCH TECHNIQUE IN COOKBOOKS THAT TALK OF MAILLARD REACTIONS AND THE LIKE. BUT IT WASN'T UNTIL OVER TWENTY YEARS AGO WHEN MY NEWLYWED WIFE SET OFF OUR FIRE ALARM THAT I WAS AWAKENED TO TRUE RURAL CAJUN BLACK IRON MAGIC.

Packing iron has a different meaning in my neck of the woods. A 10-inch (25 cm) black iron skillet and a similar-size pot with lid are found in every Cajun kitchen. Some "ironophiles" (and I am guilty) have been known to own as many as a dozen or more heavy-duty vessels. My wife, Roxanne, is the real iron maiden of our house. She lovingly maintains our growing cast of cooking vessels with skills she learned as a child. Never soak, always hand-wash, dry on the stovetop, and thinly coat it with oil before putting it away—these are the rules she adheres to.

And when I bring home a rust-laden, vintage castaway, she takes it in like a long-lost orphan child to be nurtured back to its original iron strength.

But readers, take note. It's what these cooks do with their black iron that is magical. Listen up, everybody: *black iron cooking is fundamental to understanding the essence of French Acadian culinary arts, and without it no cook can ever truly cook Cajun.* There, I've said it, and within these pages you will find many pan-seared recipes that will open up the dark world of black iron cookery, Cajun-style.

CRAWFISH-HEAD BISQUE

The essence of Cajun cooking can be found at the bottom of a black iron pot of crawfish-head bisque. No one will point to the arduous process it took to make the rich, dark roux that lies at the base of this pot, nor will they wax poetically about the crawfish stock reduction that mined the liquid gold that infuses it. Not a second thought will be given to the time it took to stuff these heads one by one, and nobody will even think to point out the painstaking care it took a farmer to raise, trap, and process the crawfish. But with just one spoonful you'll know: This is righteous bisque.

Rinse the boiled crawfish of excess spice. Separate the head from the tails and place in piles. Peel all the tail meat, cover, and refrigerate. Place the shells from the tails into a colander and rinse once again. Place in a stockpot.

Pull the leg and pincher undercarriage from the head portions, leaving an empty cavity. Place all the leg and pincher shells into the colander, retaining the heads. Rinse the leg and pincher shells and add to the stockpot. Fill the stockpot with water until it just covers the shells. Turn the heat to high and bring to a boil. Lower the heat to a simmer and cook for 1 hour. Remove the stockpot from the heat and strain 6 cups (1.4 L) of stock into a container for later use.

Place the boudin on a cutting board and remove from the casing. Move the crawfish heads to the cutting board. Using your hands, scoop a portion of boudin and stuff tightly into the empty cavity of as many heads as you can. Place into a covered container and refrigerate.

Heat the oil in a cast-iron pot with a lid over medium-high heat. Add the onions, bell pepper, celery, green onions, and parsley. Cook until the onions turn translucent, about 5 minutes, and then add the garlic and stir. Stir while adding the roux and stock. Bring to a boil and then lower the heat to a simmer. Cover and cook for 1 hour.

Add the crawfish tail meat, cover, and cook for 15 minutes more. Add the stuffed crawfish heads, cover the pot, and turn off the heat. Let rest for 15 minutes and then uncover and taste the stew. Add a pinch of the Cajun Seasoning Blend, salt, pepper, and hot sauce to your desired level of spice.

Serve the stew in shallow bowls over a mound of perfectly steamed white rice. Garnish with green onions and serve with French bread and a bottle of hot sauce on the table.

TABLE TIP

I stuff the crawfish heads with spicy pork boudin for a unique flavor contrast. Eat the stuffing by spooning it out, or like a Cajun, simply suck the stuffing out. Buy whole boiled crawfish online (Sources, page 314).

SERVES 6 TO 8

3 pounds (1.4 kg) whole boiled crawfish

3 pounds (1.4 kg) pork boudin (page 252)

2 tablespoons (28 ml) canola oil

2 cups (320 g) diced yellow onion

1 cup (150 g) diced green bell pepper

1 cup (120 g) diced celery

1 cup (100 g) diced green onion tops

½ cup (30 g) chopped flat-leaf parsley

2 tablespoons (20 g) minced garlic

1 cup (235 ml) dark roux (page 14)

Pinch of Cajun Seasoning Blend (page 13)

Kosher salt and freshly ground black pepper

Dash of hot sauce

8 cups (1.3 kg) cooked long-grain white rice

1 cup (100 g) diced green onion tops

What's That?

Bisque (*bisk*) is a rich soup elevated to center-of-the-plate status. In the city, bisque is usually cream based with rich ingredients, such as oyster and artichoke or crab and asparagus. In the countryside of Acadiana, dark roux-based versions with peppery flavors are just as common. Either way, you usually cannot go wrong when you see bisque on a menu.

PAELLA LOUISIANE

Paella? Jambalaya? It's not difficult to connect these two iconic dishes. The Spanish settled Acadiana long before the French arrived. It is easy to see the handoff of spicy ingredients that infuse the duo, but the technique is what's most defining. The paella vessel is radically different—the shallow, flat, stainless-steel pan versus the deep, black iron pot of jambalaya.

Like jambalaya, paella is all about the rice. I've used Spanish bomba rice as well as Italian arborio, but I love the Louisiana jasmine rice grown and milled by Supreme Rice in Crowley, Louisiana. When cooked down in a stock, it has a small-grain, textural quality that works well in paella. Whichever rice you use, follow the directions in adding the stock; ratios will vary.

Not only is paella similar in the ingredients used, but I also believe the custom of paella is akin to Cajun heritage. Much like our crawfish boil and Cajun boucherie, paella is a social affair that is cooked outdoors over an open fire with everyone crowded around the large pan with a spoon in hand. So, invite your friends and family for a paella party.

SOFRITO

Place a 28-inch (71 cm) paella pan over medium-high heat and add the olive oil. When hot, add the garlic, onions, and tomatoes. Sauté the ingredients until they cook down and the sofrito comes together as a paste. Add the paprika, chili powder, and cumin and stir to combine. Move the sofrito to the outer edges of the pan.

PAELLA

In a stockpot over high heat, bring the seafood stock to a boil and add the saffron. Turn off the heat and set aside.

In the paella pan over medium-high heat, add 2 tablespoons (28 ml) of the olive oil along with the celery, green onions, and bell pepper. Cook until the onions turn translucent, about 5 minutes. Move the vegetables to the outer edges of the pan with the sofrito.

Add the remaining 2 tablespoons (28 ml) olive oil to the paella pan. Season the chicken and rabbit pieces with the paprika, salt, and pepper and sauté until partially cooked and just browned, about 10 minutes. Add the pork loin, and tasso, andouille and sauté for 5 minutes.

Begin the assembly by moving the sofrito and vegetables back to the center of the pan with the meats. Add all the rice along with the seasoned seafood stock infused with the saffron and stir to incorporate evenly. Lower the heat to a simmer and cook, uncovered, for 20 minutes.

Add the rosemary and green beans to the pan. Do not stir the rice, but make sure the rice is cooking evenly and move the pan around on the heat if it is not. At this point, add the oysters on the half shell, the shrimp, crawfish, and peas, distributing evenly throughout the pan. Add the red bell pepper strips in a pattern around the top of the paella. Do not stir! Cover the pan with aluminum foil and continue to cook over low heat for about 10 minutes.

SERVES 12

SOFRITO

¼ cup (60 ml) olive oil, plus more if needed

¼ cup (40 g) chopped garlic

3 cups (480 g) diced yellow onion

3 cups (540 g) chopped ripe tomatoes

1 tablespoon (7 g) smoked paprika

1 tablespoon (8 g) chili powder

1 tablespoon (7 g) ground cumin

TABLE TIPS

★ Paella is a staged recipe with the sofrito as the foundation and each layering of flavors building depth of taste. The meats and seafood used can vary widely from this recipe, so feel free to go with what you have fresh and available.

★ I own a 28-inch (71 cm) paella pan. If your paella pan is smaller, then scale the ingredients down accordingly. The cooking time will be about the same.

PAELLA

12 cups (2.8 L) seafood stock (page 55)

1 teaspoon saffron

4 tablespoons (60 ml) olive oil, divided

2 cups (200 g) chopped celery

2 cups (200 g) diced green onion tops

2 cups (300 g) diced green bell pepper

4 skinless chicken thighs (5 ounces, or 140 g each), cut into bite-size pieces

1 whole rabbit (about 2½ pounds, or 1.1 kg), cut into bite-size pieces

2 tablespoons (14 g) smoked paprika

Kosher salt and freshly ground black pepper

1 pound (455 g) lean pork loin, cut into ¾-inch (2 cm) pieces

1 pound (455 g) tasso (preferably) or smoked ham, diced

1 pound (455 g) andouille sausage (preferably) or smoked pork sausage, sliced

6 cups (1.1 kg) white rice, such as bomba, arborio, or Supreme brand Louisiana jasmine

¼ cup (7 g) chopped fresh rosemary

12 green beans

12 oysters on the half shell

4 pounds (1.8 kg) jumbo (16/20 count) shrimp, peeled and deveined

1 pound (455 g) Louisiana crawfish tail meat

1 package (10 ounces, or 280 g) frozen peas

1 large red bell pepper, cut into strips

2 cups (120 g) chopped fresh flat-leaf parsley

6 lemons, cut into wedges

As it cooks, you should smell the rice browning in the center of the pan. This burnt center of the rice is the socarrat—the most prized part of the paella. After 10 minutes, lift the cover and see that the shrimp are pink and the oysters have curled at the edges. Taste the rice in several areas of the pan for doneness. Once all the stock is absorbed and the rice is tender, it is ready to serve.

Carry the paella pan to the serving table and let rest for 10 minutes while still covered to let the flavors meld. Once your guests are seated, lift the foil to the inevitable applause you will receive. Sprinkle the chopped parsley and serve with lemon wedges.

FRENCH ONION SOUP
(THE FRENCH LOUISIANA VERSION)

It was not France but New York where I had my first taste of an exquisitely prepared French onion soup. It was a simple chef-owned French bistro in SoHo that focused on the classics, and one taste of his rich, beefy, oniony broth was a mind-expanding experience. After dinner, while I lingered over a glass of Burgundy, the chef appeared from the kitchen. He was a crusty, well-worn Frenchman. He sat sipping a glass of *vin rouge* and, with a heavy Parisian accent, he disclosed his secrets to me. I took notes: beef bones, caramelized onions, a Gruyère gratin, and a splash of dry sherry, oh, and chicken feet. Uh, what? Yes, he told me he uses chicken feet for the gelatinous thickening they give his stock. The secret to the rich, round flavor of his beef stock was, of all things, chicken feet and a long, slow simmer.

So slip into your culinary rhythm and relax. Patience is essential.

BEEF STOCK

Preheat the oven to 400°F (200°C, or gas mark 6).

Rinse the beef bones in cold water until all the blood is removed. Assemble the bones on a large rimmed baking sheet and roast for 1 hour. Add the tomato paste and Creole mustard by brushing them onto the bones. Add the onions, celery, and carrots and continue roasting until browned, about 30 minutes. Once completely browned and caramelized, remove and let cool.

In a large stockpot over medium heat, combine all the bones and vegetables from the baking sheet. Pour off all the grease from the baking sheet. Turn a burner on high under the baking sheet and add the wine. With a spatula, scrape up the bits and pieces as you deglaze the baking sheet and reduce the wine by at least one-half. Add all the contents to the stockpot. Add the chicken feet, peppercorns, and bay leaves. Cover the contents with water. Bring the pot to a boil and then lower the heat to a simmer. Cook for 5 hours, skimming the surface to remove residual fat and scum every hour or so.

Strain the stock through a fine-mesh strainer to remove the bones and chicken feet and place into a covered container to cool. Refrigerate overnight. The next day, skim the fat from the top of the liquid. The beef stock can be used immediately or frozen for future use.

(CONTINUED)

SERVES 8

BEEF STOCK

5 pounds (2.3 kg) beef bones

2 tablespoons (32 g) tomato paste

2 tablespoons (42 g) Creole mustard or other coarse-grained mustard

2 large yellow onions, quartered

4 celery stalks, chopped into large pieces

4 carrots, chopped into large chunks

1 cup (235 ml) red wine

1 pound (455 g) chicken feet

6 black peppercorns

2 bay leaves

SOUP

Peel all of the yellow, sweet, and red onions and remove the stem parts of the leeks. Slice the yellow onions ¼-inch (6 mm) thick so that once cooked down they will hold their shape. Slice the rest of the onions thinly.

Melt the bacon fat in a large cast-iron pot over medium heat. Add all of the onions and leeks. Cook slowly and caramelize the onions to eliminate bitterness and achieve sweetness. Try not to stir too much, as it will prevent caramelization. Once the onions begin to brown, add the sugarcane molasses—a touch of Cajun country sweetness. Cooking these onions properly requires the same attention you would apply to making a dark Cajun roux.

Speaking of roux, after about 45 minutes, add the 1 tablespoon (8 g) of flour to the onions. Stir the onions and let the flour combine with the bacon grease. You want to achieve a dark caramel color to bring out all the sugars inside the onions, but stop short of burning or they will go from sugary sweet to a burnt bitterness in no time at all. Low, slow, and stirring constantly are the keys.

Transfer the onions from the pot to a platter. Turn the heat to medium-high and add the sherry to the pot. Stir with a spatula and deglaze the pot, scraping up all the browned bits along the bottom. Reduce the sherry by one-half and turn off the heat.

Add the onion mixture to a stockpot over medium heat. Add the beef stock until just covering the onion mixture. Add the thyme bundle and cook for 1 hour. After 1 hour, the soup should be well combined and thickened. Remove the bundle of thyme. Taste the soup and adjust the seasoning with salt and pepper.

Preheat the broiler. Fill individual ovenproof bowls with the soup and place a toasted baguette slice on top. Sprinkle a generous handful of Gruyère on the bread and run under the broiler until browned and gratinéed. Garnish with a small sprig of fresh thyme.

SOUP

10 large yellow onions

8 sweet onions, such as Vidalia

2 red onions

3 leek stalks, green stems removed

½ cup (103 g) bacon fat

1 tablespoon (20 g) sugarcane molasses

1 tablespoon (8 g) unbleached all-purpose flour

½ cup (120 ml) dry sherry

Fresh thyme sprigs, tied in a bundle, plus small sprigs for garnish

Kosher salt and freshly ground black pepper

8 thick slices of French baguette, toasted

3 cups (360 g) shredded Gruyère cheese

TABLE TIPS

★ Listen up: Making this beef stock from scratch is the key to this recipe. While you are at it, make enough to freeze and use for so many other gravy-laced Cajun and Creole dishes.

★ Any Latin or Asian grocery should have chicken feet.

★ Buy the finest aged Gruyère cheese you can find.

★ When I make this soup, I make a ton of it and portion and freeze the extras. It warms up beautifully in a slow cooker.

THE PRIDE OF SPEAKING FRENCH

Rosalie Fontenot Waldrop is my mother-in-law and a sweet Cajun lady who grew up in rural southwest Louisiana during a time when change threatened the traditional French Acadian way of life. In the post-war 1940s and 1950s, there was a movement afoot throughout Acadiana to eradicate the French language and homogenize Cajuns and Creoles into a more mainstream way of life. Rosalie was raised in a predominantly Cajun French–speaking family in Allen Parish. She recalls that children were punished (some made to kneel on grains of rice) for speaking anything but English in school. In those days, there was a shadow of shame cast over Cajun French traditions, and her language, customs, music, and foodways were in jeopardy.

In 1968 the Council for the Development of French in Louisiana (CODOFIL) emerged and rescued the culture from extinction, breathing pride back into Cajun ways. Today, CODOFIL is a strong political advocacy and social force in promoting the language and culture of French-speaking Louisiana. Now Cajun and zydeco music are recognized worldwide as significant and award-winning genres; and the cuisine is heralded as one of the most unique food cultures in America.

And these days, you can walk into most any small-town barbershop anywhere in Acadiana and hear the Cajun French language spoken with pride. Even in the city of Lafayette, there is a popular trend of "French tables" in small cafés where anyone can sit down and listen in on the Cajun French conversation. And best of all are the traditional music halls that host sessions of French-speaking musicians in the rural towns that dot the Cajun landscape.

BLACKENED AND SMOTHERED RIBEYES WITH RICE AND GRAVY

Just one bite and the curtain will be pulled to reveal the essence of what makes Cajun black pot cooking so mysteriously delectable. One of the familiar home-cooked Cajun dishes that shows up regularly on plate lunch menus is a simple smothered dish called steak, rice, and gravy. Usually made with inexpensive round steak, this dish is a hearty dinnertime meal that graces the table of most every Cajun home. On rare occasion, I've seen this simple dish elevated by using ribeye steak in a fork-tender version that will convert you to cast-iron cooking forever. Follow the principles of this black pot technique and you can substitute chicken, pork, or wild game with the same tasty results.

Remove the ribeyes from the refrigerator 1 hour before cooking. Season generously with salt and pepper.

Heat 2 tablespoons (28 ml) of the oil in a cast-iron pot or skillet with a heavy lid over high heat. Once the oil begins to smoke, add the steaks. Sear over high heat without turning for 1 minute. Turn the steaks to see that they have blackened. Lower the heat to medium and cook on the other side until browned. Transfer to a platter and keep warm.

In the same pot over medium heat, heat the remaining 2 tablespoons (28 ml) oil. Add the onions, celery, and mushrooms. Stir until the onions turn translucent, about 5 minutes. Lower the heat to low and add the garlic, tomatoes, and beef broth. Add a dash of hot sauce. Return the ribeyes to the pot, covering them with the vegetables. Bring to a simmer, cover, and cook for 1 hour.

Uncover the pot and check for doneness by sticking a fork into the meat to see if it is tender. Taste the gravy and season to taste with salt, pepper, and hot sauce.

For serving, mound white rice in the center of shallow serving bowls. Add a ribeye and spoon the gravy around each bowl. Garnish with a sprinkling of diced green onions. Serve with hot French bread for soppin'.

SERVES 4

4 boneless ribeye steaks (8 ounces, or 225 g each)

Kosher salt and freshly ground black pepper

4 tablespoons (60 ml) canola oil, divided

2 cups (230 g) thickly sliced yellow onion

1 cup (100 g) chopped celery

2 cups (140 g) sliced button mushrooms

2 tablespoons (20 g) minced garlic

1 cup (180 g) chopped tomatoes

1 cup (235 ml) beef broth

Dash of hot sauce

4 cups (632 g) cooked long-grain white rice

1 cup (100 g) diced green onion tops

TABLE TIP

Prime steak is not needed for this recipe. Just find an economical, well-marbled Choice or even cheaper Select grade cut of beef sliced ¾ inch (2 cm) thick.

GARFISH COURTBOUILLON

There are a few longtime Cajun classics—garfish courtbouillon is one of them—that have disappeared from restaurant menus. These are time-honored menu standards from earlier days that just don't make the cut with contemporary diners. So call me old-fashioned, but lingering over a steaming bowl of garfish courtbouillon transports me back to a time—the late 1700s, perhaps—when Cajun families arrived in Acadiana and embraced the land's bountiful indigenous ingredients. I am reminded of the centuries-old methods and long-kept traditions handed down to skilled hands that made this extraordinary dish. The Atch-afalaya Basin still produces the fish, turtle, alligator, frogs, and crawfish that are trapped or fished by those original swamp people. And little has changed; this garfish courtbouillon proves it. This is a spicy, stew-like dish that creates an addictive sauce, so be sure to serve with plenty of French bread for sopping.

Heat a cast-iron pot with a heavy lid over medium-high heat. Add the hog jowl pieces and sauté until browned, about 5 minutes. Remove the pork and reserve.

In the same pot, sauté the onions, bell peppers, and celery in the hog grease until browned, about 5 minutes. Lower the heat and add the garlic, parsley, thyme, jalapeño pepper, and tomatoes. Stir to incorporate and add the seafood stock and roux. Stir the mixture and add the bay leaf and hog jowl pieces, along with the Cajun Seasoning Blend and hot sauce. Cover and cook at a simmer for 40 minutes, stirring occasionally.

Uncover the pot and taste the mixture. Add salt and pepper to taste, along with any additional hot sauce until it achieves your desired heat level. Submerge the garfish fillets into the sauce and cover. Cook at a simmer until the fish is tender, about 20 minutes. Cover, turn off the heat, and let rest for 5 minutes before serving.

Remove the bay leaf.

For serving, mound a large portion of rice in the center of serving plates or shallow bowls and spoon the courtbouillon sauce around it, along with pieces of the garfish. Sprinkle with green onions and serve with hot French bread and more hot sauce on the side.

SERVES 4

4 strips (1 ounce, or 28 g each) of smoked hog jowl or smoked bacon, chopped

2 yellow onions, chopped

1 red bell pepper, chopped

1 green bell pepper, chopped

1 cup (100 g) chopped celery

2 cloves of garlic, minced

½ cup (30 g) chopped fresh flat-leaf parsley

1 teaspoon dried thyme

1 fresh jalapeño pepper, seeded and diced

2 cups (484 g) canned diced tomatoes, drained

4 cups (946 ml) seafood stock (page 55)

2 tablespoons (28 ml) dark roux (page 14)

1 bay leaf

1 tablespoon (10 g) Cajun Seasoning Blend (page 13)

1 teaspoon hot sauce

Kosher salt and freshly ground black pepper

2 pounds (900 g) garfish fillets or other firm white fish fillets, such as redfish or catfish

4 cups (632 g) cooked long-grain white rice

1 cup (100 g) diced green onion tops

What's That?

Courtbouillon (*coo-bee-YON*) is not to be confused with the classic French cooking liquid court-bouillon. Louisiana courtbouillon is a classic Cajun and Creole fish stew featuring tomatoes along with the trinity of vegetables (onions, bell pepper, and celery) and a good seafood stock. Redfish, usually cooked whole, is traditional, but catfish and lesser fish like garfish and gaspergou are typical in rural home cooking. It's old-school and rarely seen in restaurants these days, but if you do see it listed, order a double portion.

TABLE TIPS

★ I like the flavor of hog fat for sautéing, but feel free to substitute vegetable oil.

★ While you can use a store-bought seafood stock, I make my own easily by combining 1 cup of dried shrimp (the tiny dried shrimp you find in Asian markets) and 4 cups (946 ml) of boiling water. Let it sit for an hour and then strain off the shrimp to make a potent stock.

★ To make crab stock or crawfish stock, place crab shells or crawfish shells (rinsed of any spice) in a stockpot with enough water to cover. Simmer for at least 30 minutes to reduce the liquid and intensify the flavor. Strain off the shells and refrigerate the stock until ready to use.

★ The key to this dish is not to overcook the fish until it disintegrates into small pieces.

CREOLE OYSTER AND SPINACH SOUP

Spinach and oysters are a natural in this creamy Creole soup. As an ingredient, oysters present a contrast: They are as strong and impenetrable as they are gentle and delicate. Spinach, as a leafy vegetable, has many of the same delicate traits as oysters. You'll appreciate the balance of flavors in this bowl, which allow the briny bivalves to shine. It is a cream-based, bisque-like soup with light floral notes of anise and fresh thyme. I sometimes note in recipes that the alcohol is optional, but here it is essential. There are a variety of acceptable anise-flavored liqueurs, but Pernod is my choice here. One final recommendation: Please go easy on the hot sauce for this delicate brew.

Melt the butter in a large pan with a tight-fitting lid over medium heat. Add the onions, celery, and bell pepper and cook until the onions turn translucent, about 5 minutes. Add the garlic, thyme, Pernod, and spinach leaves. Let the alcohol burn off as the spinach begins to wilt. Add the cream and stir. Add 1 cup (235 ml) of oyster liquor from the container to the pan, reserving the oysters for later. Lower the heat to a simmer, cover the pan, and let cook for 10 minutes, stirring every 5 minutes.

Uncover the pan and stir. The spinach should be wilted, and the cream will have begun to reduce. Continue simmering the mixture as the soup thickens, about 5 minutes. Add salt, pepper, and hot sauce to taste.

Just before serving, add the oysters. Gently simmer the oysters in their creamy bath until they are delicately poached and the edges begin to curl and wrinkle, about 2 to 3 minutes. Turn off the heat.

For serving, ladle the soup into shallow bowls with several oysters in each.

SERVES 4

4 tablespoons (½ stick, or 55 g) unsalted butter

1 cup (160 g) finely diced yellow onion

½ cup (60 g) finely diced celery

½ cup (75 g) finely diced red bell pepper

1 tablespoon (10 g) minced garlic

2 tablespoons (5 g) chopped fresh thyme

½ cup (120 ml) Pernod

2 cups (60 g) fresh spinach leaves, stemmed

4 cups (945 ml) heavy cream

1 pint (455 g) shelled oysters, with their liquor

Kosher salt and freshly ground black pepper

Dash of hot sauce

TABLE TIPS

★ Plump, fresh oysters that are gently poached in the final stage of cooking are the key to this dish. Don't settle for anything but the saltiest oysters with their briny liquor. The oyster jus—a flavor-filled liquid that has a sticky feel to it—is a must-have ingredient in this bisque.

★ Serve with plenty of warm French bread and pair with a chilled sauvignon blanc.

SHORT RIB CHILI WITH JALAPEÑO CROUTONS AND CRACKLIN' CORN CAKES

In the winter, a big pot of chili on the stovetop is as common in South Louisiana as it is most anywhere else. The one I like best features ground short rib—bold, beefy, and flavorful, with a hearty, textural quality that redefines the chili experience. Along with Cajun green onion–pork sausage and Mexican beef chorizo, all that is needed is an infusion of beer thickened with a roux (made with masa corn flour). I like my chili topped three ways: Frying up sliced pickled jalapeños adds heat and crunch. A spoonful of cold crema brightened with zesty lime cools things down and plays perfectly against the heat of the dish. And a cracklin' corn cake nestled into the bowl of red to scoop it up is the pièce de résistance.

SHORT RIB CHILI

Place the short ribs on a cutting board. With a sharp boning knife, remove the meat from the bone, making sure to retain all the fat. Carefully remove all silver skin and tough sinew from the meat. Cut the beef into 1-inch (2.5 cm) cubes of even size. Refrigerate the meat.

When ready to grind (or food-process) the rib meat, place the grinder or container and blade into the freezer for 1 hour.

Assemble the grinder or food processor and begin the first grind at a very coarse grind to combine the rib meat and break down the pieces. After you have completed grinding it all, inspect the ground meat to pick out any hard pieces or sinewy cuts. Place the ground meat back into the refrigerator so that it becomes ice cold. Once cold, return the meat for another grind to achieve a smaller grind that is more typical of store-bought chili meat.

Heat a lidded cast-iron pot over medium-high heat and add 1 tablespoon (15 ml) of the oil; add the beef, green onion–sausage, and chorizo to the pot and cook until browned. Transfer to a tray and keep warm.

Add another 1 tablespoon (15 ml) of oil to the pot, if needed. Add the onions, celery, bell peppers, and garlic and sauté until the onions turn translucent, about 5 minutes. Transfer to the tray and keep warm.

Add the remaining 2 tablespoons (28 ml) of oil and the masa harina. Whisk the corn flour into the hot oil and continue stirring until it just begins to brown and you can smell toasted corn. Immediately add the beer, stirring, to stop the cooking.

Add the sautéed vegetables and the meat back to the pot and bring to a simmer. Add the cilantro, jalapeño, chipotle with adobo, Cajun Seasoning Blend, and chili powder. Stir to combine. Add the tomatoes with chiles and crushed tomatoes and combine. Cover the pot and cook on low heat for 40 minutes.

Ladle off any oil from the surface of the chili. Season to taste with salt and pepper. Add the beans (if using) and let simmer for 15 minutes.

(CONTINUED)

SERVES 4 TO 6

SHORT RIB CHILI

4 pounds (1.8 kg) bone-in beef short ribs

4 tablespoons (60 ml) vegetable oil, divided

1 pound (455 g) bulk green onion–sausage or ground pork

1 cup (225 g) Mexican beef chorizo sausage, such as Cacique brand

1 cup (160 g) diced yellow onion

1 cup (120 g) diced celery

½ cup (75 g) diced green bell pepper

½ cup (75 g) diced red bell pepper

1 tablespoon (10 g) minced garlic

3 tablespoons (22 g) masa harina corn flour, such as Bob's Red Mill

2 bottles beer (12 ounces, or 355 ml each)

2 tablespoons (2 g) chopped fresh cilantro

1 tablespoon (9 g) diced fresh jalapeño pepper, seeds and ribs removed

1 tablespoon (8 g) finely chopped canned chipotle peppers in adobo sauce with 1 tablespoon (15 ml) sauce

1 tablespoon (10 g) Cajun Seasoning Blend (page 13)

¼ cup (30 g) chili powder

1 can (10 ounces, or 280 g) mild diced tomatoes with green chiles, drained

(CONTINUED)

CREMA

In a small bowl, blend the crema and yogurt. Stir in the lime zest and juice and combine. Cover and refrigerate until ready to serve.

CRACKLIN' CORN CAKES

In a large bowl, combine the cornmeal with the oil and water; add the corn, green onions, jalapeños, cracklin's, and salt and stir to combine.

Set a large nonstick pan over medium-high heat and spray generously with nonstick spray. Once the pan is hot, add 2 tablespoons (28 g) of the batter. Fry until golden brown and cooked through, about 5 minutes. With a spatula, carefully flip to the other side and finish cooking, about 2 minutes. Repeat with the remaining batter. Transfer to a platter and keep warm.

FRIED JALAPEÑOS

Add enough oil to a stockpot to come halfway up the side of the pot and heat the oil to 375°F (190°C).

Pour out the jalapeños into a colander and drain. Whisk the buttermilk and egg together in a medium bowl until combined. Combine the flour and cornmeal in another bowl.

Dredge the sliced jalapeños first in the buttermilk mixture and then coat with the flour mixture. Add the jalapeños to the pot of hot oil and fry until golden brown, about 2 to 3 minutes. Transfer to a wire rack set over paper towels to drain. Sprinkle with salt and keep warm.

For serving, ladle the chili into large serving bowls and top with fried jalapeños. Add a corn cake to the side of the bowl. Serve the crema and lime wedges on the side.

TABLE TIPS

★ Buy the English-cut, bone-in short ribs, where the meat-to-bone weight ratio is about 50-50. Use the Mexican chorizo rather than the smoked and linked Spanish chorizo.

★ Beans or no beans in your chili is an ongoing debate, and I will leave it up to you.

★ Cajun cracklin's are readily available on my home turf, but substituting a small bag of pork rinds will give a similar crunchy, porky punch to the corn cakes.

---

1 can (28 ounces, or 785 g) crushed tomatoes

Kosher salt and freshly ground black pepper

2 cans (16 ounces, or 455 g each) red kidney beans (optional), rinsed and drained

CREMA (OPTIONAL)

½ cup (120 ml) Mexican crema

½ cup (100 g) plain Greek yogurt

1 tablespoon (6 g) grated lime zest

2 tablespoons (28 ml) freshly squeezed lime juice

CORN CAKES

2 cups (275 g) stone-ground yellow cornmeal

1 cup (235 ml) vegetable oil

1 cup (235 ml) water

2 tablespoons (20 g) yellow corn kernels

2 tablespoons (12 g) diced green onion tops

2 tablespoons (18 g) diced fresh jalapeño pepper, seeds and ribs removed

1 cup (80 g) chopped cracklin's or pork rinds

1 tablespoon (8 g) kosher salt

FRIED JALAPEÑOS

Vegetable oil, for frying

1 jar (12 ounces, or 340 g) sliced pickled jalapeño peppers

1 cup (235 ml) buttermilk

1 large egg

1 cup (125 g) unbleached all-purpose flour

1 cup (140 g) cornmeal

Kosher salt

1 lime, cut into wedges

STUFFED TURKEY WING GUMBO

The rich Creole history of South Louisiana is a spiritual mixture of heritage and customs that has become an essential ingredient of the cultural gumbo of Acadiana. Time-honored Creole traditions of zydeco music, the Acadian horse culture, and the delicious recipes handed down through generations add amazing depth to our local folkways.

It's simple food—soul food, I call it—and there are few dishes better than this one to feed the soul. But don't mistake simplicity for lack of skill. It takes a keen understanding of the balance of spices and the cooking times required to render a tough turkey appendage into a sticky, flavor-filled wing that lifts your taste buds to the high heavens.

These are wings to pray for, and the reverential treatment they are given in this recipe will make you weak in the knees. A complex, darkly divine turkey stock–infused gumbo with the added smokiness of andouille and tasso provides the base, and the braised turkey wings stuffed with onions and herbs float on top. This is a dish so regally rich and so decadently deep in flavor that you might never come up for air. Amen, and pass the napkins.

WINGS

Preheat the oven to 400°F (200°C, or gas mark 6).

Wash the turkey wings and pat dry with paper towels. Sprinkle the wings lightly with Cajun Seasoning Blend.

Heat the oil in a large cast-iron pot with a heavy lid over medium-high heat. Add the 4 wing midsection pieces. Let them brown on one side and then turn to brown the other side. Remove from the pot and let cool.

In the same pot over medium heat, add the diced onions, diced celery, and bell pepper. Stir until the onions turn translucent, about 5 minutes. Add the garlic and season the mixture lightly with more Cajun Seasoning Blend, salt, and pepper. Continue cooking and stirring until all the vegetables are browned, about 3 minutes longer. Turn the heat off and transfer the vegetable mixture to a platter. Let cool.

Place the wing midsection portions on a cutting board and using a sharp knife, make a lengthwise incision along the center (do not go all the way through) to open up a cavity. With your fingers, pull the skin and flesh of the wing midsection to widen the cavity for stuffing. With a spoon, add enough vegetable mixture to fill the inside cavity and pull the skin of the wing to close it as much as you can.

Place the stuffed wings on the bottom of a large pot. Spread the chunks of chopped onions, chopped celery, and carrots around the bottom and add enough turkey stock just to cover the wings. Cover the pan tightly with aluminum foil. Place the pan in the oven and cook for 1½ hours without opening.

(CONTINUED)

SERVES 4

WINGS

4 large turkey wings (8 ounces, or 225 g each), midsection only

2 tablespoons (20 g) Cajun Seasoning Blend (page 13)

2 tablespoons (28 ml) canola oil

1 cup (160 g) finely diced yellow onion

1 cup (120 g) finely diced celery

1 cup (150 g) finely diced green bell pepper

2 tablespoons (20 g) minced garlic

Kosher salt and freshly ground black pepper

1 yellow onion, peeled and chopped

1 celery stalk, chopped

1 carrot, peeled and chopped

8 cups (1.9 L) dark turkey stock or Dark Chicken Stock (page 215)

(CONTINUED)

Remove the pot from the oven and uncover. Test the wings for doneness by sticking a fork into the meat and pulling it apart. It should be approaching fork-tender. Continue cooking the wings, uncovered, for 30 minutes longer or until the tops begin to brown and the skin and meat become sticky and fall-apart tender. Transfer the wings to a platter.

GUMBO

Heat the oil in a large cast-iron pot over medium-high heat. Once sizzling hot, add the onions, bell pepper, and celery. Sauté until the onions turn translucent, about 5 minutes. Add the garlic and parsley and stir until combined. Add the andouille and tasso and sauté just until it begins to brown.

Add the turkey stock, season with cayenne, and stir to combine. Add the roux and stir. Bring the pot to a boil and then lower the heat to a simmer. Cover the pot and let it cook for 1 hour.

Skim the surface of any excess oil. Sample the gumbo and add salt and pepper to taste. Cover the pot and simmer for 30 minutes longer. Uncover the pot and skim the surface again of any excess oil. At this point, add the stuffed turkey wings to the pot. Cover and simmer for 15 minutes longer.

Sample the finished gumbo and season with hot sauce to taste. Ladle the gumbo into large bowls over a mound of rice, top with a stuffed turkey wing, and garnish with diced green onions.

TABLE TIPS

★ While the stuffed turkey wings are the star of this dish, feel free to add turkey meat to the gumbo for a heartier base.

★ The turkey wing braising liquid makes a terrific gravy, so make sure to save it for another dish.

GUMBO

2 tablespoons (28 ml) vegetable oil

2 cups (320 g) diced yellow onion

2 cups (300 g) diced green bell pepper

2 cups (240 g) diced celery

2 tablespoons (20 g) minced garlic

½ cup (30 g) chopped flat-leaf parsley

2 cups (16 ounces, or 455 g) sliced andouille sausage (preferably) or smoked pork sausage

1 cup (150 g) chopped tasso (preferably) or smoked ham

12 cups (2.8 L) turkey stock or Dark Chicken Stock (page 215)

1 teaspoon cayenne pepper

1 cup (235 ml) dark roux, plus more if needed (page 14)

Kosher salt and freshly ground black pepper

Dash of hot sauce

8 cups (1.3 kg) cooked long-grain white rice

1 cup (100 g) diced green onion tops

COLLARD, BLACK-EYE, ANDOUILLE, AND SWEET POTATO SOUP

In South Louisiana, a big black iron pot of collard greens and black-eyed peas is like putting the welcome mat out for family and friends. Leave your boots at the door and pull up a chair at the kitchen table for a bowl of good home cookin'.

Memories of growing up in the South are first and foremost peppered with recollections of certain foods. Beans and greens have always been at the top of my list. They are usually cooked down with smoked andouille and spiced with a vinegary pepper sauce. This version with Louisiana sweet potatoes is a simple soup, and the keys are patient cooking (low and slow) and not over-seasoning it; the andouille should do the job. The purity of the broth—the potlikker—is imperative.

In a large stockpot over medium-high heat, sauté the bacon. Once the bacon begins to brown and the fat is rendered, add the onions, celery, bell pepper, and carrots. Continue to stir until the onions turn translucent, about 5 minutes. Add the andouille and garlic as you continue to stir the ingredients.

Add the chicken stock, smoked ham hock, and bay leaves. Bring the pot to a boil and then quickly lower the heat to a simmer. Cover and simmer for 1 hour.

Add the black-eyed peas and collard greens. Stir the pot to submerge all of the greens into the liquid and cover. Cook on a low simmer for 1 hour. Lift the lid, taste the liquid, and add salt to taste.

Add the sweet potatoes and cover the pot. Continue to simmer until the sweet potatoes are tender but not falling apart, about 1 hour.

After the sweet potatoes have finished cooking, taste for seasoning. The smoked meats should have added enough flavor and spice, but add any hot sauce to your taste or pass it at the table. Remove the bay leaves and bones of the hock.

Serve in large bowls along with hot corn bread.

SERVES 4 TO 6

3 strips (1 ounce, 28 g each) of thick-cut smoked bacon, chopped

1 cup (160 g) diced yellow onion

1 cup (120 g) diced celery

1 cup (150 g) diced red bell pepper

1 cup (130 g) diced carrot

2 cups (16 ounces, or 455 g) sliced andouille sausage (preferably) or smoked pork sausage

2 tablespoons (20 g) minced garlic

10 cups (2.4 L) chicken stock

1 smoked ham hock (6 ounces, or 170 g)

2 bay leaves

1 pound (455 g) dried black-eyed peas, rinsed and picked over

1 large bunch of collard greens, woody stems removed and chopped

Kosher salt

2 cups (220 g) chopped sweet potato (bite-size cubes)

Hot sauce

TABLE TIP

The resulting potlikker is the prize. All the nutrients are contained in this magic elixir. What potlikker remains should be saved and used as a flavorful stock for making soup.

What's That?

Andouille (*ahn-DOO-ee*) is a building block of the cuisine. To say it is simply a spicy pork sausage smoked in a casing totally understates its role as a foundation for many great Cajun and Creole dishes. It is sold everywhere, and it is unquestionably the most used of all Cajun sausages as a seasoning ingredient. My favorite is found at Poche's in rural St. Martin Parish, but many other smokehouses have outstanding versions.

SHRIMP AND WHITE BEAN SOUP WITH FRIED KALE

As crisp, cool fall weather approaches Acadiana and the black pots begin coming out of hibernation, most Cajun cooks instantly think of gumbo. But there is a special one-pot dish I reserve for this time of year that celebrates the end of the shrimping season and makes special use of my stash of 16/20-count jumbos. White beans and smoky andouille bristling with the brine of Gulf shrimp and garnished with crispy fried kale is pure comfort in a bowl.

Heat the oil in a large pot with a lid over medium-high heat. Sauté the onions until they turn translucent, about 5 minutes. Add the bell pepper, carrots, ham, and andouille and cook for 5 minutes. Drain the beans and add the beans and enough water to cover to the pot. Add the bay leaves, thyme, and rosemary and lightly season with a sprinkle of salt, pepper, and Cajun Seasoning Blend. Bring to a boil and then lower the heat to simmer.

Add 2 cups (134 g) of the kale; cover the pot and cook, stirring every 15 minutes to check to see if more liquid is needed. When more liquid is needed, add the clam juice. Continue cooking until the beans are tender, about 45 minutes total.

Add the shrimp and cook until done, about 5 minutes. Turn off the heat, remove the thyme stems and bay leaves, taste the soup, and adjust the seasonings accordingly.

For the fried kale garnish, heat the oil in a pot over medium-high heat. Dry the remaining kale with paper towels to remove any moisture. Once the oil reaches 350°F (180°C), add the kale. Step back (the oil will pop and splatter) and watch as the kale fries and any remaining moisture cooks out, about 3 minutes. Transfer the crunchy kale to a paper towel–lined plate to drain.

Ladle the soup into individual bowls and garnish with fried kale leaves.

SERVES 4

2 tablespoons (28 ml) olive oil

1 cup (160 g) diced yellow onion

½ cup (75 g) diced green bell pepper

1 cup (130 g) diced carrot

1 cup (150 g) diced smoked ham

2 cups (16 ounces, or 455 g) sliced andouille sausage (preferably) or smoked pork sausage

1 pound (455 g) dried large white beans, rinsed and picked over, soaked overnight in water to cover

2 bay leaves

2 fresh thyme sprigs

1 tablespoon (2 g) chopped fresh rosemary

Kosher salt and freshly ground black pepper

Cajun Seasoning Blend (page 13)

3 cups (201 g) coarsely chopped kale, stemmed and divided

1 bottle (8 ounces, or 235 ml) clam juice

1 pound (455 g) jumbo (16/20 count) shrimp, peeled and deveined

2 cups (475 ml) vegetable oil

CHICKEN LEG FRICASSÉE

I like to call this "frickin' chicken," and if you've ever had Cajun smothered chicken in wine, you'll know exactly why: This dish is so frickin' good! Butter, garlic, and fresh herbs combine with a splash of dry white wine that pulls it all together into a distinct flavor combination. These wine-bathed chicken legs are addictive. But before you even bite into a chicken leg, dip a crusty piece of French bread into the sauce and give it a taste—sensory overload.

Heat the oil in a large skillet with a cover over medium-high heat. Once sizzling hot, add the chicken legs and brown on all sides. Remove the chicken from the skillet and keep warm.

In the same skillet over medium-high heat, add the onions, bell pepper, and celery. Sauté until the onions turn translucent, about 5 minutes. Add the garlic, parsley, and rosemary and stir until combined. Add the wine and cook until reduced by half. Add the chicken stock and roux, along with the bay leaves and Cajun Seasoning Blend. Stir to combine and bring to a boil. Immediately lower the heat to a simmer and add the potatoes and lemon slices. Distribute the chicken legs back into the skillet, cover, and cook on the stovetop for 1 hour.

Uncover and skim the surface of any excess oil. Taste the fricassée gravy and season to taste with salt, pepper, and hot sauce. Cover the pot and simmer for 15 minutes longer.

Remove the bay leaves.

Ladle the chicken legs and fricassée gravy over a mound of white rice. Garnish with a sprinkle of green onions.

What's That?

Fricassée (*FREEK-ah-say*) is a slow-simmered stew that produces an unmistakable gravy. Usually made with chicken or older hen or rooster, a fricassée renders a tough old bird tender after a long braise in stock and vegetables (sometimes thickened with a dark roux).

SERVES 4 TO 6

¼ cup (60 ml) vegetable oil

12 skin-on chicken legs

2 cups (320 g) diced yellow onion

1 cup (150 g) diced green bell pepper

1 cup (120 g) diced celery

2 tablespoons (20 g) minced garlic

½ cup (30 g) chopped flat-leaf parsley

2 tablespoons (4 g) chopped fresh rosemary

½ cup (120 ml) dry white wine

4 cups (945 ml) Dark Chicken Stock, plus more if needed (page 215)

3 tablespoons (45 ml) dark roux, plus more if needed (page 14)

2 bay leaves

1 teaspoon Cajun Seasoning Blend (page 13)

16 small new potatoes

2 slices of fresh lemon

Kosher salt and freshly ground black pepper

Dash of hot sauce

6 cups (948 g) cooked long-grain white rice

1 cup (100 g) diced green onion tops

TABLE TIP

Have plenty of hot French bread on hand for soaking up the gravy and a bottle of hot sauce (of course) on the side.

SHRIMP AND ARTICHOKE SOUP

This sumptuous shrimp and artichoke soup is an impressive start to a classic Creole dinner. You'll see it on the menus of restaurants across Louisiana, and it is just as popular in rural Acadiana lunchrooms as it is in citified New Orleans restaurants. It is casual yet elegant: simple but with a complex flavor profile. And it's easy; using canned artichokes makes this a convenient classic. Once you learn the basics of this soup, experiment by replacing the shrimp with crabmeat, oysters, or even crawfish tails.

Heat the oil and butter in a heavy pot over medium heat. Add the onions, celery, red bell pepper, and poblano pepper. Cook until the onions turn translucent, about 5 minutes, and then stir in the parsley, thyme, and garlic. Add the flour and stir to make a light blond roux, about 5 minutes. Add the wine (if using) and stir until it reduces, about 5 minutes. Add the seafood stock, milk, and cream. Stir to combine and then add the artichokes. Season with the paprika and Cajun Seasoning Blend and stir. Cook at a gentle simmer for 30 minutes.

Season to taste with salt, pepper, and a dash of hot sauce. At this point, the soup should be at a bisque-like consistency to coat the back of a spoon. If you like, turn off the heat and let sit until time to serve (up to 2 hours, or refrigerate overnight).

Just before serving, bring the soup back up to a simmer. Add the shrimp. Stir and let the shrimp cook until they turn pink, about 5 minutes. Sample one of the larger shrimp for doneness and turn off the heat. Ladle the soup into bowls and garnish each with a sprig of fresh parsley. Serve with toasted French bread rounds.

TABLE TIP

If you leave this soup on to simmer while waiting for your guests to be seated, be sure to check the thickness before serving and adjust accordingly.

SERVES 6

1 tablespoon (15 ml) olive oil

8 tablespoons (1 stick, or 112 g) unsalted butter

1 cup (160 g) diced yellow onion

1 cup (120 g) diced celery

½ cup (75 g) diced red bell pepper

1 tablespoon (9 g) diced poblano pepper

2 tablespoons (8 g) chopped flat-leaf parsley

1 teaspoon minced fresh thyme

1 tablespoon (10 g) minced garlic

2 tablespoons (16 g) unbleached all-purpose flour

½ cup (120 ml) dry white wine (optional)

2 cups (475 ml) seafood stock (page 55)

2 cups (475 ml) whole milk

2 cups (475 ml) heavy cream

2 cans (14 ounces, or 390 g) quartered artichokes (packed in water), drained

1 teaspoon smoked paprika

1 teaspoon Cajun Seasoning Blend (page 13)

Kosher salt and freshly ground black pepper

Dash of hot sauce

2 pounds (900 g) medium (41/50 count) shrimp, peeled and deveined

Fresh flat-leaf parsley sprigs

Toasted French bread rounds

BAKED POTATO, TASSO, AND LEEK SOUP IN A SEA SALT BOULE

There's nothing better than a steaming hot bowl of potato soup. Well, actually there is: baked potato, tasso, and leek soup in a French bread bowl. This blending of flavors piles on the smoky goodness of tasso and the peppery bite of leeks to the velvety warmth of creamy potatoes. And it's all served up in a garlic butter–brushed boule studded with fleur de sel. While the dramatic presentation is impressive enough, it is the heady aroma of crusty baked garlic bread that gets the juices flowing. Breaking off a hunk and dipping it into the center is heavenly. Oh yeah, soup's on.

Preheat the oven to 400°F (200°C, or gas mark 6).

Wash the potatoes and rub them with the oil. Wrap individually in aluminum foil and bake for 1 hour or until tender when poked with a skewer. Remove the foil wraps, let cool, and chop into bite-size pieces. Leave the oven on.

In a heavy pot with a lid over medium-high heat, melt ½ cup (1 stick, or 112 g) of the butter. Add the leeks, celery, bell pepper, and tasso and cook until just wilted, about 5 minutes. Add 4 tablespoons (16 g) of the parsley and the thyme and stir. Add the chicken stock and cream and blend thoroughly. Add the cheddar cheese and potatoes. Season with a dash of hot sauce, salt, and pepper. Cover and cook for 45 minutes, stirring occasionally. If the soup becomes too thick, thin it out with some of the milk.

Meanwhile, slice the top off of each boule. With your hands, pull out the soft interior bread, making a cavity. With a spoon, scrape the bottom and sides, leaving them about 1 inch (2.5 cm) thick in all directions. Melt the remaining ½ cup (1 stick, or 112 g) butter and add the minced garlic. Brush the bread exterior and the boule tops with the melted butter and bake for 20 minutes or until the edges begin to brown. Remove and brush again with the butter and sprinkle each boule with 1 tablespoon (17 g) sea salt. Keep warm until serving.

As an added topping, stir the sour cream and Parmesan cheese together in a ramekin.

For serving, ladle the hot soup into each bread bowl and garnish with the remaining 2 tablespoons (8 g) of chopped parsley. Serve each boule on a plate with the bread top alongside and garnish with the cheesy sour cream topping, if desired.

SERVES 4

4 large russet potatoes

1 tablespoon (15 ml) olive oil

1 cup (2 sticks, or 225 g) unsalted butter, divided

2 cups (178 g) sliced leeks (white part only)

2 cups (240 g) finely diced celery

1 cup (150 g) finely diced green bell pepper

2 cups (300 g) chopped tasso (preferably) or smoked ham

6 tablespoons (24 g) chopped flat-leaf parsley, divided

2 teaspoons chopped fresh thyme

4 cups (945 ml) chicken stock

2 cups (475 ml) heavy cream

½ cup (58 g) shredded white Cheddar cheese

Dash of hot sauce

Kosher salt and freshly ground black pepper

1 cup (235 ml) whole milk, if needed

4 round French bread boules

1 tablespoon (10 g) minced garlic

4 tablespoons (68 g) coarse sea salt

1 cup (230 g) sour cream (optional)

1 tablespoon (5 g) freshly grated Parmesan cheese (optional)

What's That?

Tasso (*TAH-so*) is a cured and smoked piece of boneless pork butt used much like ham in cooking. It is highly spiced with cayenne pepper and garlic. Tasso is fully cooked and is usually used as a component ingredient rather than served on its own. When I go to The Best Stop Supermarket in Scott, Louisiana, I load up on their tasso, among the best in Acadiana.

SEAFOOD PASTALAYA

I don't know the precise moment this whole pastalaya thing started, but a few years back some inventive Cajun decided to replace the rice in his jambalaya with pasta, and here we are. I was not an early adopter of this attempt to hijack the heritage of my beloved jambalaya, but after one taste of this pastalaya, I can assure you I am now on board. Briny shrimp, succulent scallops, and salty oysters infuse the flavors of the Gulf into the pasta in this creamy entrée, sending it in a totally different direction. Forget the connection to jambalaya; this one can stand on its own.

Fill a large pot halfway with water and bring to a boil over high heat. Add the salt and the pasta. Cook just until the pasta reaches al dente; immediately drain the pasta in a colander, reserving some of the pasta water for later use.

Heat the oil in a large pot over medium heat. Add the onions, celery, bell pepper, and rosemary and cook until the onions turn translucent, about 5 minutes. Add the white wine and cook until the wine reduces by half, about 5 minutes. Add the cream and bring to a boil. Decrease the heat to a simmer and continue cooking until the cream reduces and begins to thicken, about 10 minutes. If too thick, add a little pasta water.

Add the tomatoes, shrimp, scallops, and oysters along with their liquor and cook for 5 minutes.

Add the cooked spaghetti to the pot and stir to incorporate it into the hot cream mixture. Season to taste with salt, pepper, and a dash of hot sauce. Add the diced green onions and Parmigiano-Reggiano cheese and stir.

For serving, ladle the pastalaya into shallow bowls, making sure to evenly distribute the seafood. Serve with crusty French bread.

TABLE TIP

I'm suggesting genuine imported Parmigiano-Reggiano cheese as the crowning touch for this pastalaya.

SERVES 4

½ cup (144 g) salt

1 pound (455 g) spaghetti

¼ cup (60 ml) olive oil

1 cup (160 g) diced yellow onion

½ cup (60 g) diced celery

½ cup (75 g) chopped green bell pepper

2 tablespoons (4 g) chopped fresh rosemary

½ cup (120 ml) dry white wine

2 cups (475 ml) heavy cream

½ cup (75 g) yellow cherry tomatoes, halved

2 pounds (900 g) jumbo (16/20 count) shrimp, shells removed, tails left on

4 plump sea scallops or 12 bay scallops

12 oysters, plus ½ cup (120 ml) oyster liquor

Kosher salt and freshly ground black pepper

Dash of hot sauce

½ cup (50 g) diced green onion tops

¼ cup (25 g) freshly grated Parmigiano-Reggiano cheese

CREOLE SHRIMP AND ANDOUILLE JAMBALAYA

Jambalaya (*jam-buh-LYE-uh* or *jum-buh-LYE-uh*) is a rice dish of Spanish influence interpreted first in the Caribbean and then reinterpreted by Cajun and Creole cooks as a spicy mixture of Louisiana ingredients. Even the origin of its colorful name originates from the mishmash of the Spanish word *jamón* and the French *jambon*, both meaning "ham," along with the French *à la*, which translates to "in the style of," and *ya*, thought to be an African word meaning "rice."

Variations on this ever-popular one-pot entrée are cooked throughout South Louisiana with wild game versions, as well as chicken and sausage versions in the rural countryside and seafood versions along the coast.

In fact, as is the case with many Louisiana dishes, there are two distinctly different styles of jambalaya in Louisiana: Creole (with tomatoes) and Cajun (without). Perhaps it is this dish that defines the two cultures. I subscribe to the often-quoted theory that Creole jambalaya was a compromise by Spanish cooks attempting to make paella in a strange new land where saffron was nowhere to be found. Bright red tomatoes became the substitute, adding color and flavor to a defining dish.

Preheat the oven to 375°F (190°C, or gas mark 5).

In a large cast-iron pot with a tight-fitting lid over medium-high heat, fry the bacon until done. Remove the bacon, drain on paper towels, and chop into pieces. Reserve for later use.

Pour off all but 2 tablespoons (26 g) of the bacon fat from the pot. Add the onions, celery, and bell peppers to the bacon grease and cook until the onions turn translucent, about 5 minutes. Add the garlic, rosemary, andouille, and tasso and continue to sauté until the meats just begin to brown, about 5 minutes. Deglaze the pot by pouring in the beer and scraping the bits from the bottom of the pot while stirring. Add the bacon pieces back to the pot, along with the shrimp and all of the chopped tomatoes, parsley, and green onions. Add the paprika, cayenne, a couple of shakes of hot sauce, and the salt and black pepper.

Add the rice to the pot and stir until evenly distributed. Add the seafood stock and stir again. Cover the pot and bake in the oven for 1 hour. Do not stir or even raise the lid on the pot for that 1 hour. In that hour, all the flavors are melding, and the rice is cooking. At the end of the hour, take a peek, but do not stir. Make sure most of the stock has been absorbed and taste to see if the rice is cooked to at least al dente. When it is, turn off the oven, cover the pot, and leave it in the oven for another 20 minutes. Serve with crusty bread and ice-cold beer.

SERVES 4 TO 6

4 strips (1 ounce, or 28 g each) of smoked bacon, chopped

2 cups (320 g) diced yellow onion

2 cups (240 g) diced celery

1 cup (150 g) diced green bell pepper

1 cup (150 g) diced red bell pepper

2 tablespoons (20 g) minced garlic

3 tablespoons (6 g) chopped fresh rosemary

2 cups (16 ounces, or 455 g) sliced andouille sausage

1 cup (150 g) diced tasso (preferably) or smoked ham

1 cup (235 ml) beer

2 pounds (900 g) jumbo (16/20 count) shrimp, peeled, tail-on, and deveined

1 cup (180 g) chopped tomatoes

1 cup (150 g) yellow cherry tomatoes, halved

1 can (10 ounces, or 280 g) mild diced tomatoes with green chiles, drained

1 cup (60 g) chopped flat-leaf parsley

1 cup (100 g) diced green onion tops

2 teaspoons (5 g) smoked paprika

1 teaspoon cayenne pepper

Dash of hot sauce

1 teaspoon kosher salt

2 teaspoons (4 g) freshly ground black pepper

4 cups (632 g) long-grain white rice

4 cups (945 ml) seafood stock (page 55)

SWEET CORN SOUP

To me, there is something bold and regal about a freshly picked ear of yellow corn. It stands tall, wrapped tightly in a husky robe with a scruffy little tuft of brown "hair" poking out from the crown. Peeling back the layers and removing the strands of silk reveal a golden treasure chest of nuggets of tightly packed flavor. Scraping those corn kernels away from the cob as the milky juices release is a sweet prize reserved only for those in the know.

Truth be told, there is nothing mysterious about my corn soup, but I can tell you that there is something very special about the ingredients in it. The hands of Louisiana farmers harvested these ears of corn, and I can taste the quality—and the love. I urge you to make it with adherence to its simplicity and to stay true to the goodness of its fresh ingredients.

With a sharp knife, cut the corn from the husks as close to the cob as you can. Place the corn kernels in a bowl.

In a cast-iron pot over medium-high heat, melt the butter. Add the onions and celery. Stir the mixture and cook just until the onions turn translucent, about 5 minutes. Add the garlic, thyme, and corn. Stir until the corn begins to soften and then add the sugar, white pepper, cayenne, and the chicken stock. Season with salt to taste. Bring to a boil and then immediately lower the heat to a simmer. Add the half-and-half and continue cooking until the soup begins to thicken, about 35 minutes. Remove from the heat, pour into a heatproof bowl, and let cool.

Pour the cooled soup into a blender, up to the halfway point. Blend on high speed until completely smooth. Pour the mixture back into the pot. Repeat until all the soup is blended. (Or if you have an immersion blender, use that right in the pot.)

Reheat the soup over medium-high heat until it reaches a simmer. Ladle the soup into individual bowls. Garnish each with a sprig of thyme and serve with crispy crackers.

SERVES 4

8 ears yellow corn, husks and silk removed

8 tablespoons (1 stick, or 112 g) unsalted butter

1 cup (160 g) diced yellow onion

1 cup (120 g) diced celery

1 tablespoon (10 g) minced garlic

1 tablespoon (2 g) chopped fresh thyme

1 teaspoon granulated sugar

1 teaspoon freshly ground white pepper

Pinch of cayenne pepper

1 cup (235 ml) chicken stock

Kosher salt

2 cups (475 ml) half-and-half

Fresh thyme sprigs

Crispy crackers

CAJUN PHO

I am fanatical when it comes to Vietnamese pho and decided on the name for this dish as an apt description. But truth be told, to call this dish Cajun pho doesn't do it justice. This is no watered-down fusion mishmash; its pungent and pork-intensive roots are firmly planted in French Acadian terroir. Pork neck bones, with their fatty morsels of meat simmering in a smoky ham hock–infused broth and thickened gently by gelatinous pig trotters, provide the backdrop for the holy trinity of onions, celery, and bell pepper. With the carrots, star anise, and whole cinnamon sticks that lend their fragrance to the intoxicating flavors of the soup, you will begin to understand the Asian influences taking root in Acadiana. And that's not all: Like a Vietnamese pho, it is topped at the table with slivered green onions, stems of parsley and cilantro, diced jalapeño, sweet peppers, and noodles. It's enough to make you weep—or at least cry out for another bowl. Please, just one more.

BROTH

In a large stockpot, combine all of the broth ingredients. Add enough water to cover the ingredients and come halfway up the side of the pot, 6 to 8 quarts (5.7 to 7.6 L). Bring to a boil and then lower the heat to a simmer. Cook until the pork neck bone meat is tender, about 1½ hours.

Skim the surface of any fat or scum. Strain the broth and refrigerate in a covered container until chilled. Place the pork neck bones, along with any meat picked from the pig's feet and ham hocks, in a bowl; refrigerate for later. Discard the skin, fat, bones, and vegetables.

SOUP

Remove the container with the broth from the refrigerator and with a spoon, remove the fat cap from the top of the broth. Pour the broth into a large pot over medium heat and bring to a simmer. Add back the pork neck bones and reserved meat. Taste the broth and season with salt. Skim any fat or foam from the broth and let simmer for about 10 minutes.

Meanwhile, make the fried garlic condiment by placing the fried garlic in a bowl and topping it with the oil, fish sauce, and sriracha to taste. Stir to combine and let sit to absorb the flavors.

For serving, add the noodles to the bottom of large individual bowls. Pour over the steaming hot broth, along with pieces of the neck bone and other pork meat.

Garnish by topping each bowl with carrots, green onions, parsley, cilantro, a wedge of lime, and jalapeño slices, along with a mini sweet pepper. Serve with the fried garlic condiment and more sriracha sauce to top each spoonful of this delicious soup.

SERVES 4 TO 6

BROTH

6 pounds (2.7 kg) pork neck bones

4 pig's feet

2 smoked ham hocks (6 ounces, or 170 g each)

2 large yellow onions, quartered

2 celery stalks, chopped

1 green bell pepper, quartered and seeds removed

1 cup (130 g) chopped carrot

10 star anise

4 cinnamon sticks

¼ cup (60 ml) fish sauce

SOUP

Kosher salt

6 tablespoons (84 g) fried garlic

2 tablespoons (28 ml) vegetable oil

1 teaspoon fish sauce

Sriracha sauce

6 cups (840 g) cooked noodles, such as rice noodles or thin spaghetti

2 large carrots, 1 cut into ribbons and 1 julienned

1 cup (100 g) chopped green onion tops

1 bunch of fresh flat-leaf parsley

1 bunch of fresh cilantro

1 lime, cut into wedges

1 fresh jalapeño pepper, sliced

4 to 6 red and yellow mini sweet peppers

CRAWFISH ÉTOUFFÉE

Étouffée is the best way I know to highlight the unique flavor and texture of Louisiana crawfish. This buttery mixture envelops the tail meat with a rich, flavor-filled coating of golden goodness. My method is simple and classic with an emphasis on freshness and quality ingredients. From time to time, I do use frozen cooked crawfish tails, but, in season, there is no substitute for fresh-picked tail meat. When eating boiled crawfish at a restaurant, I always save the shells and take home another 5-pound (2.3 kg) order. The next day, I remove and reserve the tail meat and wash all the heads and shells of excess spice. These shell pieces are simmered in a large pot of water to reduce to the intense, fat-infused, crawfish stock that is essential for a good étouffée.

In a large cast-iron pot or skillet over medium-high heat, melt the 2 sticks (225 g) of butter. Add the onions, bell pepper, and celery and sauté until the onions turn translucent, about 5 minutes. Add the garlic, lower the heat to simmer, and stir to combine. Sprinkle the flour over the mixture, stir to incorporate, and cook the flour until it turns light brown, about 10 minutes. Add the crawfish stock and stir until you reach a stew-like thickness.

Add the crawfish tail meat; stir the mixture to combine. Simmer the crawfish in the pot for 15 minutes. Add the cayenne and season to taste with salt, pepper, and hot sauce. As a final touch, stir in the remaining 1 tablespoon (14 g) butter, along with the chopped parsley and green onions. Bring the étouffée back to a simmer and turn off the heat.

Serve in shallow bowls by ladling the étouffée over a mound of white rice. Have plenty of hot French bread and extra hot sauce on the side.

TABLE TIP

It is best to peel your own crawfish, but packaged tail meat (Louisiana, of course) is a huge time-saver and works just fine. If you use the packaged, be sure to add a little water to the fat inside the bag to get all the flavor out.

SERVES 4 TO 6

1 cup (2 sticks, or 225 g) unsalted butter, plus 1 tablespoon (14 g)

2 cups (320 g) diced yellow onion

1 cup (150 g) diced green bell pepper

1 cup (120 g) diced celery

1 tablespoon (10 g) minced garlic

¼ cup (31 g) unbleached all-purpose flour

2½ cups (570 ml) crawfish stock or seafood stock (page 55)

2 pounds (900 g) Louisiana crawfish tail meat

1 teaspoon cayenne pepper

Kosher salt and freshly ground black pepper

Dash of hot sauce

¼ cup (15 g) chopped fresh flat-leaf parsley

1 cup (100 g) diced green onion tops

6 cups (948 g) cooked long-grain white rice

What's That?

Étouffée (*AY-too-fay*) is the crown jewel (along with gumbo) of Cajun/Creole dishes and one of the simplest. By language translation, it means "smothered," but to translate this recipe into a proper Cajun/Creole stew takes a deft hand and lots of seasoned experience. The most familiar version is made with crawfish, but shrimp is quite common as well. I've found the best étouffée is usually discovered not in the fancy restaurants, but rather in the least likely backroad cafés and lunchrooms of Acadiana.

WHOLE CATFISH IN CREOLE RED GRAVY

SERVES 4

Long ago, before modern aquaculture methods created a nationwide marketplace for catfish, eating the slippery bottom dwellers was reserved for those of us who lived below the Mason-Dixon line. Back then, buying pristine packaged white fillets of the fish at the local supermarket wasn't an option; we ate whole on-the-bone catfish.

As a son of the South, I recall fishing trotlines along the Pearl River and loading the boat with catfish. Skinning a mess of flatheads and blues for dinner was a grubby task, but the payoff was well worth the effort. Dining on crispy fried whole catfish and picking the morsels of sweet, flaky flesh off the bone made for perfection on a plate.

In Creole culture, folks still prefer the whole catfish, but with a twist. Instead of frying, these cats are cooked down in steamy red tomato gravy spiced with a heavy dose of cayenne, onions, and peppers. Spooned over a mound of white rice, it's fall-off-the-bone goodness in a bowl.

Heat the oil in a cast-iron pot with a lid over medium-high heat. Add the onions, celery, and bell peppers and sauté until the onions turn translucent, about 5 minutes. Add the garlic, parsley, and andouille and cook for 3 minutes. Add the wine and seafood stock, along with the whole tomatoes, diced tomatoes with chiles, and tomato paste. Stir to combine and bring to a boil.

Lower the heat to a simmer and add the roux and bay leaves. Stir in the salt, white pepper, and cayenne. Toss in the lemon slices. Cover and simmer for 30 minutes longer.

Uncover and stir and using the edge of the spoon, break up any large pieces of whole tomato. Add the catfish and cover them in the sauce. Simmer for another 45 minutes. Lift the lid and inspect to make sure the catfish is tender and easily pulls away from the bone with the tug of a fork. Sample the sauce and adjust the seasoning to your taste.

Remove the bay leaves.

For serving, remove the catfish from the pot and bone them. Use the back of a spoon to gently push the fillet away from the dorsal fin and use a fork or knife to slide the fillet off the vertebrae, discarding the bones. Ladle the Creole red gravy into bowls over the rice and top with portions of the catfish. Garnish with the green onions. Serve with crusty French bread and hot sauce on the side.

2 tablespoons (28 ml) vegetable oil

2 cups (320 g) diced yellow onion

2 cups (120 g) diced celery

1 cup (150 g) chopped green bell pepper

½ cup (75 g) chopped red bell pepper

1 tablespoon (10 g) minced garlic

½ cup (30 g) chopped flat-leaf parsley

1 cup (8 ounces, or 225 g) sliced andouille sausage (preferably) or smoked pork sausage

1 cup (235 ml) dry white wine

2 cups (475 ml) seafood stock (page 55)

1 can (28 ounces, or 785 g) whole peeled tomatoes

1 can (10 ounces, or 280 g) mild diced tomatoes with green chiles, drained

1 can (6 ounces, or 170 g) tomato paste

2 tablespoons (28 ml) dark roux (page 14)

2 bay leaves

1 tablespoon (8 g) kosher salt

1 tablespoon (6 g) freshly ground white pepper

1 teaspoon cayenne pepper

2 lemon slices

2 whole catfish (2 pounds, or 900 g each), skinned and cleaned with heads removed

4 cups (632 g) cooked long-grain white rice, such as Supreme brand

½ cup (50 g) diced green onion tops

A LITTLE LAGNIAPPE ON THE SIDE

CHAPTER

FOUR

THE CONCEPT OF LAGNIAPPE (*LON-yop* OR *LAN-yap*) IS A KEY TO UNDERSTANDING CAJUN CULTURE. IT IS A SIMPLE, OFTEN USED, CAJUN FRENCH TERM THAT MEANS "A LITTLE SOMETHING EXTRA." TO ME, IT REPRESENTS THE GENEROUS NATURE OF CAJUNS WHO LIKE TO SHARE THEIR GOD-GIVEN GIFTS.

Lagniappe in these pages means an extra sampling of the cuisine of South Louisiana that will help you to understand and appreciate what makes Acadiana so beautiful and unique. Small plates, dips, sides, sandwiches, appetizers, handheld snacks, party foods, and, of course, pickles are all at the heart of the joie de vivre that makes Cajun country so much fun. Every good cook in Acadiana has an arsenal of these explosively flavorful recipes that are either culinary traditions or creative expressions of the talent of the region.

As a cook, I appreciate the seasonality of food, and here in Acadiana we tend to define the year by food: Fall is for oysters, winter is for wild game, spring is for crawfish, and summer—well, that is for Creole tomatoes, Sugartown watermelon, sweet corn, shrimp, and crabs, too. But once the season fades, you miss those tastes. Preserving the seasonal best is where canning and pickling come in. And I've learned a trick or two.

My wife, Roxanne, tells stories of growing up on the prairie of Jeff Davis Parish in the western part of South Louisiana. The flatland is home to rice farming, and she has fond memories of swimming in the rice pumps along the parish highway north of Jennings. Her Paw Paw Fontenot was a proud farmer who had the only windmill on the stretch of road to Hathaway. Her grandmother was an expert at farm cooking, pickling, and crafting. My wife recalls how she always said that the way to stretch the harvest through to winter was "puttin' up what God blessed us with."

Cajun folks never waste a thing, and the Fontenot family added on a spare room to the main farmhouse that served as a canning pantry. The walls were lined with beets, zucchini, okra, peppers, cucumbers, and the like; anything and everything was saved for a bath of vinegary, sweet brine and wound up in a Ball jar.

SPICY PICKLED WATERMELON RIND

Pickled watermelon rind is seen throughout the Deep South, but leave it to Cajun cooks to introduce a fiery kick of heat to the mix. You can slice the rinds down to the white or leave a little of the pink melon for contrast. Some add green food coloring, but I prefer it au naturel. You really can't mess this up.

Place the watermelon rinds and salt in a large container with a lid. Add enough water to just cover the rinds. Stir until the salt has dissolved. Cover the container and refrigerate overnight.

The next day, remove the rinds from the refrigerator. Pour the rinds into a colander and rinse with cold water until all the salt is removed. Put the rinds in a large pot and cover with water. Bring the pot to a boil over high heat and then lower the heat to a simmer. Cook for 1 hour. Turn off the heat, drain the rinds, and transfer them to a container. Place in the refrigerator to cool.

Put the vinegar and sugar in a large pot over high heat. Bring the liquid to a boil and add the rinds. Once the water comes to a boil again, lower the heat to a simmer and add all of the spices, along with a dash of hot sauce. Cover the pot and simmer for 1 hour over low heat.

After an hour, the liquid should have reduced slightly and begun to thicken. The rinds should have a translucent pickle-like look. Pour the rinds, along with the pickling liquid, into a tightly lidded container and let come to room temperature.

At this point, you have two options. You can place the lidded container in the refrigerator and store your pickled rinds for a couple of months. If you want to keep them longer, I recommend you follow safe canning instructions for sterilizing in canning jars.

Serve these pickles with sandwiches or just for snacking. I like to make them a center of attraction on a well-stocked charcuterie board with various meats and sausages.

MAKES 2 QUARTS (1.9 L)

5 cups (750 g) watermelon rinds, cut into strips and cubes

1 cup (288 g) salt

2 quarts (1.9 L) apple cider vinegar

1½ cups (300 g) granulated sugar

3 tablespoons (15 g) coriander seeds

4 star anise

3 tablespoons (9 g) dill seeds

3 tablespoons (33 g) brown mustard seeds

3 tablespoons (33 g) yellow mustard seeds

3 tablespoons (18 g) ground allspice

4 bay leaves

3 tablespoons (15 g) white peppercorns

2 tablespoons (14 g) cardamom seeds

2 tablespoons (8 g) whole cloves

2 cinnamon sticks

1 tablespoon (4 g) red pepper flakes

Dash of hot sauce

ZUCCHINI PICKLES

Zucchini make excellent pickles, as do yellow summer squash and mirliton (chayote squash). Try this simple 1-2-3—brine, boil, and pickle—process on any of them. Feel free to vary the spice—either add more sweetness or add more hot sauce for an edgier layer of heat.

With a sharp knife, slice the zucchinis into rounds to your desired thickness.

Peel and slice the onions thinly. Put the zucchini and onions in a large bowl. Sprinkle the salt over the zucchini and onions and mix. Refrigerate for 1 hour.

In a saucepan over medium-high heat, combine the vinegars, sugar, spices, and hot sauce. Bring the ingredients to a boil. Remove the zucchini and onions from the refrigerator and rinse off the salt. Add the zucchini and onions to the saucepan. Once it resumes a boil, turn off the heat and let cool to room temperature.

Refrigerate the pickles and their liquid in a tightly covered container. If you plan to preserve your zucchini pickles, follow canning instructions carefully for sterilizing the canning jars.

MAKES 1½ QUARTS (1.4 L)

4 pounds (1.8 kg) zucchini

2 red onions

¼ cup (32 g) kosher salt

3 cups (700 ml) sugarcane vinegar

3 cups (700 ml) white vinegar

2 cups (400 g) granulated sugar

1 tablespoon (11 g) mustard seeds

1 tablespoon (5 g) black peppercorns

1 tablespoon (4 g) red pepper flakes

Dash of hot sauce

FRIED PICKLED OKRA WITH SRIRACHA MAYO

In the South, frying most anything is acceptable, and I am hard-pressed to find any ingredient that doesn't taste better in a crackling golden brown crust. Two of my favorite fried treats are cornmeal-coated okra and a platter of hot-and-crunchy fried dill pickles. When I thought about these together, a lightbulb went off and a flash of culinary brilliance came over me: fried pickled okra. Hey, why not? Add a spiced creamy dipping sauce to round out the flavor contrast and we're talking Deep Dixie, deep-fried goodness.

Pour out the okra pods into a colander set in a bowl. Transfer the pods from the colander to a cutting board, reserving the bowl of pickle juice for later. Slice each okra pod lengthwise through the middle, exposing the inside. Lay the pods on paper towels and let drain of excess pickling liquid.

Crack the eggs into a bowl and add the half-and-half and hot sauce. Whisk to combine to a batter consistency. Sift the flour into another bowl and remove any lumps. In a third bowl, combine the cornmeal and Cajun Seasoning Blend. Line up the three bowls. Toss the okra first in the flour mixture, then in the egg mixture, and finally in the cornmeal. Be sure to coat each piece evenly in the final coating. Place on a platter.

Meanwhile, make your dipping sauce by combining the mayonnaise and sriracha in a bowl. Add 2 tablespoons (28 ml) of the reserved pickled okra juice, along with the cayenne. Whisk the ingredients until fully incorporated. Pour into a serving bowl.

In a pot over medium-high heat, pour enough canola oil to submerge the okra. When the oil reaches a temperature of 375°F (190°C), you are ready to fry. Test the first okra pod in the oil to ensure that your grease is hot enough. Add the remaining okra pods in batches and fry until golden brown and crispy, about 3 to 5 minutes. Transfer to a wire rack set over paper towels and let any excess oil drain. Serve immediately with the sriracha dipping sauce.

SERVES 4

1 jar (16 ounces, or 454 g) pickled okra (at least 12 whole okra pods)

2 large eggs

¼ cup (60 ml) half-and-half

Dash of hot sauce

1 cup (125 g) unbleached all-purpose flour

1 cup (140 g) yellow cornmeal

2 tablespoons (20 g) Cajun Seasoning Blend (page 13)

1 cup (225 g) mayonnaise

¼ cup (60 g) sriracha sauce

2 tablespoons (28 ml) dill pickle juice

1 teaspoon cayenne pepper

Canola oil, for frying

SPICY CREOLE SHRIMP DIP

Certain traditions make family gatherings special. And, of course, in the Graham family, those traditions involve food. My brother Jackie's shrimp dip is based on a traditional Creole rémoulade. While similar to that sauce, the base of this dip is a zestier version infused with extra horseradish, Creole mustard, and hot sauce. As with any combination, you can adjust the ingredients to your taste, but I urge you to follow this one to a tee the first time out. This dip is guaranteed to clear up any sinus problem you might have, and I can assure you it is also addictive. Thank you, brother.

★ ★ ★ ★ ★

Fill a large pot to the halfway point with cold water and add the eggs. Turn the burner to high and bring the water to a boil and then immediately turn off the heat. Cover the pot and let sit for 12 minutes. Remove the hard-boiled eggs from the water (keep the water in the pot) and rinse the eggs under cold water. Peel the eggs and dice. Place the diced eggs in a bowl, cover, and refrigerate.

Bring the same pot of water back to a boil over high heat. Add the shrimp. Bring the water back to a boil and cook for about 5 minutes. Remove one of the larger shrimp and test for doneness. If fully cooked, turn off the heat. Immediately drain the shrimp in a colander. Rinse with cold water to stop the carryover cooking, drain again, and pat with paper towels to dry. Place in the refrigerator to cool.

Combine the Creole mustard, horseradish, canola oil, and lemon juice in a large bowl. Add the onions, bell pepper, and celery and stir. Add the diced eggs and stir to distribute evenly throughout the mixture. Add salt, pepper, and hot sauce to your taste.

Make sure the shrimp are dry or your dip will be watery. Add the shrimp and stir to distribute evenly throughout the mixture. Cover and refrigerate until chilled (or up to overnight).

For serving, fill a bowl with the dip and place on a tray surrounded by Ritz crackers.

What's That?

Rémoulade (*RIM-a-lod* or *ROM-a-lod*) is a cold, mayonnaise-based sauce preparation. The Louisiana version of the classic French sauce is infused with lots of spicy flavors. You can't make a respectable Louisiana rémoulade without horseradish and Creole mustard. There are many variations, from the classic white rémoulade of the fine Creole restaurants of the French Quarter to spicier Cajun versions seen along the bayou.

MAKES ABOUT 6 CUPS

4 large eggs

2 pounds (900 g) small (61/70 count) shrimp, peeled and deveined

1 jar (16 ounces, or 455 g) Creole mustard or other coarse-grained mustard

1 jar (5¼ ounces, or 150 g) prepared horseradish

1 cup (235 ml) canola oil

1 tablespoon (15 ml) freshly squeezed lemon juice

1 cup (160 g) finely diced yellow onion

1 cup (150 g) finely diced green bell pepper

1 cup (120 g) finely diced celery

Kosher salt and freshly ground black pepper

Dash of hot sauce

Ritz crackers

TABLE TIPS

★ Make sure you use pure prepared horseradish and not the mayo-like creamy stuff.

★ The recipe is easy to scale up by doubling or tripling all of the ingredients.

★ You can make this ahead and it will keep for at least a week. In fact, it is even better if made at least 2 days before serving.

FRIED OYSTER AND CRAWFISH CAESAR SALAD

Caesar salad is a thing of beauty, but finding a well-made Caesar these days is next to impossible. The chaining of American restaurants has led to all sorts of tame and lame versions of America's classic dishes, and my beloved Caesar is one of the casualties.

In this version, I return to the basics and put a South Louisiana spin on it. I adhere to classic Caesar rules but for three additions—smoked oysters, fresh Louisiana oysters, and crawfish. I supplement my anchovy-infused dressing with the addition of canned smoked oysters to add a briny, smoky flavor. And crowning the salad with crisp, fried Louisiana oysters and crawfish tails is a no-brainer.

CAESAR SALAD AND DRESSING

Leave a few of the lettuce leaves whole and tear the rest into bite-size pieces. Place in a bowl and refrigerate.

To coddle the eggs, put the eggs in a pot of water and bring to a boil. Immediately turn off the heat and let the eggs cook for no more than 1 minute. Remove the eggs and rinse under cold water. Peel the eggs and scoop out the cooked whites and the runny yolks into the container of a blender.

Add all of the anchovies, along with their oil, and one-half of the drained smoked oysters to the blender container. Add the Worcestershire, Creole mustard, and Tabasco and squeeze in the lemon juice, removing any seeds. Add 2 tablespoons (10 g) of the Parmigiano-Reggiano cheese. Turn the blender on low.

While the blender is on low, drizzle in the olive oil until an emulsion forms and all the ingredients are incorporated. Taste the dressing for balance and flavor and season with salt and pepper as desired. Add more olive oil to round out the flavors and thin out the dressing, if needed.

FRIED OYSTERS AND CRAWFISH

In a pot or skillet over medium-high heat, bring the canola oil to a temperature of 375°F (190°C).

Beat the eggs in a medium bowl. In another bowl, stir together the cornmeal, flour, and Cajun Seasoning Blend. Toss the oysters gently in the eggs to coat them and then toss in the cornmeal to coat them evenly. Add the oysters to the hot oil and fry until golden brown, about 3 to 5 minutes. Remove and drain on paper towels. Sprinkle lightly with salt.

Add the crawfish tails to the bowl with the eggs and then toss them into the bowl with the cornmeal to coat evenly. Add the crawfish to the hot oil and fry until golden brown, about 3 to 5 minutes. Remove and drain on paper towels. Sprinkle lightly with salt.

SERVES 4

CAESAR SALAD AND DRESSING

2 heads of romaine lettuce

4 large eggs

1 tin (2 ounces, or 55 g) flat anchovies

1 tin (3½ ounces, or 100 g) smoked oysters, drained

¼ cup (60 g) Worcestershire sauce

2 tablespoons (42 g) Creole mustard or other coarse-grained mustard

2 teaspoons (10 ml) Tabasco sauce

1 large lemon, halved

1½ cups (150 g) freshly grated Parmigiano-Reggiano cheese, divided

1½ cups (355 ml) extra-virgin olive oil, plus more as needed

Kosher salt and freshly ground black pepper

2 cups (60 g) croutons

1 cup (150 g) yellow cherry tomatoes, halved

FRIED OYSTERS AND CRAWFISH

4 cups (946 ml) canola oil

3 large eggs

2 cups (275 g) cornmeal

1 cup (125 g) unbleached all-purpose flour

2 tablespoons (20 g) Cajun Seasoning Blend (page 13)

12 oysters

Kosher salt

1 pound (455 g) Louisiana crawfish tails

TABLE TIPS

★ Find a high-quality Parmigiano-Reggiano, not the stuff in the green can. The same with the croutons—it's ridiculously easy to make your own, and once you do, you will never use store-bought again.

★ The coddled (between raw and soft-boiled) eggs are classic but optional.

★ This recipe makes more dressing than you will need, so save the rest for your next Caesar.

For assembling the salad, remove the torn lettuce from the refrigerator and with paper towels, dry up any moisture that has accumulated at the bottom of the bowl. Add the croutons. Pour over just enough of the dressing to coat the lettuce. Add half of the remaining cheese. With two large spoons, toss the lettuce and the croutons with the dressing. Add more dressing if needed or reserve the remaining dressing for another use. Sprinkle on the remaining cheese and a grind of black pepper.

On individual chilled dinner plates, arrange the whole romaine leaves and the dressed greens and croutons. Place several of the sliced cherry tomatoes around the plate and top with several of the fried oysters and crawfish.

CHEESY BEEF AND POTATO SKILLET

This beefed-up skillet sauté with the Cajun holy trinity of aromatic vegetables will appeal to the hearty meat-and-potatoes crowd. Think nachos meets potato skins with some spinach dip thrown in for good measure—my three favorite snack foods in one steaming hot pan. The fried potato rounds are just big enough to scoop up a mouthful of cayenne-spiced beef and onions topped with the melted pepper Jack. Another ice-cold beer, please.

Preheat the oven to 400°F (200°C, or gas mark 6).

Heat 2 tablespoons (28 ml) of the oil in a 10-inch (25 cm) cast-iron skillet with a tight-fitting lid over medium-high heat. Add the potato rounds and cook until browned on both sides and cooked through. Transfer to a paper towel–lined platter to drain away any excess oil. Sprinkle with salt and pepper and keep warm.

To the same skillet over medium-high heat, add the remaining 2 tablespoons (28 ml) oil along with the onions, bell pepper, and celery. Sauté until the onions turn translucent, about 5 minutes. Add the ground meat and the garlic; season with cayenne and a dash of hot sauce. Once the meat and onions are browned, after about 8 minutes, add the spinach and beer. Cover and let the steam cook down the spinach, about 5 minutes.

Remove the cover and let the beer cook away. Lower the heat, add the jalapeño peppers, and sprinkle the pepper Jack cheese around the outer edge of the pan. Add the potato rounds around the edges of the pan and bake for 12 minutes or until the cheese is melted. Serve straight from the skillet, with ice-cold beer.

SERVES 4 TO 6

4 tablespoons (60 ml) vegetable oil, divided

2 large russet potatoes, sliced into rounds

Kosher salt and freshly ground black pepper

1 large yellow onion, chopped into bite-size chunks

1 large red bell pepper, seeded and chopped into bite-size chunks

1 celery stalk, chopped

1 pound (456 g) ground beef

1 tablespoon (10 g) minced garlic

1 teaspoon cayenne pepper

Dash of hot sauce

1 cup (30 g) fresh spinach leaves, stemmed

¼ cup (60 ml) beer

2 tablespoons (18 g) pickled jalapeño pepper slices with juice

2 cups (230 g) freshly grated pepper Jack cheese

What's That?

The holy trinity: The French have their mirepoix, the Spanish have their sofrito, and South Louisiana has the holy trinity—celery, onions, and green bell pepper. It is the foundation of most every Cajun recipe. I don't know the origin of the colorful name for these base ingredients (some say it was Chef Paul Prudhomme), but it certainly connects back to the Catholic traditions and religious culture of the area. And you would be hard-pressed not to find a refrigerator full of those three primary vegetables in any Cajun kitchen. Slicing and dicing the holy trinity is an essential skill in learning to cook Cajun.

TABLE TIP

This recipe is perfect for a 10-inch (25 cm) pan, so scale the ingredients up if your pan is larger.

CRAWFISH-STUFFED BEET-BOILED EGGS

I lay this egg platter out on the buffet table early before Easter dinner, but it is just as tasty any time of year. A crawfish-laced stuffing piped into the crevice of a perfectly boiled egg is tasty and colorful enough, but dyeing these eggs beforehand in a bath of beet juice is divine. It's quite simple; the only problem is in controlling how many of these your guests stuff down before the main meal hits the table.

Fill a large pot halfway with water, add the eggs, and cover. Bring to a boil over high heat. Once the water begins boiling, turn off the heat and cover; let the eggs sit in the water for 12 minutes. Drain and rinse the eggs under cold water until cooled. Peel each egg by cracking on all sides and ends and rolling the cracked egg gently between the palms of your hands to loosen the shell. The egg should peel easily. Repeat with the remaining eggs.

Stack the eggs in a narrow upright glass container or jar. Pour over the red pickling liquid from the jar of beets (reserve the beets for another use) until all of the eggs are submerged. Cover the container and let sit for about 1 hour, gently shaking every 15 minutes to evenly redistribute the beet juice around the eggs. (Note: The longer you let the eggs sit, the deeper the red juice will penetrate the whites.)

Drain the beet juice from the container. Transfer the eggs to a cutting board, being careful not to spill any juice onto your counter. Slice the eggs in half lengthwise and transfer the yolks to a large bowl. Reserve the dyed, egg white halves.

Remove the par-cooked crawfish tails from the package and place in a saucepan with just enough water to cover the crawfish. Over high heat, bring the water to a simmer and then turn off the heat. Drain the crawfish and reserve 16 of the whole tails for garnish. Finely chop the remaining crawfish tails and add to the bowl with the egg yolks. Mix in the mayonnaise, Creole mustard, paprika, celery salt, and green onions.

Reserve some of the dill fronds for garnish and finely chop the remaining dill. Add the chopped dill to the bowl. Add a dash of hot sauce and mix. Season with salt and pepper to taste.

For serving, neatly scoop a generous portion of the egg and crawfish mixture into the egg white halves; be careful to leave a clean edge around the white. Place the stuffed halves on a white platter. Crown each with a whole crawfish tail and a feathery dill frond. Serve at room temperature.

SERVES 8

8 large eggs

1 jar (16 ounces, or 455 g) pickled red beets

1 pound (455 g) Louisiana crawfish tail meat

1 cup (225 g) mayonnaise

1 tablespoon (21 g) Creole mustard or other coarse-grained mustard

1 teaspoon smoked paprika

1 teaspoon celery salt

2 tablespoons (12 g) finely diced green onion tops

1 small bunch of fresh dill

Dash of hot sauce

Kosher salt and freshly ground black pepper

TABLE TIP

Be forewarned: Red beet juice will stain anything it comes into contact with, including your hands and your counter. Wear disposable gloves and work in the sink to prevent staining.

BEER-BATTERED GROUPER CHEEKS WITH SWEET POTATO CHIPS

I like to call this dish "cheeks and chips": my Cajun take on English fish and chips. Off-shore fishermen know the morsels of flaky white meat hiding in the head of a big grouper are good eating. With a dredge in a beer-soaked batter, these cheeks fry up golden brown. And when combined with a mound of crispy sweet potato chips, well, all you need is another ice-cold beer.

Combine the flour, baking powder, Cajun Seasoning Blend, and salt in a large bowl. Slowly add the beer while whisking to combine and to eliminate any lumps. Add the fish to the batter and gently toss to coat.

Fill a large pot filled with oil and bring to a temperature of 350°F (180°C). One at a time, carefully add the battered fish cheeks. Do not crowd the pot or they will stick together. Fry until the pieces are golden brown and crispy, about 6 to 8 minutes. Drain on a wire rack and season with salt immediately. Once all the fish is fried, move them to a platter and keep warm.

For the potato chips, add the sweet potato slices to the hot oil. Fry until golden brown and crispy, about a minute or two. Remove and drain on paper towels and season with salt immediately.

Serve the fish and chips with lemon wedges, your favorite dipping sauce, and malt vinegar, if you like.

SERVES 4

1½ cups (188 g) unbleached all-purpose flour

1 teaspoon baking powder

1 tablespoon (10 g) Cajun Seasoning Blend (page 13)

1 teaspoon salt, plus more to taste

1½ cups (355 ml) beer, chilled

2 pounds (900 g) grouper cheeks (about 24)

Canola oil, for frying

4 large sweet potatoes, sliced into very thin rounds

Lemon wedges

TABLE TIPS

★ Any good seafood market should be able to source grouper cheeks, but if you cannot, any firm white fish fillet will be a good substitute.

★ Sweet potatoes are dense in texture, so slice them very thinly to fry crispy. Make more chips than you think you will need—they are addictive.

SAVORY MIRLITON PANCAKES WITH CAJUN SOY DIPPING SAUCE

I first discovered this Korean savory pancake technique at the Covington, Louisiana, farmers' market. The zucchini version I tasted had folks lined up for it, and my Cajun combination featuring Louisiana mirliton squash will have your guests salivating for more. Make plenty. And be sure to experiment with other julienned vegetables using this technique.

CAJUN SOY DIPPING SAUCE

Combine the garlic, green onions, soy sauce, Worcestershire, and honey in a bowl. Stir to combine. Taste and add hot sauce to your desired level of heat. This sauce should be prepared at least 1 hour before serving, covered, and refrigerated.

MIRLITON PANCAKES

Put the mirliton, green onions, carrots, and jalapeño pepper in a large bowl and stir to combine.

Put the flour in a large bowl. In a small bowl, whisk together the egg and ½ cup (120 ml) of the cold water. Add to the flour. Add the Cajun Seasoning Blend. Continue whisking and add more of the cold water until the batter thins out to a liquid that will just coat the back of a spoon.

Add enough oil to a large nonstick pan to coat the bottom and place over medium-high heat. Once the oil is hot, spread one-quarter of the vegetable mixture evenly across the bottom of the pan. Ladle in enough of the batter to just barely spread over all of the vegetables. Let it cook until browned, about 5 minutes, and flip to the other side. Brown on that side and slide the pancake onto a plate and keep warm. Repeat with the remaining ingredients to make 4 pancakes. Sprinkle lightly with salt.

With a sharp knife or scissors, cut the pancakes into 4 equal-size wedges and stack on the platter. Serve with the Cajun Soy Dipping Sauce on the side.

SERVES 4 TO 6

CAJUN SOY DIPPING SAUCE

1 teaspoon finely minced garlic

1 teaspoon finely diced green onion tops

½ cup (120 ml) soy sauce

1 tablespoon (15 g) Worcestershire sauce

1 teaspoon honey

Dash of hot sauce

MIRLITON PANCAKES

1 mirliton (chayote squash), seeded and julienned

1 cup (100 g) diced green onion tops

½ cup (65 g) julienned carrot

1 tablespoon (9 g) chopped fresh jalapeño pepper

1 cup (125 g) unbleached all-purpose flour

1 large egg, beaten

1 cup (235 ml) cold water, divided

1 tablespoon (10 g) Cajun Seasoning Blend (page 13)

Canola oil, for frying

Kosher salt

What's That?

Mirliton (*merl-uh-TAWN* or *mel-e-TAWN*) is technically a chayote squash, with roots in Latin America. It's a pear-shaped, green squash used in many Cajun and Creole dishes. Mostly stuffed with crab or shrimp dressing, mirliton is often seen on holiday tables. Over the years, it has found a prominent place in Acadiana cuisine.

CHIC STEAK SANDWICH

In 1946, my father's restaurant in Bogalusa, Louisiana—the Acme Café—was the epitome of a sleepy small-town diner but for one big difference: It was located across the street from one of the nation's largest paper mills, employing more than 4,000 hungry workers. The Acme was a 24-hour, 7-days-a-week operation, and for breakfast, lunch, dinner, and the hours in between, my father served up Southern specialties that developed a wide following.

One of the most popular items on the menu—the Chic Steak Sandwich—was invented out of necessity. Chicken fried steak was a popular menu item, but in those days, the cost of beef put a sandwich version out of reach. Pork was the answer. Cutting ¾-inch-thick (2 cm) slices of the lower-priced pork loin and running them twice through a tenderizing machine created a magnificent sandwich cut—tender, tasty, and huge. Fried with a dredge of flour and simple seasonings and served on a sesame bun along with a slather of mayo and pickle slices, the Chic Steak Sandwich was a big hit.

SERVES 4

2 quarts (1.9 L) canola oil

2 cups (250 g) unbleached all-purpose flour

2 tablespoons (20 g) Cajun Seasoning Blend (page 13)

4 slices of pork loin (¾ inch, or 2 cm thick), tenderized

Kosher salt and freshly ground black pepper

4 large sesame seed buns

1 cup (225 g) mayonnaise

2 cups (144 g) shredded iceberg lettuce

8 slices of ripe tomato

1 cup (143 g) dill pickle rounds

In a large skillet over medium-high heat, begin heating the oil. Combine the flour and Cajun Seasoning Blend in a shallow bowl.

Sprinkle the pork loin slices with salt and pepper; dredge in the flour to coat each side thoroughly, removing any excess.

Once the oil reaches 350°F (180°C), add the pork loin slices and fry until golden brown on each side. Transfer to a paper towel–lined platter and keep warm.

For assembly, open the buns and slather both halves with mayonnaise; add the shredded lettuce and 2 tomato slices, along with some pickle slices, to the bottom half. Top with the fried pork loin and close the sandwich. Serve with potato chips or French fries.

TABLE TIP

Buy boneless pork loin chops and ask your butcher to run them through the tenderizer twice, rotating the chops 90 degrees on the second pass.

CRAB, SPINACH, AND ARTICHOKE DIP

Spinach and artichoke dip is always a crowd favorite, but adding lump blue crabmeat brings a touch of elegance that will leave you happy to be singing the blues. Hot, creamy, and stepped up with just enough heat to get your undivided attention, this dip works in pitch-perfect, three-part harmony: Wilted spinach, chunky artichoke hearts, and succulent blue crab make sweet music in a black iron skillet.

Preheat the oven to 450°F (230°C, or gas mark 8).

Heat the oil and butter in a 10-inch (25 cm) cast-iron skillet over medium-high heat. Add the onions, bell pepper, and celery and cook just until the onions turn translucent, about 5 minutes. Add the parsley and minced garlic and stir to combine. Sprinkle the flour over the vegetables and cook for 3 minutes, stirring constantly. Add the half-and-half and continue stirring as the mixture thickens. Add the spinach and artichokes, stirring until the spinach begins to wilt into the hot liquid. Season with the white pepper, granulated garlic, Cajun Seasoning Blend, a dash of hot sauce, and salt and pepper to taste. Add the pepper Jack cheese and stir. Continue cooking until the cheese is melted and all is combined, about 5 minutes.

At this point, you will see just how thick the mixture is and be able to adjust accordingly. It should be thick enough (not runny) to be scooped up with a tortilla chip. If too thick, thin the mixture by gradually adding the cream until it thins out. If too thin, thicken by mixing equal parts of cornstarch and water to make a slurry and add the slurry to the mixture.

Add the crabmeat to the skillet and stir it into the spinach mixture, trying not to break up the lumps.

Bake until the dip is bubbling hot, about 12 minutes. Serve right away with tortilla chips or crackers.

TABLE TIPS

★ Be sure to make this in a cast-iron skillet. The heavy iron retains more heat than a regular pan, keeping the dip hot for much longer.

★ My recipe is moderately spicy. If you like it even hotter, try adding some diced jalapeño peppers and an extra dash of hot sauce.

SERVES 6 TO 10

1 tablespoon (15 ml) olive oil

1 tablespoon (14 g) unsalted butter

2 cups (320 g) diced yellow onion

1 cup (150 g) diced green bell pepper

1 cup (120 g) diced celery

½ cup (30 g) chopped flat-leaf parsley

1 tablespoon (10 g) minced garlic

½ cup (63 g) unbleached all-purpose flour

2 cups (475 ml) half-and-half

1 pound (455 g) fresh spinach leaves

2 cans (12 ounces, or 340 g) whole artichoke hearts packed in water, drained

1 teaspoon freshly ground white pepper

1 teaspoon granulated garlic

1 tablespoon (10 g) Cajun Seasoning Blend (page 13)

Dash of hot sauce

Kosher salt and freshly ground black pepper

2 cups (230 g) freshly grated pepper Jack cheese

1 cup (235 ml) heavy cream, or as needed

2 tablespoons (16 g) cornstarch

2 tablespoons (28 ml) cold water

8 ounces (225 g) white lump crabmeat, picked over for shells and cartilage

CRAWFISH POTATO SKINS

So, here's the thing: Baked potato artistry is not as simple as it appears. Do it right and it is sublime; skip a few steps and you fall short. Just find a large russet potato, scrub it, oil it, poke it, wrap it, and bake it in a hot oven. It's pretty straightforward, huh?

Down on the bayou, we have a take on the term *loaded* that sends this simple spud soaring into the high heavens. Crawfish is that singular ingredient that defines good Cajun cooking, and when baked inside a creamy, cheesy potato, it's time to lock and load. With this multilayered method, I combine the interior of the baked potatoes with butter, cheese, and the rich fat of plump Louisiana crawfish tail meat. Then it's all stuffed inside the hollowed-out potato skins and baked again. This is one savory, saucy mouthful, superb as a two-bite party snack or a side dish with a grilled ribeye. No half-baked idea here: Give it a try and you'll never look at a baked potato the same way again.

Preheat the oven to 350°F (180°C, or gas mark 4).

Using a fork, poke a few holes in each side of the potatoes to allow moisture to escape during cooking. Slice in half vertically, coat the potatoes with the olive oil, and put the two halves back together. Wrap the potatoes individually in aluminum foil. Bake until completely tender, about 1 hour.

Unwrap and scoop out the inside flesh of the potato halves without breaking through the outer skin. Chop the flesh of the potatoes into small pieces. Keep warm.

Increase the oven temperature to 400°F (200°C, or gas mark 6) and line a baking sheet with parchment paper. Melt the butter in a skillet over medium-high heat. Add the onions, celery, and green onions. Cook until the onions turn translucent, about 5 minutes. Add the garlic, Cajun Seasoning Blend, and hot sauce. Season to taste with salt and pepper. Turn off the heat and add the crawfish tails, along with the scooped-out potato flesh. Mix thoroughly to combine, add the cheddar cheese and sour cream, and mix again. Stuff the crawfish mixture into the potato shells and place on the prepared baking sheet. Bake until the cheese is melted and the tops begin to brown, about 30 minutes.

Serve on a platter with extra hot sauce on the side.

SERVES 4

4 small baking potatoes

1 tablespoon (15 ml) olive oil

8 tablespoons (1 stick, or 112 g) unsalted butter

½ cup (80 g) diced yellow onion

½ cup (60 g) diced celery

2 tablespoons (12 g) diced green onion tops

1 teaspoon minced garlic

1 tablespoon (10 g) Cajun Seasoning Blend (page 13)

Dash of hot sauce

Kosher salt and freshly ground black pepper

1 pound (455 g) Louisiana crawfish tail meat

1 cup (115 g) shredded Cheddar cheese

2 tablespoons (30 g) sour cream

TABLE TIPS

★ The small russet potatoes make this version perfect for a party, but with large potatoes, this becomes an entrée portion.

★ Packaged crawfish tails have added flavor—juice and fat—inside the bag. Be sure to scoop it all out and add it to your potato mixture. If you can't find crawfish tails, you can substitute shrimp.

BROILED MARINATED CRAB CLAWS

Cracked open to reveal the morsel of sweet meat hidden inside, the upper pincher portion of the Louisiana blue crab claw is a delicacy found throughout the coastal region. One-pound containers packed with these little fingers of crabmeat are sold everywhere, and most seafood restaurant menus feature a platter of fried crab claws at the top of the appetizer column. But these claws are different. They'll grab your full attention with a pool of spicy, anchovy-infused, garlicky marinade, and then pull you in with a dusting of Parmesan cheese and a quick run under the broiler. Crack open another cold beer and dive in.

Place all of the ingredients except for the Parmesan cheese in a large bowl and combine. Cover and chill for 2 hours, stirring every 30 minutes.

Preheat the oven to broil.

Place the crab claws and their marinating liquid in a large ovenproof skillet. Sprinkle evenly with the Parmesan cheese and place under the broiler on the highest rack. Watch carefully as the marinating liquid begins to sizzle and the cheese melts, about 3 to 5 minutes. Remove and serve immediately with ice-cold beer and French bread for sopping up the sauce.

TABLE TIP

Cracked blue crab claws are readily available in most seafood markets (or you can order them from your local fishmonger), but feel free to crack your own. Also feel free to try this recipe with king crab legs or stone crab claws.

SERVES 4

½ cup (120 ml) olive oil

Juice of 1 large lemon

¼ cup (25 g) diced green onion tops

1 tablespoon (9 g) capers, coarsely chopped

1 tablespoon (2 g) fresh thyme leaves

1 tablespoon (15 g) Worcestershire sauce

1 tablespoon (21 g) Creole mustard or other coarse-ground mustard

1 teaspoon minced garlic

1 teaspoon finely minced anchovy

1 teaspoon red pepper flakes

1 teaspoon Cajun Seasoning Blend (page 13)

Dash of hot sauce

Freshly ground black pepper

1 pound (455 g) cracked blue crab claws

2 tablespoons (10 g) freshly grated Parmesan cheese

PECAN-CRUSTED OYSTERS WITH MEYER LEMON AIOLI

I love the versatility in taste and texture of briny Louisiana oysters. Baked, stewed, flame-grilled in their shell, or just plain raw, oysters can take on a variety of flavors. But when battered with cornmeal laced with finely ground toasted pecans, fried to a crispy golden brown, and dipped in a fragrant lemon-kissed aioli, oysters become addictive. I love the bright taste of Meyer lemon here, but regular lemon will work as well.

MEYER LEMON AIOLI

Place the egg yolks, both mustards, garlic, rosemary, and lemon juice in a food processor. Pulse until combined and then slowly drizzle in the olive oil while processing. Use just enough of the olive oil to form a smooth emulsion and then turn off the processor. Season with salt and white pepper to taste. Cover and refrigerate until ready to serve.

PECAN-CRUSTED OYSTERS

Fill a pot halfway with oil, set over medium-high heat, and bring to 375°F (190°C).

Combine the cornmeal, flour, pecans, and Cajun Seasoning Blend in a medium bowl. Add the oysters and coat on all sides with the dry mixture. Add them a few at a time to the hot oil, but do not crowd the pot. Once crispy and golden brown on both sides, about 4 to 5 minutes total, transfer to a paper towel–lined platter. Keep warm and repeat until all the oysters are fried.

Serve immediately by mounding the oysters on a platter with a bowl of the Meyer Lemon Aioli on the side for dipping. Squeeze the lemon wedges over the oysters and garnish with the rosemary sprig.

TABLE TIPS

★ Toast your pecans in a cast-iron skillet over medium heat, or in a 350°F (180°C) oven, until they darken slightly and smell aromatic.

★ If you are not a fan of using raw eggs, then make this sauce by eliminating the eggs and olive oil and add the seasonings to a base of 1 cup (225 g) jarred mayonnaise.

SERVES 4 TO 6

MEYER LEMON AIOLI

4 egg yolks

1½ tablespoons (23 g) Dijon mustard

1½ tablespoons (32 g) Creole mustard or other coarse-ground mustard

1 teaspoon finely minced garlic

1 tablespoon (2 g) finely minced fresh rosemary

¼ cup (60 ml) freshly squeezed Meyer lemon juice

¾ cup (175 ml) extra-virgin olive oil

Kosher salt and freshly ground white pepper

PECAN-CRUSTED OYSTERS

Canola oil, for frying

1 cup (140 g) yellow cornmeal

½ cup (63 g) unbleached all-purpose flour

½ cup (48 g) finely ground toasted pecans

1 tablespoon (10 g) Cajun Seasoning Blend (page 13)

36 oysters in the shell

Meyer lemon wedges

Fresh rosemary sprigs

SOFTSHELL CRAB BÁNH MÌ

For obvious reason, here in South Louisiana, a bánh mì sandwich is referred to as a Vietnamese po'boy. It doesn't take a great stretch of the imagination to see the similarities in the two sandwiches, both built upon a similar French bread loaf. But delving deeper, the two have even more in common than just bread.

Like the early French Acadians coming to Louisiana in the late 1700s, a century later the French came to Vietnam during the Indochine era of 1887 to 1946. Their influence on the culinary culture of Southeast Asia was unmistakable. French bread baking, and the introduction of cooking methods for dishes such as liver pâté and even mayonnaise, became intermingled with local tastes and techniques. Like the Cajun and Creole cultures of Acadiana, over time unique recipes linking the two cultures became mainstream—the bánh mì sandwich being a prime example.

Bánh mì is Vietnamese for "bread," and the use of the ubiquitous French baguette led to its current sandwich interpretation. The classic bánh mì is a combination of meat—usually pork—with a slathering of pâté, crowned with pickled vegetables and fresh herbs.

For my Cajun version, I'm going with a focus on softshell crab. Fried crispy golden brown, the crab is set on a bed of crunchy slaw and topped with pickled red onions, carrot, and cucumber. With a slathering of spicy mayonnaise replacing the liver pâté for a more mainstream Southern taste, this Vietnamese po'boy—uh, bánh mì—has just the right balance of flavors.

CABBAGE SLAW AND PICKLED VEGETABLES

Place all of the vinegars and the honey in a large bowl. Stir to combine, add the cabbage, and stir again. Pour off all of the vinegar mixture into another bowl. To the cabbage, add the mayonnaise and blend until incorporated. Cover the cabbage and refrigerate.

Add the carrots, cucumber, and onions to the bowl containing the vinegar mixture. Add a pinch of salt to the bowl and stir to coat all of the vegetables with the vinegar mixture. Cover and refrigerate for at least 1 hour.

SPICY MAYO

Combine all of the ingredients thoroughly in a bowl. Cover and refrigerate.

SOFTSHELL CRAB AND ASSEMBLY

Preheat the oven to 200°F (93°C). Fill a deep pot with enough oil to come halfway up the side of the pot. Bring to a temperature of 375°F (190°C) over medium-high heat.

Slice open the bread loaves lengthwise through the middle and place on a baking sheet. About 15 minutes before serving, place the bread in the oven to warm.

In a shallow container, blend the flour and Cajun Seasoning Blend. In another shallow container, whisk together the half-and-half, buttermilk, and hot sauce.

SERVES 4

CABBAGE SLAW AND PICKLED VEGETABLES

¼ cup (60 ml) white vinegar

¼ cup (60 ml) apple cider vinegar

¼ cup (60 ml) sugarcane vinegar

1 teaspoon honey

2 cups (150 g) shredded napa cabbage

1 tablespoon (14 g) mayonnaise

1 large carrot, peeled and julienned

1 cucumber, peeled and sliced

1 small red onion, sliced

Pinch of salt

SPICY MAYO

1½ cups (340 g) mayonnaise

1 tablespoon (15 g) sriracha sauce

1 teaspoon ketchup

1 teaspoon Worcestershire sauce

1 teaspoon Cajun Seasoning Blend (page 13)

½ teaspoon freshly squeezed lemon juice

SOFTSHELL CRAB AND ASSEMBLY

Canola oil, for frying

4 French bread loaves or po'boy bread (6 inches, or 15 cm each)

2 cups (250 g) unbleached all-purpose flour

2 tablespoons (20 g) Cajun Seasoning Blend (page 13)

1 cup (235 ml) half-and-half

1 cup (235 ml) buttermilk

1 tablespoon (15 ml) hot sauce

4 large softshell blue crabs (1 pound, or 455 g total), cleaned

Kosher salt and freshly ground black pepper

1 cup (16 g) fresh cilantro leaves

¼ cup (25 g) diced green onion tops

2 fresh jalapeño peppers, sliced

1 lime, quartered

TABLE TIPS

★ Try to find the large soft-shells [about 6 inches (15 cm) across], which will fit the bread nicely. If yours are smaller, I recommend two per sandwich.

★ The vegetables I use for pickling are usually what I have on hand; you could easily use radishes or daikon, as well as any number of other vegetables.

Rinse the crabs and pat dry with paper towels to remove any moisture. Sprinkle the crabs with salt and pepper, place in the liquid and turn to coat, and then dredge in the seasoned flour, coating both sides. Shake off any excess flour from each crab and place in the hot oil, being careful not to crowd the pot. Fry the crabs until golden brown on both sides, about 5 minutes. Transfer to a paper towel–lined platter and keep warm. Repeat until all the crabs are cooked.

Remove the hot French loaves from the oven and slather the insides with the spicy mayonnaise. Add a portion of cabbage slaw and then top with a softshell crab. Drain the pickled vegetables. Add equal amounts of onions, cucumber, and carrots to the sandwich. Garnish with cilantro, diced green onions, and sliced jalapeños. Serve with more of the spicy mayonnaise on the side and lime quarters for squeezing.

CRAWFISH-STUFFED ARTICHOKE

Large globe artichokes shout at me in the produce section of my local market and I cannot resist—not ever.

In Louisiana, stuffing artichokes is a uniquely New Orleans thing. At the close of the 1800s, boatloads of Sicilians came into the city and coastal South Louisiana along with many immigrants from Catholic Mediterranean countries. They brought their customs and beliefs along with a treasure trove of recipes. While the artichoke is not typically known as a French Acadian delicacy, it has found its way into the playbook of many bayou cooks with a unique variation on the stuffing featuring crawfish.

The thought process behind this recipe is straightforward; take an ordinary artichoke and make it colorful and festive with fresh Louisiana crawfish tail meat, fragrant extra-virgin olive oil, grated Parmigiano-Reggiano cheese and herbs nestled among the leaves.

Preheat the oven to 400°F (200°C, or gas mark 6).

Slice the stem portion of the artichoke off at the bottom so that it will stand vertically. Cut off the top inch (2.5 cm) of the artichoke and use scissors to trim the points off the leaves.

In a large pot with heavy lid, add the artichoke. Add enough water to cover the artichoke and pour in the salt. Slice 1 lemon into halves and squeeze into the pot to keep the artichoke from discoloring. Turn the burner on high heat and bring to a boil. Lower the heat to a simmer and cover the pot. Cook until tender but not falling apart, about 20 minutes. Check for doneness (the leaves should effortlessly pull out and a knife should easily pierce the bottom). Remove from the hot water and quickly submerge into ice-cold water for 5 minutes as an added means to preserve color. Remove and drain.

In a large mixing bowl, add the bread crumbs. Mix in all the ingredients except the olive oil and crawfish. Cut the remaining lemon in half and squeeze half the lemon into the mixing bowl. Slowly drizzle olive oil while stirring to achieve a wet consistency, about ½ cup (120 ml). Add the crawfish tail meat to the container of a food processor and pulse until coarsely chopped. Add the crawfish to the mixing bowl and mix together.

Starting from the bottom, pack the mixture into each leaf until every leaf is stuffed. Any remaining mixture should fill the center cavity area. Place the whole crawfish into the center cavity with its head and claws poking out. Drizzle the entire stuffed artichoke with the remaining olive oil, squeeze the remaining half of lemon over top, and bake in a 400°F (200°C, or gas mark 6) oven for 15 minutes or until browned on top. Let sit for 1 hour minimum before serving.

SERVES: 2

1 large artichoke

½ cup (144 g) salt

2 large lemons

2 cups (230 g) finely ground unseasoned bread crumbs

1 tablespoon (9 g) garlic powder

1 tablespoon (7 g) onion powder

1 tablespoon (3 g) dried oregano

1 tablespoon (10 g) minced garlic

1 cup (100 g) finely grated Parmigiano-Reggiano cheese

Dash of hot sauce

1 tablespoon (4 g) red pepper flakes

Kosher salt and freshly ground black pepper

1 cup (236 ml) extra-virgin olive oil, divided

1 pound (455 g) Louisiana crawfish tail meat

1 whole crawfish, for garnish (optional)

TABLE TIPS

★ My recipe is for one artichoke, but I suggest making several because they will go fast and are just as good—or maybe even better—days later.

★ Be careful not to pulverize the crawfish into mush; the texture of coarsely chopped tail meat is essential.

★ Fresh Louisiana crawfish, high-quality artichokes, and using lots of herbaceous extra-virgin olive oil are the keys to this appetizer. Also, be sure to let the stuffed artichoke sit for a while, if not overnight, before serving to distribute the flavors within the leaves. Crawfish can be substituted with crabmeat or shrimp.

FARM FRESH

CHAPTER

FIVE

MUCH IS WRITTEN ABOUT LOUISIANA CUISINE, AND MOST OF THE FOCUS IS ON OUR EXCEPTIONAL GULF SEAFOOD, UNIQUE SMOKED SAUSAGES, AND ONE-OF-A-KIND CRAWFISH. BUT THERE IS A LIGHTER SIDE TO SOUTH LOUISIANA, WITH ORGANIC FARMING AND ARTISANAL CRAFT-MAKING BRINGING NEW PRODUCTS AND INGREDIENTS TO MARKET.

In the South, we are blessed with short winters. We are thawed out by the end of March, and farm-fresh vegetables begin showing up soon after. It is my favorite season in Acadiana. Every Saturday morning at the Lafayette Farmers' and Artisans' Market at the Horse Farm, local growers and producers gather to share their skills and talents with a community that understands and appreciates their gifts. The Horse Farm, smack-dab in the middle of Lafayette, is undergoing a renaissance as a central park project that has ignited the passion of the community. As a thriving outdoor market complete with a lively jam session of Cajun accordions and fiddles, the Horse Farm is more a celebration of Acadiana's joie de vivre than just a marketplace.

This farmers' market is different from the run-of-the-mill roadside market. It is full of personality and self-expression reflected by the many skilled artisans representing their local farm communities. From nearby St. Martinville, Mary Patout runs Mary Mary Markets, where she blends her fresh-grown herbs and sprouts into seductive condiments like her peppery handmade beer mustard. Inglewood Farm comes to the market with a variety of mixed greens, heirloom tomatoes, spring onions, and the like. They grow fresh produce year-round in their hothouse, and when they happen to have their unique variety of organic radishes or mild hakurei turnips, I load up. I love to talk food with these knowledgeable folks, and I never fail to learn a culinary trick or two while discovering a surprising new ingredient for my Acadiana table.

TOMATO FLATBREAD WITH PICKLED SHRIMP AND CREOLE MUSTARD VINAIGRETTE

To celebrate the farm-fresh best that graces the tables of Acadiana, I've sourced local products for a simple yet splendid flatbread salad—a free-form salad that can take on endless variations depending on your access to fresh ingredients. Just think of it as a work of art with crispy flatbread as your canvas and paint on the vibrant and tasty colors of spring.

Fresh tomatoes, red onions, and edible primrose flowers (with a taste much like mild lettuce) colorfully pop in this salad. I buy fresh organic herbs from Mark and Mary Hernandez, who run City Farm and who are always at my local Lafayette Farmers and Artisans Market at the Horse Farm. Pickling fresh Gulf shrimp is a cinch, and the addition of a spicy Creole mustard vinaigrette with its zesty finish adds a bright counterbalance.

PICKLED SHRIMP

Squeeze the juice of the lemons and limes into a large container with a cover. Whisk in the vinegar and olive oil. Add the onions, celery, both peppers, garlic, cilantro, red pepper flakes, and hot sauce and stir. Add a pinch of salt and a grind of black pepper to taste. Add the shrimp and stir to combine. Cover and refrigerate for at least 8 hours or up to overnight.

CREOLE MUSTARD VINAIGRETTE

In a small bowl, combine the vinegars, lemon juice, honey, and Creole mustard. While whisking, drizzle enough olive oil into the container until it begins to emulsify. Season to taste with salt and black pepper. Cover and refrigerate until ready to serve.

SALAD

In a large bowl, toss the salad greens, tomatoes, and onions with just enough of the Creole Mustard Vinaigrette to coat the leaves.

Arrange the flatbreads on a large platter. Add a portion of the salad to each flatbread, evenly distributing the tomatoes and onions. Add 3 pickled shrimp to each flatbread salad.

Pinch off the fronds of the dill stems and sprinkle over the salad. Spread the alfalfa sprouts over the flatbreads. Place the basil leaves and flowers in various places on the salad. Season with a few grinds of black pepper to taste.

For serving, I recommend presenting the platter in the center of the table with individual plates and the remaining vinaigrette on the side so guests can spoon over as much as they like.

SERVES 4 TO 6

PICKLED SHRIMP

4 lemons

2 limes

1 tablespoon (15 ml) sugarcane vinegar

1 cup (235 ml) extra-virgin olive oil

¼ cup (40 g) diced yellow onion

¼ cup (30 g) diced celery

¼ cup (38 g) diced green bell pepper

1 tablespoon (9 g) finely diced fresh jalapeño pepper

2 tablespoons (20 g) minced garlic

2 tablespoons (2 g) chopped fresh cilantro

1 teaspoon red pepper flakes

1 teaspoon hot sauce

Kosher salt and freshly ground black pepper

24 jumbo (16/20 count) shrimp, peeled and deveined

CREOLE MUSTARD VINAIGRETTE

¼ cup (60 ml) white wine vinegar

2 tablespoons (28 ml) balsamic vinegar

1 tablespoon (15 ml) freshly squeezed lemon juice

½ teaspoon honey

2 tablespoons (42 g) Creole mustard or other coarse-grained mustard

½ cup (235 ml) extra-virgin olive oil, plus more if needed

Kosher salt and freshly ground black pepper

SALAD

1 cup (55 g) loosely packed spring mix salad greens

2 large ripe tomatoes, thickly sliced

1 small red onion, sliced into rings

8 large cracker-style flatbreads

½ cup (5 g) loosely packed fresh dill

½ cup (17 g) loosely packed alfalfa sprouts

½ cup (12 g) loosely packed fresh basil leaves

12 small primrose flowers or any colorful edible flower

Freshly ground black pepper

TABLE TIP

Get creative: I find colorful and mild-flavored edible primrose flowers at my local market, but you may already have edible flowers (pansies or nasturtiums, perhaps) in your garden. Fresh ripe tomatoes are all-important for this dish, so be sure to build your flatbread salad with that foundation.

ASPARAGUS WITH SHRIMP CREOLAISE

Some vegetables scream flavor, and then there are those that speak softly. Asparagus whispers. I've had a love affair with asparagus all my life and continuously stalk the purest expression of its full flavor potential. I've eaten well-crafted asparagus preparations in France, in Napa, and in many of the best restaurants on both coasts. I love them all. This technique celebrates asparagus, elevating it with Creole inspiration and shining a light on this astonishing ingredient. With a delicately spiced sauce (not a nostril-flaring hit of horseradish), the briny sweetness of the shrimp shines in this balanced combination.

DRESSING

In a bowl, combine the Creole mustard and mayonnaise, along with the onions and celery. Whisk in the lemon juice and olive oil. Season with oregano, salt, and pepper. Cover and refrigerate until ready to serve.

SALAD

Using a vegetable peeler, scrape the peeling from the lower portion of each asparagus stalk, removing the tough exterior.

Fill a large pot with enough water to come up to 4 inches (10 cm) on the side of the pot. Add the salt, cover, and place over high heat. Once the water comes to a boil, add the asparagus and cook for 4 minutes. Turn off the heat and let sit for another 4 minutes. With a slotted spoon, transfer the asparagus to a container of ice water. Let the asparagus cool and then drain. Move the asparagus to a paper towel–lined platter.

In the same pot, bring fresh water to a boil. Add the eggs. Once the water comes to a boil, turn off the heat and cover. Let the eggs sit in the water for 12 minutes. With a slotted spoon, transfer to a colander. Run cold water over the eggs until cooled. Peel the eggs and chop. Cover and refrigerate.

In the same pot, bring the water back to a boil. Add the crab boil seasoning and shrimp and bring the water back to a boil. Turn off the heat and cover the pot. Let the shrimp cook in the seasoned water for 5 minutes and then drain in a colander. Run cold water over the shrimp to stop the cooking. Move to a paper towel–lined platter.

For serving, arrange the asparagus on a large serving platter. Add one-half of the shrimp and one-half of the chopped boiled eggs to the dressing. Stir to incorporate. Spoon the dressing over the asparagus spears. Spoon the additional one-half of the chopped egg over the dressing and place the remaining one-half of the shrimp on top. Sprinkle with the green onions. Squeeze a wedge of lemon over the asparagus and serve the remaining lemon wedges on the side. Sprinkle with salt and a grind of black pepper to taste.

SERVES 4

DRESSING

2 tablespoons (42 g) Creole mustard or other coarse-grained mustard

¼ cup (60 g) mayonnaise

¼ cup (40 g) finely diced yellow onion

2 tablespoons (15 g) finely diced celery

Juice of 1 lemon

2 tablespoons (28 ml) extra-virgin olive oil

1 teaspoon dried oregano

Kosher salt and freshly ground black pepper

SALAD

24 green asparagus spears

½ cup (144 g) salt

4 large eggs

¼ cup (60 ml) liquid crab boil seasoning or (38 g) Cajun Seasoning Blend (page 13)

1 pound (455 g) small (61/70 count) shrimp, peeled and deveined

½ cup (50 g) diced green onion tops

1 lemon, cut into wedges

TABLE TIPS

★ Find the thick green asparagus spears, not the thin variety. Trim the woody ends
and peel back the bottom half of the stalks. Be careful not to overcook—cooked
asparagus should snap to attention and never limp into action.

★ This dressing is akin to a classic French ravigote rather than a traditional rémoulade. You can feel free to adjust the dressing to your taste and preference for heat
and spice. Horseradish or diced jalapeño pepper would give it zing, but in that
case, I suggest the dish become an appetizer portion rather than a main dish.

SQUEEZEBOX SWEET POTATOES WITH SUGARCANE CREAM SAUCE

Listening to chank-a-chank, Cajun French songs featuring a classic squeezebox accordion, is a Sunday morning ritual for me and my dog, Molly. With the radio blaring, we take a ride to the local markets and farm stands for Sunday dinner ingredients. In the autumn months, two classic Southern staples are sure to show up on the dinner table: yams and pecans. The farms around St. Landry Parish are famous for growing the sweetest yams in the country, and a bit farther north is Cane River pecan country.

While the tried-and-true baked sweet potato casserole topped with chopped pecans and marshmallows is a familiar holiday course, I embarked on a journey to combine these ingredients into a new interpretation. It was the image in my mind of that squeezebox that got my creative juices flowing as I recalled seeing techniques using the Hasselback method of serving potatoes cut into thin rounds that unfold for a delightful accordion-style presentation. Why not use that trick on sweet potatoes?

SUGARCANE CREAM SAUCE

In a saucepan over medium heat, melt the butter. Add the brown sugar and molasses, stirring until the sugars melt and begin to sizzle. Immediately pour in the cream and whisk vigorously as you add the rum (if using). Turn the heat off and continue whisking as the sauce comes together. Remove from the stovetop and keep warm until serving.

SWEET POTATOES

Preheat the oven to 400°F (200°C, or gas mark 6). Line a baking pan with aluminum foil.

Using a pair of chopsticks as a guide, place a potato between the sticks on a cutting board. Using a sharp, thin-blade knife, cut down into the potato crosswise until you hit the chopstick. Continue slicing across the potato in ⅛-inch (3 mm) intervals. The slices should create a fan-like, accordion-style pattern across the potato. Repeat with the second potato; transfer to the prepared baking pan.

In a saucepan over medium heat, bring the butter and olive oil to a low sizzle. Add the rosemary and sauté briefly to release the flavor. Add the brown sugar and molasses, along with a sprinkle of sea salt and the pecans.

Spoon the sauce over the potatoes, making sure to work the pecan pieces down into the potatoes to help separate the segments. Cover the baking pan with another piece of foil and seal tightly. Bake for 1½ hours. At around the halfway point, check the potatoes and carefully fan out the round segments so that they cook in an even accordion-fold pattern during the remaining time in the oven.

For serving, place on a platter and drizzle over some of the Sugarcane Cream Sauce.

SERVES 4

SUGARCANE CREAM SAUCE

8 tablespoons (1 stick, or 112 g) unsalted butter

¼ cup (60 g) dark brown sugar

2 tablespoons (40 g) sugarcane molasses

1 cup (235 ml) heavy cream

2 tablespoons (28 ml) dark rum (optional)

SWEET POTATOES

2 very large sweet potatoes

6 tablespoons (¾ stick, or 85 g) unsalted butter

6 tablespoons (90 ml) olive oil

2 tablespoons (4 g) finely chopped fresh rosemary, plus 1 sprig for garnish

¼ cup (60 g) firmly packed dark brown sugar

2 tablespoons (40 g) sugarcane molasses

Coarse sea salt

½ cup (55 g) chopped pecans, toasted

SWEET POTATO OR YAM?

Before we go any further, let's sort out the confusion. Louisiana yams are sweet potatoes—usually the Beauregard variety grown in rich South Louisiana soil. Back in the 1930s, Louisiana decided to brand its crops of sweeter and moister orange-fleshed sweet potatoes as yams. The name stuck, and now we commonly refer to them with both terms. Only in Louisiana.

TABLE TIPS

★ If you need to reheat just before serving, feel free to microwave on high until heated.

★ Of course, the rum is an optional ingredient, but I highly suggest it for flavor and punch.

ZEPHYR AND ZUCCHINI CASSEROLE

When fresh, nothing beats squash sautéed down into a flavorful casserole. Zephyr is a hybrid of the yellow crookneck, with a yellow stem and pale green blossom end. It has a sweet, nutty flavor that works in a variety of cooking methods. And no one grows tastier squash than my friend Brian Gotreaux. Every summer, Gotreaux Family Farm shows up at Lafayette's Hub City farmers' market with bushel baskets of beautiful zephyr squash and zucchini that are a favorite combination of mine. This zesty Cajun-spiced casserole features contrasts in flavors with the fragrant notes of peppers and spices topped by the creamy finish of cheese.

Preheat the oven to 300°F (150°C, or gas mark 2).

Rinse the squash and slice into ¼-inch-thick (6 mm) rounds. To reduce their moisture content, sprinkle the squash pieces lightly with salt and place on a wire rack over a paper towel–lined baking sheet. Let the squash sit at room temperature for 30 minutes and then blot dry.

In a large cast-iron skillet with a heavy lid over medium-high heat, heat 2 tablespoons (28 ml) of the oil. Add the ground chuck, Cajun Seasoning Blend, and pepper. Sauté until browned, about 8 minutes, and then transfer the meat to a platter with a slotted spoon. Keep warm.

Return the skillet to medium-high heat and add the remaining 2 tablespoons (28 ml) oil. Once the oil is hot, add the squash, onions, celery, bell pepper, poblano pepper, and garlic. Sauté until the onions are browned and all the vegetables have begun to cook through, about 10 minutes.

Add the water to the pan and cover with the lid. Let the mixture steam for 3 minutes and then turn off the heat. Remove the cover and stir with a flat spatula, releasing the bits and pieces from the bottom of the pan.

Return the meat to the pan, season with hot sauce, and stir to combine. Add the Monterey Jack cheese to the top of the casserole and cover with the lid. Bake for 20 minutes. Uncover the pan and bake for another 10 minutes.

For serving, bring the skillet to the table family-style. Spoon the squash casserole onto side plates to accompany another dish or serve in larger portions as a main dish.

SERVES 4 TO 6

4 medium zephyr squash (preferably) or yellow crookneck squash

4 medium zucchini

Kosher salt

4 tablespoons (60 ml) canola oil, divided

1 pound (455 g) ground beef chuck

1 tablespoon (10 g) Cajun Seasoning Blend (page 13)

1 teaspoon freshly ground black pepper, or to taste

1 medium yellow onion, diced

½ cup (60 g) diced celery

2 large green bell peppers, seeded and chopped into large pieces

2 medium poblano peppers, seeded and chopped into large pieces

1 tablespoon (10 g) minced garlic

½ cup (120 ml) water

1 tablespoon (15 ml) hot sauce

1 cup (115 g) freshly grated Monterey Jack cheese

TABLE TIPS

★ Certainly you can use regular yellow summer squash in this recipe, but try to find the flavorful zephyr variety. I look for the medium-size squash with a firm texture rather than the larger, more fibrous mature squash.

★ One of the keys to cooking squash is reducing the water content. The inner flesh of a squash is spongy and should never be rinsed once cut. A sprinkle of salt and a half hour on a wire rack will purge some of the water content. The flesh will then be drier and absorb flavor from the moisture content of your added ingredients.

★ The tame poblano peppers add a subtle spiciness to this dish that works well, but feel free to go even hotter with fresh jalapeño peppers.

CHARRED PERSIMMON SALAD WITH AGAVE NECTAR VINAIGRETTE

Not everyone is lucky enough to have a persimmon tree in their backyard, but my friend Walter Adams is and does. His quaint maison in rural St. Martin Parish is just a short drive from me, which is even luckier, because I love persimmons. They have a tart, mouth-puckering, astringent sweetness, unlike any other fruit I've tasted. I don't see them often, but early in the fall I seek them out, and it is good to have a friend like Walt.

This salad is all about simplicity of preparation and a concentrated focus on the fruit. It is a perfect small plate accompaniment to a heartier meat entrée or a lighter fish entrée. Charring ripe fruit in cast iron is a dramatic method of adding flavor and contrast, and when you taste these scorched persimmon slices, you will find the complexity of the fruit hidden within. The agave nectar works to create a platform for the tartness, and the pomegranate seeds are exclamation points for a whimsical touch.

AGAVE NECTAR VINAIGRETTE

In a bowl, combine the lemon juice, agave nectar, Dijon mustard, and salt. While whisking, add enough olive oil to create an emulsion. Cover and keep at room temperature until serving.

SALAD

Slice the persimmons into 6 thick rounds each, leaving the peel on. Position each round on the cutting board and brush with a coating of olive oil. Sprinkle each round with sugar and then evenly scatter the rosemary over the tops.

In a cast-iron skillet over medium-high heat, arrange the sliced persimmon rounds sugar-side down. Watch carefully as the fruit grills and the edges begin to blacken. Lift the edges with a spatula to check to see if the sugar is caramelizing and beginning to blacken. Just as the slices take on a darkened color, transfer them from the pan to a platter and keep warm.

Place a spoonful of the Agave Nectar Vinaigrette on each serving plate and tilt the plate until it runs to the edge decoratively. Place a mound of lettuce on one side of each plate and layer 6 charred persimmon slices on top. Add some pomegranate seeds and a rosemary sprig for garnish, along with a sprinkling of salt.

SERVES 4

AGAVE NECTAR VINAIGRETTE

2 tablespoons (28 ml) freshly squeezed lemon juice

¼ cup (84 g) agave nectar

2 teaspoons (10 g) Dijon mustard

1 teaspoon kosher salt

½ cup (115 ml) extra-virgin olive oil, plus more if needed

SALAD

4 ripe persimmons

¼ cup (60 ml) extra-virgin olive oil

3 tablespoons (39 g) granulated sugar

2 tablespoons (4 g) chopped fresh rosemary

2 cups (110 g) spring mix lettuce

3 tablespoons (33 g) pomegranate seeds

4 small fresh rosemary sprigs

Kosher salt

TABLE TIP

Persimmons come in two varieties—Fuyu and Hachiya. You could use either, but the ones I used here happened to be the astringent Hachiya variety, and I allowed them to ripen to the stage just before they turn gelatinous. I like their bitterness balanced by the addition of sugar and rosemary. The Fuyu variety would work as well, but they are crisp and less tannic and would need to grill longer to soften. The key is to achieve a blackened crust to the exterior edges of the persimmon. Experiment with both varieties and you will become a persimmon fan like me.

STUFFED ROSA BIANCA EGGPLANT

Like bell peppers, stuffed eggplant is a very common Acadiana dish. I am fascinated with heirloom varieties like the violet-streaked Rosa Bianca eggplants that farmer Molly Daigle brings every year to the local Lafayette Farmers and Artisans Market at the Horse Farm. Grown in her rich St. Landry Parish soil at Prudhomme City Farms near Eunice, Rosa Bianca eggplant is a Sicilian variety with a mild, creamy flavor—just right for cooking whole. The medium-size Rosa Bianca is missing the bitterness of traditional eggplant and has far fewer seeds. These Italian heirloom vegetables are an example of the farm-to-table movement sweeping South Louisiana and bringing unique varieties of produce to market. Armed with a few pounds of Grant Cannatella's fennel-infused sausage and my fresh Rosa Bianca eggplant, it's time to celebrate the Italian side of Cajun.

Preheat the oven to 350°F (180°C, or gas mark 4).

Remove the skin from the onions and slice in half. Slice off the stem end of each pepper and slice in half lengthwise, removing the seeds. Sprinkle with salt and pepper and reserve for later.

Holding each eggplant on its side, slice off the top one-third lengthwise just above the stem. Remove the top portion and with a sharp paring knife or teaspoon, remove the pulp from the cavity of the eggplant, being careful not to break through the skin of the eggplant. Chop the top portion of the eggplant and the pulp into 1-inch (2.5 cm) pieces and reserve. Transfer the hulled-out eggplants to a platter, coat lightly with 1 tablespoon (15 ml) olive oil, and season with salt and pepper.

Heat 2 tablespoons (28 ml) of the olive oil in a large ovenproof skillet over medium-high heat. Add the onions, celery, peppers, and reserved chopped eggplant pulp. Sauté until the onions turn translucent and the eggplant softens, about 5 minutes. Add the garlic, rosemary, parsley, and Cajun Seasoning Blend. Add ½ cup (120 ml) of the chicken stock and simmer just until the liquid is absorbed, about 5 minutes. Transfer to a large bowl and keep warm.

Add 2 tablespoons (28 ml) of olive oil to the skillet. Add the Italian sausage and cook until just beginning to brown, about 5 to 7 minutes. Transfer to the bowl with the vegetables.

Spoon just enough of the cooked rice into the meat mixture to balance the mixture without being too ricey. Sprinkle with salt and pepper. Spoon the stuffing mixture into the inside of each eggplant cavity. Drizzle 1 tablespoon (15 ml) of the olive oil over the stuffing and sprinkle with the Pecorino Romano cheese.

Arrange the stuffed eggplants in the skillet. Add the pieces of onion and Marconi peppers around the eggplants in the pan. Drizzle the onions and peppers with the remaining 1 tablespoon (15 ml) olive oil and add the remaining ½ cup (120 ml) chicken stock to the pan. Cover the pan with aluminum foil and bake for 30 minutes. Remove the foil and bake for another 15 minutes, uncovered, until the eggplants are tender and the stuffing is browned.

For serving, move the pan to the table, family-style. Serve with crusty Italian bread and red wine.

SERVES 4

5 large yellow onions

6 large red and green Marconi peppers or bell peppers

Kosher salt and freshly ground black pepper

4 Rosa Bianca eggplants or medium purple eggplant

7 tablespoons (105 ml) extra-virgin olive oil, divided

1 cup (160 g) diced yellow onion

½ cup (50 g) chopped celery

½ cup (75 g) diced red and green Marconi peppers or bell peppers

2 tablespoons (20 g) minced garlic

2 tablespoons (4 g) chopped fresh rosemary

2 tablespoons (8 g) chopped flat-leaf parsley

2 tablespoons (20 g) Cajun Seasoning Blend (page 13)

1 cup (235 ml) chicken stock

1 pound (455 g) bulk sweet Italian sausage

2 cups (316 g) cooked long-grain white rice

½ cup (50 g) freshly grated Pecorino Romano cheese

TABLE TIP

Find bulk Italian sausage or buy the links and remove from the casings.

CANNATELLA'S ITALIAN GROCERY

Italian culinary influence is evident in classics like the famous muffuletta sandwich and the crabmeat-stuffed artichoke that are now so meshed into our South Louisiana foodways. Sicilians immigrated up the Atchafalaya River to Acadiana years after the French Acadians. Most never made it past Morgan City, but a few, like the Cannatella family, settled in the town of Melville, in St. Landry Parish. For the past ninety years, four generations of Cannatellas have been making sweet Italian sausage from a secret family formula. Until his recent passing, eighty-five-year-old Pete came in every morning to add just the right amount of fennel to his sausage. His sons, Brian and Grant, carry on the family legacy. They operate a well-run, ultra-clean operation turning out some tasty old-country products.

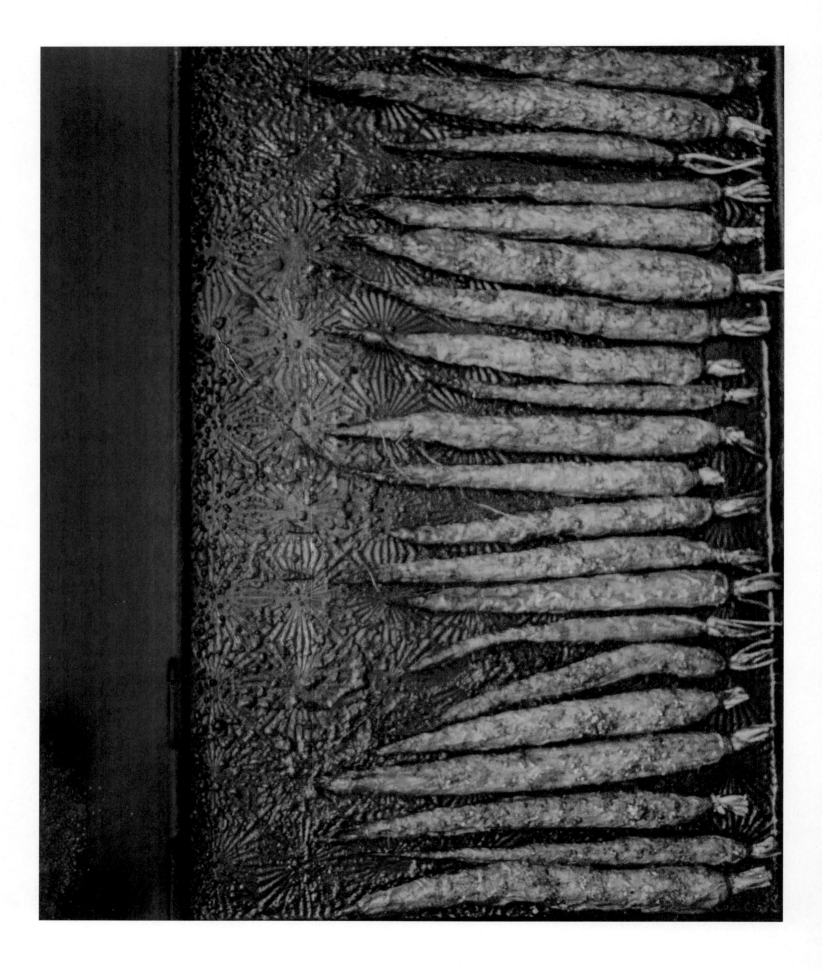

SWEET HEAT CARROTS

This classic combination defines simplicity, yet creates complex flavors of opposite extremes. These carrots—butter-slicked and punched with a jolt of sweet heat—are a complement to any entrée or a showcase for a holiday buffet table. My seasoning blend combines a light brown sugar and cumin base with more familiar South Louisiana spices such as cayenne. It is a balanced spice rub that works well in a number of uses from grilled pork chops to roasted butternut squash, and it should be a staple of your flavor arsenal.

SWEET HEAT SEASONING

Mix all of the ingredients together and store in an airtight jar.

CARROTS

Preheat the oven to 400°F (200°C, or gas mark 6).

Place the carrots on a large baking sheet, drizzle the melted butter over the top, and roll the carrots to coat with the butter. Sprinkle liberally with the Sweet Heat Seasoning. Bake for 45 minutes or until the carrots are tender.

TABLE TIPS

- ★ Be sure to buy young, thin carrots of approximately the same size so that they will cook evenly. Peeling these young carrots is optional.

- ★ I like to use the granulated Domino pourable light brown sugar to prevent clumping in the spice mix.

SERVES 4 TO 6

SWEET HEAT SEASONING (MAKES JUST OVER ½ CUP)

2 tablespoons (30 g) light brown sugar

2 tablespoons (14 g) ground cumin

1 tablespoon (6 g) ground coriander

1 tablespoon (8 g) chili powder

1 tablespoon (7 g) sweet paprika

1 teaspoon ground cinnamon

1 teaspoon ground allspice

1 teaspoon ground ginger

½ teaspoon cayenne pepper

½ teaspoon ground turmeric

½ teaspoon ground cloves

CARROTS

24 young carrots, stems removed

4 tablespoons (½ stick, or 55 g) unsalted butter, melted

SWEET DUMPLING SQUASH STUFFED WITH JASMINE RISOTTO

Much like acorn squash, dumpling squash are sweet and make an excellent vessel for stuffing. A squash risotto stuffing made with Louisiana-grown jasmine rice, along with fresh herbs and artisanal goat cheese, makes this dish perfect for a cozy dinner on a crisp fall evening.

Preheat the oven to 375°F (190°C, or gas mark 5). Line a baking sheet with parchment paper.

Cut the tops off the squash and scrape out the membrane and all seeds. Reserve the tops of the squash for garnish. Place the squash on the prepared baking sheet and bake for 30 minutes or until the squash just begins to soften. Remove and let cool.

Using a spoon, remove most of the flesh from the squash, being sure to keep the outer hull of the squash intact. Chop the squash flesh until almost a purée. Reserve the chopped squash and cover the shells of the squash.

In a large pot, heat the olive oil over medium heat. Add the onions and one-half of the green onions. Sauté until they turn translucent, about 5 minutes. Add the garlic, the reserved squash purée, the rosemary, thyme, allspice, and white pepper.

Add the rice and sauté until you begin to smell a nutty aroma, about 5 minutes. Add the white wine and bring to a boil. Lower the heat to a simmer and let some of the alcohol burn off before adding the first ladle of chicken stock. As the rice absorbs the stock, continue adding more until the rice is tender, about 30 minutes. Turn off the heat and add the parsley and goat cheese. Season with salt to taste. Stir, cover, and remove from the stovetop.

Fill each squash vessel with the risotto and place on a foil-lined baking sheet. Melt the butter in a small skillet and add the bread crumbs, stirring until the butter is absorbed. Sprinkle the stuffed squash with the bread crumb mixture. Return the squash to the oven until heated through and the bread crumbs brown on top. Garnish with green onions.

SERVES 4

4 sweet dumpling squash or acorn squash

2 tablespoons (28 ml) olive oil

½ cup (80 g) diced yellow onion

½ cup (50 g) diced green onion

1 tablespoon (10 g) minced garlic

1 tablespoon (2 g) chopped fresh rosemary

1 tablespoon (2 g) chopped fresh thyme

1 tablespoon (6 g) ground allspice

1 tablespoon (6 g) freshly ground white pepper

2 cups (340 g) Supreme brand Louisiana white jasmine rice or arborio rice

½ cup (120 ml) dry white wine

3 cups (700 ml) chicken stock

2 tablespoons (8 g) chopped fresh flat-leaf parsley

½ cup (75 g) fresh goat cheese

Kosher salt

1 tablespoon (14 g) unsalted butter

1 cup (50 g) panko bread crumbs

½ cup (50 g) diced green onion tops

TABLE TIP

I urge you to seek out the Supreme brand Louisiana jasmine rice developed by the Louisiana State University AgCenter. It has an arborio-like creamy consistency that works perfectly in this risotto. Don't rinse the rice before cooking because it is the creaminess of the release of starch into the wine and stock that achieves the thick, soupy texture.

TURNIP AND SMOKED HAM HOCK STEW WITH ROSEMARY PESTO

In the autumn months, turnips turn up on Acadiana tables and reflect the love affair that the entire American South has with this folksy ingredient. I call this a stew because of the hearty consistency of the vegetables and meat, but feel free to refer to it as a soup if you like. The smokiness of ham hocks adds a heartiness to the dish, and if you've never cooked with them, you will discover their potent flavor potential here. Refrigerate leftover rosemary pesto in a jar with a tight-fitting lid for up to 2 months.

ROSEMARY PESTO

Place the rosemary, pecans, Pecorino Romano cheese, and garlic in a blender. On medium speed, slowly drizzle in enough of the olive oil to form a thick paste. Season with salt and pepper to taste. Pour into a covered container and keep at room temperature until serving.

STEW

Preheat the oven to 400°F (200°C, or gas mark 6).

Remove the root ends of the turnips and peel. Slice the turnips into bite-size chunks. Chop the turnip greens into bite-size pieces.

Fill a large pot with enough water to fill the pot to the halfway point and bring to a boil over high heat. Add the turnips and greens and bring back to a boil. Once the water is boiling, cook for 1 minute, and then drain the turnips and greens in a colander; discard the water. Reserve the turnips and greens for later.

In the same pot over medium heat, cook the chopped bacon until browned. Add the onions to the pot and cook until just beginning to brown. Add the apple and garlic and continue cooking for 1 minute. Add the turnips and greens and continue cooking for 1 minute. Add the chicken stock and ham hocks. Season lightly with salt and pepper. Lower the temperature to a simmer and cook for 1 hour, stirring every 15 minutes.

Remove the ham hocks and discard the fat, skin, and bone, returning the smoked meat to the pot.

Place the bread rounds on a baking sheet and spread with the butter. Bake until the tops are browned.

For serving, ladle the turnip stew into shallow bowls and top with a French bread crouton. Spoon over a portion of the Rosemary Pesto and serve more on the side.

SERVES 4

ROSEMARY PESTO

1 cup (32 g) loosely packed fresh rosemary leaves

¼ cup (25 g) pecans, shelled

¼ cup (25 g) freshly grated Pecorino Romano cheese

2 cloves of garlic, peeled

½ cup (115 ml) extra-virgin olive oil, plus more if needed

Kosher salt and freshly ground black pepper

STEW

4 young turnips, with greens attached

4 strips (1 ounce, or 28 g each) of bacon, chopped

1 cup (160 g) chopped yellow onion

1 apple, cored and chopped

2 cloves of garlic, chopped

4 cups (946 ml) chicken stock

2 smoked ham hocks (6 ounces, or 170 g each)

Kosher salt and freshly ground black pepper

4 sliced French bread rounds (1 inch, or 2.5 cm thick)

4 tablespoons (½ stick, or 55 g) unsalted butter, softened

FROM BITTER TO BETTER

I like cooking with turnips and enjoy their strong taste that is unlike most any other root vegetable. But some folks turn up their nose at the mere whiff of a pot of turnips and greens simmering on the stovetop. Here's the deal for cooking turnips: First, find good turnips that are fresh and young with healthy green leaves attached. Next, discard the first round of boiling water. During the second round of simmering in water or stock, add a pinch of sugar or an apple (I chose the apple). The first boil removes most of the turnip bitterness, and the apple adds an element of sweetness.

WHITE ASPARAGUS AND CRABMEAT AU GRATIN

Years ago, I rarely saw white asparagus in South Louisiana markets, but these days it is everywhere. I decided to combine it with crabmeat in a classic Creole au gratin (*oh-GROT-ten* or *oh-GRAH-tan*), a casserole preparation method seen throughout Louisiana in both upscale and rural versions. The two variations in pronunciation are usually reflective of the French authenticity of where you happen to be dining, but the key to any gratin is a topping of cheese, browned and bubbling. In my interpretation, white asparagus is paired with plump nuggets of white lump crabmeat nestled in a creamy pool of Cheddar-infused sauce is an over-the-top way of enjoying this vegetable. This is a delicate dish that show-cases the tender asparagus and sweet crabmeat, so go easy on the hot sauce.

Preheat the oven to 400°F (200°C, or gas mark 6).

With kitchen twine, tie the asparagus in bunches. Fill a deep pot with a tight-fitting lid with just enough water to submerge the lower two-thirds of the asparagus spears and bring to a boil. Stand the asparagus bundles up in the water with the tender tip ends above the water line. Cover, lower the heat to a simmer, and cook until just tender, about 10 minutes. Remove the asparagus, remove the strings, and drain on paper towels until completely dry.

Melt the butter in a large saucepan over medium heat. Add the onions and sauté until they turn transparent, about 5 minutes. Add the flour to the mixture and whisk for 3 to 5 minutes, stopping before it begins to brown. Add the milk and continue to whisk until it is incorpo-rated and starts to thicken. Add the wine and lemon juice and continue to whisk. Add the thyme, garlic, white pepper, Cajun Seasoning Blend, and a dash of hot sauce. Lower the heat to a simmer and continue stirring until it thickens enough to coat the back of a spoon. (If too thick, add a bit more milk.) Season with salt to taste. Turn off the heat and keep warm.

Place a few asparagus spears in each of 4 shallow, individual, ovenproof ramekins. Top with a portion of the crabmeat and spoon over the white sauce. Top each ramekin with a generous amount of Cheddar cheese. Move the ramekins to a baking sheet and bake for about 20 minutes or until the sauce is bubbling and the cheese begins to brown. Garnish each ramekin with a sprig of fresh thyme and serve with French bread or warm croissants.

TABLE TIPS

★ White asparagus should be peeled because it tends to be a bit woodier toward the butt end.

★ I'm going with white Cheddar for an all-white presentation, but any good melting cheese (Gruyère, Swiss, or Gouda, for example) would work well.

SERVES 4

24 spears white asparagus, ends peeled

2 tablespoons (28 g) unsalted butter

1 cup (160 g) finely diced white onion

2 tablespoons (16 g) unbleached all-purpose flour

1 cup (235 ml) whole milk, plus more if needed

½ cup (120 ml) dry vermouth or white wine (optional)

1 tablespoon (15 ml) freshly squeezed lemon juice

1 teaspoon chopped fresh thyme

1 teaspoon minced garlic

1 teaspoon freshly ground white pepper

1 teaspoon Cajun Seasoning Blend (page 13)

Dash of hot sauce

Kosher salt

1 pound (455 g) white lump crabmeat, picked over for shells and cartilage

2 cups (240 g) freshly grated white Cheddar cheese

4 fresh thyme sprigs

CABBAGE JAMBALAYA

Cabbage shows up frequently in my culinary repertoire, but this jambalaya version is my latest favorite. It combines the best of a traditional Cajun dirty rice dressing cooked down with cabbage and seasonings like smoked ham hocks and chunks of tangy andouille sausage. Some simply call this cabbage dressing or smothered cabbage. Whatever you call it, this is a full-flavored, one-dish meal or a savory side dish to serve with chicken or pork.

Place the cabbage, ham hocks, and chicken stock in a large pot with a heavy lid. Turn the heat to high and bring to a boil. Immediately lower the heat to a simmer and cook, covered, for 1 hour or until the cabbage is tender. Turn off the heat and pour off all the braising liquid, reserving the liquid.

Remove the bones from the ham hocks and break up the meat; add the meat back to the pot. Add the onions, celery, bell pepper, and rice dressing mix to the pot. Stir to combine. Add the rice, andouille, Cajun Seasoning Blend, a dash of hot sauce, and salt and pepper to taste. Pour 4 cups (946 ml) of the reserved cabbage braising liquid into the pot and stir to evenly combine.

Turn the heat to high and once it begins to boil, lower the heat to a simmer. Place the lid on the pot and simmer for 45 minutes or until the rice is fully cooked. Taste and add more hot sauce, salt, and pepper, if needed.

SERVES 6 TO 10

2 large heads of green cabbage, cored and chopped

2 large smoked ham hocks (6 ounces, or 170 g each)

8 cups (1.9 L) chicken stock

2 cups (320 g) diced yellow onion

1 cup (120 g) diced celery

1 cup (150 g) diced green bell pepper

2 containers (16 ounces, or 455 g) rice dressing mix (Sources, page 314)

4 cups (632 g) long-grain white rice

2 cups (16 ounces, or 455 g) chopped andouille sausage (preferably) or smoked pork sausage

1 tablespoon (10 g) Cajun Seasoning Blend (page 13)

Dash of hot sauce

1 tablespoon (8 g) kosher salt

1 tablespoon (6 g) freshly ground black pepper

TABLE TIPS

★ This dish should be spicy, but I urge you to correct the seasoning toward the end of cooking, as the rice dressing mix and andouille will add heat.

★ I like this jambalaya in the Cajun style (without tomatoes), but I will admit that a can of Ro*Tel diced tomatoes with green chiles would be a tasty Creole-style addition.

★ Using frozen rice dressing mix—Savoie's is my favorite—is a shortcut to making this recipe tasty and no-hassle. It is a uniquely Louisiana product spiked with seasonings, pork, liver, and a whole host of funky Cajun ingredients. I urge you to try it in this dish.

CRAWFISH-STUFFED TOMATOES

I am pitting two traditional South Louisiana ingredients against each other to see which one excels. On one side is the Creole tomato—a familiar summertime standout—going head-to-head with Cajun crawfish tails, which, thanks to farming and processing, are pretty much a year-round staple. This is a well-matched brawl of cultural standouts: Savory versus sweet, juicy meets chewy—but heads or tails, you're the winner.

In a large bowl, whisk the mayonnaise, Creole mustard, vinegar, lemon juice, cilantro, onions, celery, and green onions until combined. Add the white pepper, a dash of hot sauce, and the crawfish tails. Taste and adjust the seasoning with salt and black pepper.

Cut the stem from each tomato. Slice each tomato into quarters, being careful to stop before slicing all the way through. Fan out the quarters to form a pocket. Using a spoon, add a portion of the crawfish tail mixture into each tomato until fully stuffed. Cover and refrigerate until chilled, about 1 hour.

For serving, arrange the salad greens on a platter and arrange the stuffed tomatoes on top. Garnish with whole boiled crawfish (if using) and present family-style along with crackers.

SERVES 6

1 cup (225 g) mayonnaise

1 tablespoon (21 g) Creole mustard or other coarse-grained mustard

2 tablespoons (28 ml) sugarcane vinegar

2 tablespoons (28 ml) freshly squeezed lemon juice

½ cup (8 g) chopped fresh cilantro

1 cup (160 g) finely diced yellow onion

1 cup (120 g) finely diced celery

½ cup (50 g) diced green onion tops

½ teaspoon freshly ground white pepper

Dash of hot sauce

1 pound (455 g) Louisiana crawfish tail meat

Kosher salt and freshly ground black pepper

6 large ripe tomatoes

4 cups (220 g) mixed salad greens

Whole boiled crawfish (optional)

BAKED MIRLITON SQUASH WITH SHRIMP STUFFING

Whether as a side dish or a main course, these shrimp-stuffed mirlitons are delicious. I like how the smoky tasso ham balances the briny taste of the shrimp in this stuffing. These little pear-shaped green squash have a taste like zucchini and are a South Louisiana culinary treasure. You'll see them cooked in a variety of ways, with seafood stuffing being the most common. Making them is a cinch, and once you learn the basic technique, you'll be thinking of other stuff to stuff. A casserole version of this recipe is a popular holiday dish in Louisiana.

Preheat the oven to 375°F (190°C, or gas mark 5). Line a baking sheet with parchment paper.

Bring a pot of water to a boil and add the mirliton halves. Cook for about 20 minutes or until tender when pierced with a skewer. Remove, pat dry, and let cool. With a teaspoon, carefully scoop out the inner pulp and seeds of the mirliton without puncturing the skin. Chop the pulp and reserve for later. Move the hollowed-out mirliton shells to a paper towel–lined platter to drain.

Heat the olive oil and butter in a large skillet over medium-high heat. Add the onions, celery, green onions, bell pepper, garlic, and parsley. Cook until the onions turn translucent, about 5 minutes. Add the tasso, lower the heat, and cook for 5 minutes. Add the wine and cook for 5 minutes longer. Add the mirliton pulp, shrimp, and lemon juice and cook for another 5 minutes. Season with cayenne, white pepper, and a dash of hot sauce. Add salt and black pepper to taste. Add the bread crumbs and slowly pour in the chicken stock while stirring. As the bread crumbs absorb the liquid, the stuffing should become moist, but not runny. Add more stock if needed to achieve a moist stuffing consistency.

Arrange the mirliton shells on the prepared baking sheet and spoon in a generous mound of the stuffing. Top with more bread crumbs and the melted butter and cover with aluminum foil. Bake for 30 minutes. Uncover and bake for another 15 minutes or until browned. Serve as a side dish or with a salad as a main course.

TABLE TIPS

* In addition to shrimp, I've made this stuffing with crawfish tails and with crabmeat—all good.

* The key to a good stuffing is enough moisture to keep the bread crumbs from drying out.

SERVES 4

2 large mirliton (chayote squash), halved lengthwise

2 tablespoons (28 ml) olive oil

4 tablespoons (½ stick, or 55 g) unsalted butter

½ cup (80 g) finely diced yellow onion

2 tablespoons (15 g) diced celery

2 tablespoons (12 g) diced green onion tops

2 tablespoons (19 g) diced green bell pepper

1 tablespoon (10 g) minced garlic

1 tablespoon (4 g) chopped flat-leaf parsley

1 cup (150 g) chopped tasso (preferably) or smoked ham

½ cup (120 ml) dry white wine

1 cup (255 g) chopped shrimp

1 tablespoon (15 ml) freshly squeezed lemon juice

1 teaspoon cayenne pepper

1 teaspoon freshly ground white pepper

Dash of hot sauce

Kosher salt and freshly ground black pepper

2 cups (230 g) bread crumbs, plus more for topping

1 cup (235 ml) chicken stock, plus more if needed

2 tablespoons (28 g) unsalted butter, melted

BLACKENED BRUSSELS SALAD

For a long time, I never met a Brussels sprout that I liked. Just a whiff of those little stink bombs boiling in a pot would send me running for the door. But what the process of blackening the surface of a Brussels sprout does to the flavor of this vegetable is nothing short of miraculous. What I recall years ago to be tasteless, waterlogged little cabbages are magically transformed into crunchy, charred flavor explosions delivering a wallop of vibrant savoriness.

If charring the Brussels wasn't enough to deliver a nutty oomph to the heart of this salad, I am combining them with kale. Rounding out the zing and zest of this salad are little cubes of pepper Jack cheese for a creamy surprise. Toasted almonds give it a crown of crispness. The lemon-based dressing gets a counterbalance of Creole mustard for a jolt of Louisiana flavor. This course is superb as a side accompaniment or as a centerpiece salad entrée.

BRUSSELS SPROUTS

Fill a pot halfway with water and bring to a boil. Add the Brussels sprouts. Cook for 5 minutes and then remove and drain on a paper towel–lined platter. Dry thoroughly.

Heat the olive oil in a large cast-iron skillet over medium-high heat. Add the Brussels sprouts with their cut-side down. Cook until they begin to brown around the edges, about 10 minutes. Turn the sprouts one at a time and continue cooking until they have roasted to a dark brown with blackened edges, about 5 minutes. Transfer to a large bowl.

Add the kale, tomatoes, bell peppers, parsley, red onions, rosemary, pepper Jack cheese, almonds, and raisins to the bowl and toss to combine. Keep at room temperature.

DRESSING

In a small bowl, whisk the lemon juice, vinegar, and Creole mustard. While whisking, slowly drizzle enough of the olive oil until it forms an emulsion. Season to taste with salt and black pepper.

For serving, add 2 to 3 tablespoons (28 to 45 ml) of the dressing to the salad, along with a grind of black pepper, and toss well. Serve with the rest of the dressing on the side.

TABLE TIP

Any leftover salad should be refrigerated; it is just as good served cold the next day.

SERVES 4

BRUSSELS SPROUTS

4 cups (352 g) Brussels sprouts, trimmed and halved lengthwise

2 tablespoons (28 ml) olive oil

4 cups (268 g) chopped fresh kale, woody stems removed

1 cup (150 g) yellow cherry tomatoes, halved

½ cup (46 g) assorted colors (red, yellow, orange) bell peppers, sliced

½ cup (30 g) chopped flat-leaf parsley

½ cup (58 g) thinly sliced red onion

1 tablespoon (2 g) chopped fresh rosemary

½ cup (60 g) diced pepper Jack cheese

½ cup (55 g) slivered almonds, toasted

2 tablespoons (18 g) golden raisins

DRESSING

2 tablespoons (28 ml) freshly squeezed lemon juice

2 tablespoons (28 ml) white wine vinegar

1 tablespoon (21 g) Creole mustard or other coarse-grained mustard

½ cup (120 ml) extra-virgin olive oil, plus more if needed

Kosher salt and freshly ground black pepper

GRIDDLED CANTALOUPE AND GOAT CHEESE SALAD

This cantaloupe salad is the bomb—ripe cantaloupe fused with creamy goat cheese, fresh rosemary, microgreens, and toasted Louisiana pecans. Charred on black iron, the fruit releases a blast of heat and sweet. And, when bombarded with the dark flavor of pepper-flecked, honey-infused balsamic vinegar, well, you've got a taste explosion.

Place the vinegar, honey, and red pepper flakes in a saucepan over medium heat. Slowly simmer the mixture until it reduces to a syrupy consistency, about 10 minutes. Remove from the heat and keep warm.

Combine the brown sugar, cinnamon, and chili powder in a small bowl. Lay the cantaloupe slices out on a cutting board. Sprinkle generously on both sides with the spice mixture.

Heat the olive oil in a large cast-iron skillet or griddle over medium-high heat. Add the cantaloupe slices to the hot skillet, along with the pecans and rosemary. Griddle the cantaloupe until the juices begin to caramelize the spice-infused flesh and the pecans toast, about 10 minutes.

Arrange the lettuce leaves and goat cheese on a large platter. Place the cantaloupe and pecans over the lettuce and chunks of goat cheese. Sprinkle lightly with salt. With a spoon, lightly drizzle the balsamic reduction over the entire platter. Garnish with rosemary sprigs.

SERVES 4

1 cup (235 ml) balsamic vinegar

1 tablespoon (20 g) honey

1 teaspoon red pepper flakes

1 tablespoon (15 g) light brown sugar

1 tablespoon (7 g) ground cinnamon

1 tablespoon (8 g) chili powder

1 large ripe cantaloupe, seeds removed and sliced into 8 segments

1 tablespoon (15 ml) olive oil

1 cup (100 g) pecan halves

2 tablespoons (4 g) chopped fresh rosemary

2 cups (110 g) loosely packed spring mix lettuce

1 cup (150 g) fresh goat cheese, chopped into chunks

Kosher salt

Fresh rosemary sprigs

GRILLED BABY EGGPLANT WITH PARSLEY-PECAN PESTO

Eggplant is a workhorse vegetable in the Cajun and Creole culinary world. Whether it's fried, stuffed, sautéed, or gratinéed, it is in demand. The basic method of grilled eggplant is elemental, but this recipe explores the potential of this blank-canvas vegetable with grand results. With a brushstroke of extra-virgin olive oil and fresh-squeezed lemon, along with the hot licks of a smoky flame, these babies need just one final touch: a drizzle of garlic-infused parsley-pecan pesto.

PARSLEY-PECAN PESTO

Place the parsley, garlic, pecans, and salt in a blender container. Turn the blender on at the lowest speed while slowly beginning to drizzle in the oil. Gradually increase the speed and continue adding the oil just until the ingredients are pulverized, but before it becomes a paste. Stop the blender and stir in the Parmesan cheese. Using a rubber spatula, transfer the Parsley-Pecan Pesto to a bowl, cover, and chill.

SALAD

Preheat a gas grill to high. Slice the eggplants in half lengthwise. With a sharp knife, score the inside flesh in a crisscross pattern, being careful not to cut all the way through. Drizzle with 3 tablespoons (45 ml) of the olive oil and sprinkle with salt and pepper.

Place the red bell peppers on the grill directly over the flame and allow the fire to blacken the exterior of the peppers on all sides. Move the blackened peppers to a paper bag or a covered container to allow the steam to soften the skins. Remove the blackened outer skin. Cut the peppers into large slices and arrange on a platter.

Place the eggplant and lemon halves on the grill, flesh-side down. Grill until softened and cooked through, about 10 minutes. Add to the platter, along with the tomatoes and parsley. Drizzle with the remaining 1 tablespoon (15 ml) olive oil. Season to taste with salt and pepper, along with a squeeze of lemon juice. Serve with the Parsley-Pecan Pesto on the side.

SERVES 4

PARSLEY-PECAN PESTO

3 cups (180 g) firmly packed fresh flat-leaf parsley

2 cloves of garlic, peeled

½ cup (55 g) toasted pecans

1 teaspoon kosher salt

½ cup (120 ml) extra-virgin olive oil, plus more if needed

2 tablespoons (10 g) freshly grated Parmesan cheese

SALAD

3 baby eggplants

4 tablespoons (60 ml) extra-virgin olive oil

Kosher salt and freshly ground black pepper

3 red bell peppers

2 lemons, halved

1 cup (150 g) sliced mixed red and yellow cherry tomatoes

4 fresh flat-leaf parsley sprigs

SUMMER CORN AND SHRIMP SALAD WITH DILL VINAIGRETTE

By midsummer, I yearn for the taste of sweet summer corn. And, with Louisiana's shrimping season at peak production, I can't think of anything that epitomizes the flavors of summer like this salad. It marries the bright freshness of summer corn with the briny sweetness of Gulf shrimp.

DILL VINAIGRETTE

In a small bowl, whisk the lemon juice, vinegar, and sugar. While whisking, slowly drizzle in enough of the olive oil until an emulsion forms. Add the chopped dill, along with a sprinkle of salt and pepper to taste. Stir the vinaigrette, cover, and refrigerate until serving.

SALAD

Heat the olive oil in a large skillet over medium-high heat. Add the shrimp and sauté until the shrimp turn pink and are just cooked through, about 5 minutes. Sprinkle lightly with salt and a pinch of white pepper. Let cool in the refrigerator.

Fill a large pot halfway with water and bring to a boil over high heat. Lower the heat to a simmer. Add the corn and parboil for just 5 minutes. Drain and let cool.

With a sharp knife, cut the corn from the cobs, scraping close to the cobs to release all the juices. Coarsely chop the mint leaves and place in a large bowl, along with the green onions and red onions. Add the corn kernels and the shrimp. Toss with some of the Dill Vinaigrette, cover, and refrigerate for at least 1 hour.

Sprinkle with black pepper to taste and serve the remaining vinaigrette on the side.

SERVES 4 TO 6

DILL VINAIGRETTE

1 tablespoon (15 ml) freshly squeezed lemon juice

1 teaspoon white wine vinegar

Pinch of granulated sugar

½ cup (120 ml) extra-virgin olive oil, plus more if needed

1 tablespoon (4 g) chopped fresh dill

Kosher salt and freshly ground black pepper

SALAD

2 tablespoons (28 ml) olive oil

1½ pounds (680 g) jumbo (16/20 count) shrimp, peeled, tail-on, and deveined

Kosher salt and freshly ground white pepper

6 ears of yellow corn, husks and silk removed

1 cup (96 g) loosely packed fresh mint leaves

1 cup (100 g) sliced green onion tops

1 cup (115 g) thinly sliced red onion

Freshly ground black pepper

ACADIANA'S EVOLVING FOODWAYS

Here at the halfway point in your journey through *Acadiana Table*, you will by now have seen a few dishes that are not what you thought would fit in with the Cajun and Creole traditions. Perhaps they push past the Louisiana boundaries of the cuisine and tread into unfamiliar territory. And, if so, then I've done my job.

Over the years, I've written much about Louisiana's food culture, and I've received lots of feedback from readers. In a nutshell, my perspective on our culinary world has inspired many, riled some, and confused others. To many, my stories are steeped in a cultural reverence for the old-school classics and the time-honored traditions of our foodways. And to some, my words and methods distort historical perspective by adding a contemporary way of thinking about tried-and-true Cajun and Creole cooking. And to add to the confusion, they are both right.

You see, here in Louisiana, there is a prevailing attitude among culinary preservationists that authenticity trumps innovation. Anyone who dares to challenge the long-held methods of our beloved Cajun and Creole cuisine is ridiculed and called out. Hogwash! While I do hold dear the tenets and long-held beliefs of our culture, I still explore the boundaries with new ideas. While I write with pride about traditional roux making, I still open a jar on occasion. To me, new ways don't replace old beliefs, but rather they build on them.

I contend that the entire culinary foundation of our beloved cuisine is a slow, inevitable evolution of the cultural influences that have shaped the genre of cooking that we hold so dear. Spanish, French, African, German, and Italian are just a few of the influences in the gumbo pot we treasure. Over recent years, we've seen Vietnamese and other Asian cultures take a seat at our homegrown table with dishes that add to our eclectic menu. And lately, we've seen Latin flavors like cumin and annatto commingling with our beloved cayenne. Bacon-wrapped jalapeños stuffed with Cajun sausage have become ubiquitous on Louisiana grills, Cajun bánh mì sandwiches are elbowing po'boys for position on menu chalkboards, and our beloved baked oyster repertoire has broken tradition with a Croatian char-grilled makeover. All across Louisiana, chefs and home cooks alike are experimenting with new flavors, new methods, and new attitudes.

My point is this: For food culture to stay relevant, it must evolve. For a genre of cooking to maintain its momentum, it must embrace new ideas that build on its foundation. For Cajun and Creole culinary culture to reach new generations, it must be open to new attitudes that add to its rich heritage. Preserving the past is noble. Building on that past is the key to saving it.

THE CAJUN/CREOLE COAST

CHAPTER

SIX

FROM DULAC TO GRAND CHENIER AND ALL ALONG THE COAST OF SOUTH LOUISIANA, THERE ARE FISHERMEN, HARVESTERS, AND PROCESSORS WHO MAKE THEIR LIVING OFF THE WATERS OF THE GULF. THESE FAMILIES HAVE WEATHERED NATURE'S FURY AND MAN-MADE DISASTERS OF ALL KINDS, BUT THEY HAVE REMAINED RESILIENT. I'VE GOTTEN TO KNOW MANY OF THESE FAMILIES, AND I CAN TELL YOU THAT THEY ARE TRULY DEDICATED TO THE MISSION OF PRESERVING A WAY OF LIFE THAT IS A TIME-HONORED TRADITION IN LOUISIANA.

Buying seafood straight from the source ensures you get the freshest available—along with a boatload of stories. You see, I like to shake the hand of the fishermen that trawled the shrimp, harvested the oysters, reeled the finfish, or trapped the crabs that go into my pot.

Understand that the word *seafood* in South Louisiana can mean a lot more than the usual shrimp and crabs from the coastal Gulf region. In fact, a steady supply of seafood comes from well inland (more than 50 miles [80 km] from the nearest saltwater). It is brought to market by the fishermen and trappers who ply the backwaters of the nearby Atchafalaya Basin and farm the freshwater ponds of rural Acadiana, making their living off of indigenous species.

Even turtle meat is considered a seafood delicacy. It's often found in the white-tablecloth restaurants of New Orleans, as well as on the rural lunchroom tables around Acadiana. But that's where the similarities end. Cooking styles with turtle as the central ingredient are a prime introduction to the differences in citified Creole cooking and more rustic Cajun. Here's the story in a nutshell, or more accurately, a turtle shell.

One particular Friday morning, as I drove past a little seafood market on the highway heading west out of Opelousas, I did not have turtle on my mind. It was the colorful exterior signage on the building that caught my eye, and I made a U-turn to get a quick photo. I had taken a few shots when the door burst open, and a most attractive lady in pink rubber boots emerged with a big smile and inquisitive look. I was about to meet Sharon Sebastien, the owner of Sebastien's West End Seafood.

When I told her who I was, she invited me to come inside and learn more about her world of seafood. As I gazed in awe at the chalkboard menu on the wall, I was in heaven. Gou, garfish, snapping turtle (live and dressed), spotted catfish (nuggets or steaks), collar bone, frog legs, alligator, and crawfish were just a few of the marquee items on the product listing. Sharon explained each one to me in detail, and we talked about the sourcing of these fresh products. But she omitted to tell me the details about turtle.

"Come with me if you want some good pictures," she said. I followed her. There in the back room, sprawled out on a brightly lit stainless-steel table, was an enormous live snapping turtle on its back viciously scratching at the air with its sharp-clawed feet. And a short, stout man wielding a hatchet was about to end its life. Troy Deville is a Cajun fishmonger and an expert at dismantling a basin turtle. A stoic, soft-spoken man, Troy needed few words to describe his next order of business—swinging a death blow to the critter's vice-jawed, snapping head so he could begin work.

Methodical is the best word to describe the process of cleaning a freshly killed Atchafalaya Basin turtle. Once the lethal head was neutralized, the meat was sliced under and around the shell, cutting the belly shell free from the sinew and muscles that hold it in place. It was a total surprise to see the large quantity of meat inside. Snapping turtle is both fished and farmed for its meat, and a 40-pound (18 kg) snapper can yield as much as 15 to 20 pounds (7 to 9 kg) of quality turtle meat. At $9.99 per pound, it is a very profitable business.

I continued snapping away with my camera as Troy hacked, sawed, and filleted through the turtle. This is messy work, and by the end of the process, I understood why he wore the long bib apron and white rubber boots. With blood splattering everywhere, I wished I had done the same. But oh well—my turtle tutorial was well worth the cost of a pair of khakis.

Turtle soup, simmered down in a rich sherry-infused sauce and topped with chopped hard-boiled egg, is the most common interpretation of this ingredient in Creole haute cuisine. It is a mainstay of New Orleans restaurants like Galatoire's, Antoine's, and Commander's Palace. While I order it often, I am more inclined to belly up to a big steaming bowl of turtle sauce piquante—the rustic Cajun stew using the same key ingredient.

Sauce piquante is a rural preparation. It is often seen in Acadiana and interpreted with various wild ingredients: alligator, rabbit, or turtle are the most prevalent. The common denominator is taming a wild taste with a rich, zesty sauce. Unlike gumbo, sauce piquante does not always use a roux but almost always has tomatoes as a base ingredient. With its stew-like consistency, a well-prepared sauce piquante is the best way I know to crown a mound of white rice.

It's time for turtle.

SNAPPING TURTLE SAUCE PIQUANTE

This is a template sauce piquante recipe, so feel free to adapt it for rabbit, alligator, or most any wild game. I prefer using boneless turtle meat, but if your meat contains bones, then please advise your guests to watch out for the small bone fragments.

Cut the turtle meat into bite-size pieces. Sprinkle generously with salt and pepper. Place the turtle meat in a large covered container and pour over 2 of the bottles of beer and the buttermilk. Cover and refrigerate for a minimum of 2 hours or up to overnight.

Heat 2 tablespoons (28 ml) of the oil in a large cast-iron pot (or Dutch oven) with a tight-fitting lid over medium-high heat. Remove the turtle meat from the container and pat dry with paper towels, removing all of the marinade liquid from the meat. In batches, add the meat to the hot oil and brown on all sides. Repeat until all the meat is seared, transferring batches to a platter.

Add the remaining 2 tablespoons oil (28 ml) to the pot and, once it is hot, add the onions, bell pepper, and celery. Stir the pot to prevent browning. Cook until the onions turn translucent, about 5 minutes. Add the parsley and garlic and stir. Season with the white pepper, paprika, and cayenne. Add the jalapeño pepper, chopped tomatoes, tomatoes with chiles, tomato paste, honey, and Worcestershire and stir. Add the remaining 1 bottle of beer and the chicken stock, and then stir in the roux until dissolved and the pot begins to boil. Lower the heat to a simmer and add the turtle meat, smoked sausage, and bay leaves to the pot. Cover and cook for 1 hour, stirring every 10 to 15 minutes.

Add the chopped rosemary, thyme, basil, and one-half of the green onions. Cover and cook for another 20 minutes. Taste the sauce and adjust the seasoning with salt, pepper, and hot sauce. Taste the turtle meat for tenderness and cook longer, if needed.

Remove the bay leaves.

For serving, ladle the turtle sauce piquante over a mound of rice in a shallow bowl and garnish with the remaining green onions. Serve with crusty French bread and ice-cold beer.

SERVES 4 TO 6

2 pounds (900 g) boneless snapping turtle meat

Kosher salt and freshly ground black pepper

3 bottles (12 ounces, or 355 ml each) of beer

2 cups (475 ml) buttermilk

4 tablespoons (60 ml) canola oil, divided

2 cups (320 g) diced yellow onion

2 cups (300 g) diced green bell pepper

2 cups (240 g) diced celery

1 cup (60 g) chopped flat-leaf parsley

2 tablespoons (20 g) minced garlic

1 teaspoon freshly ground white pepper

1 teaspoon smoked paprika

1 teaspoon cayenne pepper

1 fresh jalapeño pepper, diced, seeds and ribs removed

2 cups (360 g) chopped ripe tomatoes

2 cans (10 ounces, or 280 g each) mild diced tomatoes with green chiles, drained

2 tablespoons (32 g) tomato paste

1 tablespoon (20 g) honey

1 tablespoon (15 g) Worcestershire sauce

2 cups (475 ml) chicken stock

½ cup (120 ml) dark roux (page 14)

2 cups (450 g) sliced smoked pork sausage

3 bay leaves

2 tablespoons (4 g) chopped fresh rosemary

2 tablespoons (5 g) chopped fresh thyme

2 tablespoons (6 g) chopped fresh basil leaves

2 cups (200 g) diced green onion tops, divided

Dash of hot sauce

6 cups (948 g) cooked long-grain white rice

TABLE TIPS

★ The jalapeño pepper adds fresh heat to this spicy dish, so go easy on the hot sauce.

★ The touch of honey balances out the acidity of the tomatoes—be sure to include it.

CRAB-STUFFED ROULADE OF POMPANO

I love grilling fish over an open flame, but truth be told, there are times that this trend gets in the way. Baking is oftentimes the preferred method for cooking a very special fillet of fish. For instance, take pompano, a fish that is prized by those in the know along the coast of Louisiana. The succulent, white flakes of this delicate fish do not take kindly to the grill, and to layer smoke into this pristine sweet flesh just makes no sense. This elegant, yet simple, method showcases the flavors of two of the most delicate Gulf seafood ingredients, pompano and blue crab. How can you go wrong?

Preheat the oven to 350°F (180°C, or gas mark 4). Grease 8 cups of a standard muffin tin with butter.

Using paper towels, pat the fish fillets dry; sprinkle lightly with salt and pepper.

Melt the butter in a large skillet over medium heat. Add the onions, celery, bell peppers, and green onions. Cook until the onions turn translucent, about 5 minutes. Add the garlic, thyme, wine, and cream. Let cook until the wine and cream begin to reduce and thicken, about 5 to 8 minutes. Season with the lemon juice, Cajun Seasoning Blend, and hot sauce. Remove the mixture from the heat. Add the crabmeat and stir gently to incorporate. Slowly add the bread crumbs just until the mixture reaches a moist stuffing consistency.

Arrange one of the pompano fillets in each greased muffin cup, around the sides of the cup like a tube. Spoon a portion of the crabmeat stuffing into the muffin cup of each fish fillet. Bake until the fish is cooked through, about 15 minutes. Watch carefully to avoid overcooking.

For serving, slide a knife around each roulade until it loosens from the muffin cup and then gently lift it out. Serve two of the roulades on each plate and garnish with a sprig of thyme. Simple steamed vegetables go well with the delicate flavors of this dish.

TABLE TIP

This technique of baking stuffed fish roulades in a muffin pan is one that I have applied to other delicate fish fillets, such as speckled trout and flounder. Be sure to grease the muffin pan thoroughly and run a knife around the edges before removing to prevent the fish from flaking apart. You can use a toothpick to hold the fish together, but I've found that it usually isn't necessary with this technique.

SERVES 4

8 pompano fillets (6 ounces, or 170 g each), trimmed and bones removed

Kosher salt and freshly ground black pepper

4 tablespoons (½ stick, or 55 g) unsalted butter

1 cup (160 g) finely diced yellow onion

1 cup (120 g) finely diced celery

½ cup (75 g) diced red bell pepper

½ cup (75 g) diced green bell pepper

½ cup (50 g) diced green onion tops

1 tablespoon (10 g) minced garlic

2 tablespoons (5 g) chopped fresh thyme

½ cup (120 ml) white wine

½ cup (120 ml) heavy cream

Juice of 1 lemon

1 tablespoon (10 g) Cajun Seasoning Blend (page 13)

Dash of hot sauce

8 ounces (225 g) white lump crabmeat, picked over for shells and cartilage

1 cup (115 g) unseasoned bread crumbs, plus more if needed

Fresh thyme sprigs

CRAWFISH AND ASPARAGUS TART

I am a sucker for custard tarts of most any kind. Whether savory or sweet—a quiche or a quickie dessert—egg custard is a versatile way to showcase star ingredients. I usually like my asparagus with a thumb-size thickness, but when I saw the stacks of pencil-thin green asparagus at my local farmers' market, I decided to pair it with Louisiana crawfish in a cheesy custard. Using store-bought piecrust makes this convenient, and I always have a few crusts tucked away in my freezer. This is a perfect brunch dish or a light evening dinner paired with a salad and glass of chardonnay. Try this elegant and easy Louisiana crawfish dish and once you've mastered the basics of custard tarts, let your creativity run wild. Louisiana crawfish tails make this dish unique, but crabmeat or small shrimp will work just as well.

Preheat the oven to 350°F (180°C, or gas mark 4). Spray the inside of a 5 x 14 x 1-inch (13 x 36 x 2.5 cm) tart pan with a removable bottom with nonstick spray. Line a baking sheet with aluminum foil.

On a dry surface sprinkled with flour, remove the two piecrusts from their tins and combine into one large ball of dough. Chill for 15 minutes. On the floured surface, roll out the dough into a long rectangle to fit your tart tin. Using the rolling pin sprinkled with flour, roll the pastry dough onto the pin and drape over the tart pan. With your fingers, press the dough into and along the sides of the pan. Crimp away any excess dough. Use any remaining dough to fill in along the edges or the bottom where the dough may have pulled away. Make sure there are no holes in the dough and that the edges come to the top inside edge of the pan. Place the tart tin into the refrigerator to chill.

Bring a large pot filled with at least 3 inches (7.5 cm) of water to a boil over high heat and then submerge the asparagus and cook until tender. Remove from the heat and immediately plunge into cold water to stop the cooking and retain the color. With a pair of kitchen shears, trim the woody ends of the asparagus spears. Move to a paper towel to drain.

Whisk the eggs, cream, buttermilk, and sour cream in a large bowl until combined. Add the vermouth (if using), along with the salt, white pepper, thyme, and Parmesan cheese. Stir to combine.

Move the tart pan to the prepared baking sheet and sprinkle the pastry dough with an even layer of the Cheddar cheese. Carefully pour enough egg custard mixture into the dough-lined pastry pan to fill three-quarters full. Take a cluster of 4 or 5 asparagus spears and position them in the custard with the tips facing outward. Repeat in clusters until all the asparagus spears are placed. With a spoon, evenly distribute the crawfish tails and cherry tomato halves in the custard. Add any additional custard mixture to bring the filling to the top of the crust.

Bake for about 45 minutes or until the egg custard is set and the crust is crisp and golden brown. Let rest for at least 15 minutes before cutting. Serve hot or at room temperature.

SERVES 4 TO 6

2 frozen ready-made, deep-dish piecrusts (9 inches, or 23 cm each), thawed

Unbleached all-purpose flour, for rolling

1 bunch (12 to 16 spears) of thin asparagus

4 large eggs

½ cup (120 ml) heavy cream

½ cup (120 ml) buttermilk

1 tablespoon (15 g) sour cream

2 tablespoons (28 ml) dry vermouth (optional)

1 teaspoon kosher salt

1 teaspoon freshly ground white pepper

1 tablespoon (2 g) chopped fresh thyme

2 tablespoons (10 g) freshly grated Parmesan cheese

1 cup (120 g) freshly grated white Cheddar cheese

1 cup (225 g) Louisiana crawfish tail meat

12 cherry tomatoes, halved

BUY LOUISIANA CRAWFISH

Oh, for the love of crawfish. The sweet little crustaceans show up every spring to spice up our Acadiana tables and are gone by the heat of summer. At least, that was the way it used to be years ago before farming, processing, and retail distribution transformed a natural rite of spring into a year-round industry.

You see, there are two sources for Louisiana crawfish—wild-caught basin crawfish and those that are farmed in flooded rice fields. There are still many trappers in the Atchafalaya swamp running their crawfish traps to bring a steady local supply to market. But it takes an organized aquaculture industry of crawfish farming and peeling plants to bring Louisiana's catch to the rest of the world. It's big business, and it's under attack.

If water conditions (too much or too little rain), temperature (too hot or too cold), or costs (boats, fuel, traps, and bait) weren't enough to deal with, imported Chinese crawfish tails—with radically inferior taste and texture—flood the market at prices less than half that of Louisiana tails. And these frozen imports are sold under deceptive Cajun-sounding brand names, resulting in unwary shoppers grabbing them from the supermarket case without the slightest glance to the fine print designating their Asian point of origin.

No matter the price difference, I am passionately loyal to buying only Louisiana crawfish and I urge you to join me. The reason is twofold. First, you are purchasing an American-sourced catch of the highest-quality taste and texture. Second, you are helping support a vital industry and important cultural foodway. The many Cajun families fishing the basin and farming the crawfish fields will thank you—and so will I.

SPECKLED TROUT AND SHRIMP CHOWDER

I grew up fishing the coastal saltwater flats of Lake Borgne in the southeastern corner of Louisiana. We fished the brackish waters at the mouth of the East Pearl River for redfish, flounder, and speckled trout. This chowder is a delicate dish, with the tender and tasty white-fleshed fillet of speckled trout coupled with tender Gulf shrimp. It must be cooked quickly to ensure maximum flavor and texture.

Peel the shrimp and refrigerate. Add the heads and shells to a large pot. Cover with water and bring to a boil. Lower the heat to a simmer and cook for 30 minutes. Strain the shrimp stock and reserve.

Melt the butter in a medium pot over medium heat. When the butter is sizzling, add the onions, celery, and smoked sausage. Cook until the onions turn translucent, about 5 minutes, and then add the garlic, parsley, and 1 cup (100 g) of the green onions. Cook and stir for 5 minutes to combine.

Add the flour to the vegetables and stir continuously until the flour cooks slightly to make a blond roux. Add the wine and 4 cups (946 ml) of the reserved shrimp stock. Continue cooking and stirring over low heat until the mixture thickens, about 5 minutes.

Add the milk, along with the cooked potatoes and corn. Continue cooking over low heat for 30 minutes or until it reaches a thick chowder consistency. Season with salt and pepper and add hot sauce to taste.

Add the shrimp and speckled trout. Stir until all the seafood is submerged and let simmer for 15 minutes or until the seafood is cooked through.

Ladle the chowder into bowls and sprinkle with the remaining ½ cup (100 g) green onions. Serve with hot French bread and extra hot sauce on the side.

SERVES 6 TO 8

4 pounds (1.8 kg) jumbo (16/20 count) shrimp, head-on

2 tablespoons (28 g) unsalted butter

1 cup (160 g) diced yellow onion

1 cup (120 g) diced celery

1 cup (150 g) diced mild smoked pork sausage

1 tablespoon (10 g) minced garlic

½ cup (30 g) chopped fresh flat-leaf parsley

1½ cups (150 g) diced green onion tops, divided

3 tablespoons (23 g) unbleached all-purpose flour

¼ cup (60 ml) dry white wine

2 cups (475 ml) whole milk

2 cups (450 g) chopped cooked red potatoes

1 cup (154 g) yellow corn kernels

Kosher salt and freshly ground black pepper

Dash of hot sauce

2 pounds (900 g) speckled trout fillets, cut into chunks

TABLE TIP

Get in the habit of buying head-on, shell-on shrimp whenever possible. While you can use already peeled shrimp, it's the shells and heads that are the keys to a good seafood stock, which is crucial to the flavor of this recipe.

SHRIMP-STUFFED AVOCADO SALAD

Sometimes I choose to call food fancy for no reason other than it doesn't fit into the conventional repertoire of the Cajun and Creole food I revere. But fancy is okay with these stuffed avocados. They will tingle your taste buds and lighten up your day with a balanced combination of ingredients. Speaking of ingredients: The simpler the list, the more important it is to have the freshest available. This is one of those times. Ripe (but still firm) avocados along with briny, sweet shrimp are a must; anything less won't do.

Place the water, lemon juice, hot sauce, and salt in a pot and bring to a boil. Add the shrimp and cook until done, about 5 minutes. Drain in a colander, rinse with cold running water to stop the cooking, and drain again. Place in a bowl, cover, and refrigerate until ready to use.

In a large bowl, whisk the mayonnaise, Creole mustard, vinegar, and lemon juice. Add the parsley, red onions, celery, and green onions and stir to combine. Add the pepper, a dash of hot sauce, and a sprinkle of salt. Taste and adjust the seasonings as you like.

Cut the avocados in half lengthwise and remove the pits. With a spoon, remove the pulp from each half and reserve the empty avocado halves. Cut the pulp into bite-size cubes and add it to the bowl with the dressing. Add the shrimp to the bowl and combine gently until evenly incorporated.

Spoon a large portion of the shrimp-and-avocado mixture into each avocado half. Cover and refrigerate until chilled, about 1 hour.

For serving, place the stuffed avocado halves on a plate with a bed of the mixed salad greens. Garnish with the lemon slices.

TABLE TIPS

★ This shrimp salad is remarkably versatile and also makes a tasty sandwich served on a freshly baked croissant.

★ Buy ripe but firm avocados that are not mushy. If you slice your avocados ahead of time, be sure to toss them in lemon juice to prevent them from turning brown.

★ Feel free to replace the shrimp with crabmeat or even crawfish tails.

SERVES 3 TO 6

8 cups (1.9 L) water

1 tablespoon (15 ml) freshly squeezed lemon juice

1 tablespoon (15 ml) hot sauce

2 tablespoons (36 g) salt

1 pound (455 g) medium (41/50 count) shrimp, peeled and deveined

1 cup (225 g) mayonnaise

1 tablespoon (21 g) Creole mustard or other coarse-grained mustard

1 tablespoon (15 ml) white wine vinegar

2 tablespoons (28 ml) freshly squeezed lemon juice

½ cup (30 g) chopped flat-leaf parsley

1 cup (160 g) finely diced red onion

1 cup (120 g) finely diced celery

½ cup (50 g) diced green onion tops

1 teaspoon freshly ground black pepper

Dash of hot sauce

Kosher salt

3 medium ripe but firm Hass avocados

2 cups (110 g) firmly packed mixed salad greens

1 lemon, sliced

SEAFOOD-STUFFED POBLANOS WITH MANGO SALSA

Southwest Louisiana shares a border with Texas, and many of our treasured Cajun foods make their way across the state line. But from time to time, we import a technique or two from our Texas friends. This seafood-stuffed poblano pepper is one of those. The peppery spice of Cajun cuisine mingles nicely with the chile-infused Latin flavors in this stuffed poblano. Be forewarned: This is fiery fare that I tame down just a bit with a fresh citrus salsa featuring sweet ripe mango.

MANGO SALSA

Combine all of the ingredients in a large bowl. Stir to mix thoroughly, cover, and refrigerate for at least 2 hours or up to overnight.

POBLANOS

Preheat the oven to 375°F (190°C, or gas mark 5). Line a rimmed baking sheet with parchment paper.

To remove the skins from the poblanos, place them directly over the open flame of a gas grill or gas stovetop burner and gently turn them on all sides with tongs. Or for an electric stove, broil in the oven on the top rack until charred and blistered, about 12 minutes. Once blackened, move the peppers to a large bowl covered with plastic wrap to trap the steam. After 10 minutes, the peels should rub right off with a paper towel. Using a sharp knife, slice down the center of each poblano. Make another slice across the top in a "T" pattern. Open up the pocket and fold back the sides without breaking the pepper. Remove the seeds and any membrane. Set aside.

Heat the oil in a large skillet over medium-high heat. Add the tasso, onions, and celery. Cook until the onions turn translucent, about 5 minutes. Add the green onions, cilantro, and tomatoes with chiles. Turn off the heat and add the cooked rice, along with the Monterey Jack cheese, sour cream, and Cajun Seasoning Blend. Mix to evenly distribute all the ingredients. Season to taste with salt, pepper, and hot sauce. Fold in the crawfish, shrimp, and crabmeat and mix gently.

Arrange the poblano peppers on the prepared baking sheet. Open the pocket and spoon in as much of the seafood-rice stuffing as you can. Add a small amount of water in the bottom of the pan, about ½ cup (120 ml). (This will keep the bottom of the peppers from burning and also steam them to soften.) Cover the pan tightly with aluminum foil and bake until the peppers are tender, about 20 minutes. Check to see that the peppers are tender and if not, continue baking for another 10 minutes or until done. Serve with the Mango Salsa on the side.

SERVES 4

MANGO SALSA

1 cup (175 g) diced ripe mango

2 tablespoons (2 g) chopped fresh cilantro leaves

2 tablespoons (20 g) finely diced red onion

1 tablespoon (8 g) finely diced celery

1 tablespoon (9 g) finely diced red bell pepper

1 teaspoon finely diced fresh jalapeño pepper

1 tablespoon (15 ml) freshly squeezed lime juice

1 tablespoon (15 ml) extra-virgin olive oil

1 teaspoon salt

POBLANOS

4 large fresh poblano peppers

1 tablespoon (15 ml) canola oil

2 tablespoons (19 g) diced tasso (preferably) or smoked ham

1 cup (160 g) diced yellow onion

½ cup (60 g) diced celery

2 tablespoons (12 g) diced green onion tops

2 tablespoons (2 g) chopped fresh cilantro leaves

½ cup (121 g) canned mild diced tomatoes with green chiles

2 cups (316 g) cooked long-grain white rice

2 tablespoons (14 g) freshly grated Monterey Jack cheese

1 tablespoon (15 g) sour cream

1 teaspoon Cajun Seasoning Blend (page 13)

Kosher salt and freshly ground black pepper

Dash of hot sauce

1 cup (225 g) Louisiana crawfish tail meat

1 cup (225 g) diced shrimp

½ cup (225 g) white lump crabmeat, picked over for shells and cartilage

TABLE TIPS

★ I like how all three kinds of seafood work together in this dish, but feel free to improvise with any combination you like.

★ The cheese and sour cream are here mostly to help bind the rice mixture but not to overwhelm the seafood taste.

CRAWFISH-STUFFED SHRIMP WITH CREOLE RICE

I first tasted crawfish-stuffed shrimp some thirty years ago at the Blair House, an acclaimed French Acadian restaurant in my hometown of Lafayette, Louisiana. The door to that establishment has long since closed, but the memory lingers on. I recall how delicate it was. Not the usual heavy-handed interpretation—stuffed, battered, breaded, and fried to a dense, overdone crispness—but soft and airy, with the moist stuffing crowning the tender shrimp underneath. It was glorious.

This recipe is a re-creation from my memory of that amazing meal. Food memory is a curious and fleeting thing. There are days that I have trouble recalling what I had for breakfast, but I can describe every taste, texture, and aroma of a plate of food I devoured at a restaurant in 1985. Food is just that way—either memorable or not. This dish, pairing rich crawfish-stuffed shrimp with creamy Creole rice, is one that is indelibly inscribed in my memory banks with precise and measured detail.

CREOLE RICE

Heat the olive oil in a large skillet over medium-high heat. Sauté the onions and celery until the onions turn translucent, about 5 minutes. Add the tomatoes, parsley, wine, and chicken stock. Stir to incorporate and bring to a boil. Lower the heat to a simmer and add the rice. If the leftover rice is hard, break it up with your hands or the flat side of a spatula (do not rinse the rice). The extra-starchy rice will begin to soften and thicken the mixture.

Stir in the paprika, tomato paste, cream cheese, and cherry tomatoes. Cook on low for 5 minutes. If you need more liquid, add more stock. At this point, the rice will begin to take on the texture of a creamy risotto and the rich color of a Creole jambalaya. Season with hot sauce, salt, and pepper to taste. Turn off the heat and keep warm until serving.

SHRIMP

Preheat the oven to 400°F (200°C, or gas mark 6). Line a baking sheet with parchment paper.

Using a sharp paring knife, butterfly the shrimp by slicing lengthwise from the tail into the meat along the inner curl, stopping short of cutting all the way through. Fold the flaps to reveal a flat surface for stuffing. Refrigerate for later.

Melt the butter in a skillet over medium-high heat. Sauté the onions and celery for 5 minutes or until the onions turn translucent. Add the garlic, parsley, rosemary, cayenne, salt, and pepper. Stir to incorporate. Add the vermouth and crawfish tails and cook for 5 minutes. Add the Parmesan cheese and one-half of the bread crumbs. Stir and add more bread crumbs if the mixture is too watery. As you incorporate the bread crumbs, feel free to add a bit of water to thin it out. The mixture should have a moist consistency but still be tight enough to keep its shape when stuffed into the shrimp.

SERVES 4

CREOLE RICE

1 tablespoon (15 ml) olive oil

1 cup (160 g) diced yellow onion

½ cup (60 g) diced celery

1 cup (180 g) chopped roasted tomatoes

2 tablespoons (8 g) chopped flat-leaf parsley

2 tablespoons (28 ml) white wine

½ cup (120 ml) chicken stock, plus more if needed

3 cups (474 g) leftover cooked white rice

1 teaspoon paprika

2 tablespoons (32 g) tomato paste

2 tablespoons (30 g) cream cheese

½ cup (75 g) yellow cherry tomatoes, halved

Dash of hot sauce

Kosher salt and freshly ground black pepper

SHRIMP

12 colossal (8/10 count) shrimp, peeled, tail-on, and deveined

8 tablespoons (1 stick, or 112 g) unsalted butter

1 cup (160 g) finely diced yellow onion

½ cup (60 g) finely diced celery

1 tablespoon (10 g) minced garlic

2 tablespoons (8 g) chopped flat-leaf parsley

1 tablespoon (2 g) chopped fresh rosemary

1 teaspoon cayenne pepper

1 teaspoon kosher salt

1 teaspoon freshly ground black pepper, or to taste

2 tablespoons (28 ml) dry vermouth or white wine

1 cup (225 g) Louisiana crawfish tail meat, chopped

2 tablespoons (10 g) freshly grated Parmesan cheese

2 cups (230 g) fresh bread crumbs

TABLE TIPS

★ I like roasting my own tomatoes, but feel free to use canned fire-roasted tomatoes. Just be sure to drain the excess liquid from the can before adding.

★ If you have trouble finding crawfish tails, this stuffing works equally well with crabmeat.

Lay the shrimp on the prepared baking sheet, pocket side up. Place a tablespoon (15 g) of stuffing onto the flat tail of each shrimp and form it into a mound. With the leftover stuffing, go back to each shrimp and add more until it is all used up. Bake for 20 minutes or until the shrimp are cooked through and the tops begin to brown.

For each serving, place a mound of Creole Rice on a plate and line 3 shrimp up on top.

SNAPPER IN CREOLE TOMATO BROTH

Sometimes culinary subtlety takes over my more adventurous side. Softly simmered Gulf snapper fillets and Louisiana shrimp come to life in this pool of chicken stock perfumed with the essence of sweet Creole tomatoes. When elevated ever so gently with slices of sweet pepper, fresh basil leaves, and crisp asparagus tips and awakened with a spritz of fresh lemon juice, this fish is in the swim of things.

Bring the chicken stock to a boil in a large pot over medium-high heat. Add the tomato and lower the heat to a simmer. Cook for 5 minutes or until the skin begins to pull away from the tomato. Remove the tomato and peel off the skin. Cut the tomato in half, return to the simmering stock, and cook for 10 minutes.

Using a strainer, remove the tomato, along with any seeds and pulp. Taste the stock and add a bit of salt, if needed. The stock should now be fragrant with the essence of the tomato only. Return the stock to a simmer and add the carrots, asparagus tips, and peppers. Cook for 5 minutes and then transfer the vegetables to a bowl of ice water to preserve their color.

Add the fish fillets to the simmering stock and cook until fork-tender, about 5 minutes. (The cooking time will vary depending on the thickness of your fillets.) Remove the fillets and place in individual serving bowls.

Add the shrimp and cook until they turn pink and are done, about 3 to 5 minutes. Remove the shrimp and place in the bowls.

Add a portion of carrots, asparagus tips, peppers, cherry tomato halves, and basil leaves to each bowl. Arrange the ingredients so that they are scattered throughout the bowl.

Bring the stock back to a boil and then ladle the hot broth into each bowl. Add a basil leaf and a thin slice of lemon to the edge of each bowl. Serve immediately.

SERVES 4

8 cups (1.9 L) chicken stock

1 large ripe tomato

Kosher salt

1 cup (65 g) julienned carrots

1 bunch of asparagus, tips removed (reserve stalks for another use)

4 yellow mini sweet peppers, sliced into rings and seeds removed

4 snapper fillets (8 ounces, or 225 g each), bones removed, or other flaky white finfish fillets

8 jumbo (16/20 count) shrimp, peeled, tail-on, and deveined

1 cup (150 g) cherry tomatoes, halved

4 fresh basil leaves

4 lemon slices

TABLE TIPS

★ Go easy on the salt and any other spices you might be tempted to introduce to this recipe. The beauty of this dish is that it forgoes heavy doses of seasoning and relies on maintaining the integrity of the fresh ingredients. That said, it is dependent on sourcing the freshest fish you can find. Any delicate white flaky fish will work.

★ I tried this dish using seafood stock, but I much prefer the subtle chicken stock flavored with tomato.

GRILLED REDFISH WITH SHRIMP BUTTER

Redfish are everywhere in South Louisiana waters, and anyone with a fishing rod (or a fishing friend) has easy access to this tasty finfish. Regulations on size and limits protect the species, and after you've had one bite, you'll know why. The simplicity of prepping and the ease of cooking is why this dish is a favorite of Louisiana fishing camp cooks. This is a classic preparation of grilling fish "on the half shell" where the skin, and especially the scales, act as a barrier to keep the fish moist and prevent overcooking. My buttery, caper-laden shrimp sauce finishes it with flair. Here's the beauty of this method: The butter will cause the fire to flame up, creating a charring effect, but the tender, flaky fish is protected by its natural heat shield. You will need to ask your fishmonger to prepare the fish for you this way, filleted but with skin and scales left on.

Preheat a gas grill or prepare a medium fire in a charcoal grill.

Inspect the fish fillets by feeling the flesh with your fingers and remove any bones with a pair of pliers. Rinse the fillets and dry on paper towels. Sprinkle the flesh side lightly with salt and pepper.

Put the butter, garlic, lemon juice, parsley, and capers in a medium saucepan over medium heat. When the butter melts, reduce the heat to low and add the shrimp. Cook until the flavors come together and the shrimp turn pink, about 5 minutes. Turn off the heat and keep warm.

Place the redfish fillets directly on the grill grates, skin-side down. Brush with some of the butter sauce and close the grill cover. The flame should subside when the cover is closed tight; after 5 minutes, lift the cover. Brush again with the butter sauce and close the cover to cook for another 5 minutes.

Inspect the fish for doneness (it will not take long) by sticking a knife under the flesh to see that it lifts off the skin easily. When done, transfer to a platter. Leave the fillets as is, or slide a spatula under the fish and remove it carefully from the skin and scales without breaking the flesh. Drizzle with the warm butter sauce and place 3 shrimp on top of each fillet for serving.

SERVES 4

4 redfish fillets (10 to 12 ounces, 280 to 340 g each), skin and scales on

Kosher salt and freshly ground black pepper

1 cup (2 sticks, or 225 g) unsalted butter

2 tablespoons (20 g) minced garlic

2 tablespoon (28 ml) freshly squeezed lemon juice

1 tablespoon (4 g) chopped flat-leaf parsley

1 tablespoon (9 g) chopped capers

12 jumbo (16/20 count) shrimp, peeled and deveined

TABLE TIPS

★ Redfish is the classic ingredient, but any flaky white fish (such as red snapper or black drum) with scales will work. Just be sure to have your fish market prep the fillets by leaving the skin and scales on.

★ I use shrimp in my sauce simply because I usually have leftover live bait shrimp, but feel free to add crabmeat or crawfish as a delicious variation.

BEWARE THE DEAD MAN

Summer days spent crabbing at my family's camp near Slidell, Louisiana, are some of my most vivid childhood memories. All I needed was a string and a chicken neck to load a 5-gallon (19 L) bucket in an afternoon. I recall sitting on the dock as the adults drank beer, and we all cleaned a huge pile of big blues for making a crab gumbo. "Pull out the dead man!" my dad cautioned, and with wide-eyed attention, I listened.

Cleaning crabs is pretty easy work: After killing the crabs with a short parboil, it is simply a matter of removing the back and pulling out most of the funky stuff along with the eyes. But most important is the "dead man": the feathery gill sacks that line the inside cavity. It is said that anyone who eats those would surely be a dead man. Although not exactly true, this 10-year-old wanted to live a long life, and I wasn't about to cross my dad—or the dead man.

POTATO CHIP-FRIED SHRIMP BOATS

Fried shrimp is a popular Cajun dish, and the inspiration for my take on this South Louisiana classic is twofold: the shrimp boats lining the docks of the Acadiana fishing village of Delcambre and Zapp's, the iconic potato chip of Louisiana. Grinding up a bag of the spicy Cajun Crawtators, I discovered the perfect layer of flavor and crunch to envelop my jumbos. A hollowed-out loaf of French bread became the perfect vessel for my seafood catch. With spiral-cut potato strings, creamy coleslaw, and horseradish-infused cocktail sauce, you're ready to set sail.

COCKTAIL SAUCE

Whisk all of the ingredients together in a bowl. Portion into 4 individual serving bowls and refrigerate until ready to serve.

CREAMY SLAW

Put the cabbage and carrots in a large bowl. Stir in the remaining ingredients and toss to combine. Cover and refrigerate for at least 1 hour before serving.

BREAD BOATS

Preheat the oven to 350°F (180°C, or gas mark 4).

With a bread knife, slice off the top portion of each loaf, revealing the soft inside. With your hands, scoop out the bread, being careful not to penetrate the bottom.

Mix the butter with the garlic and spread evenly along the inside walls of the loaves. Lightly sprinkle with the Parmesan cheese and salt to taste. Place the loaves and their tops in the oven and bake until browned and crusty, about 7 minutes. Keep warm until serving.

POTATO STRINGS

Pour enough oil into a large pot to come halfway up the side of the pot. Bring the oil to a temperature of 350°F (180°C).

Working in batches, add the potatoes and fry until golden brown, about 3 minutes. Using a slotted spoon or skimmer, transfer to a paper-towel–lined platter to drain. Lightly sprinkle with Cajun Seasoning Blend to taste and keep warm until serving.

(CONTINUED)

SERVES 4

COCKTAIL SAUCE

2 cups (480 g) ketchup

2 tablespoons (30 g) prepared horseradish

1 tablespoon (15 g) Worcestershire sauce

1 teaspoon freshly squeezed lemon juice

1 teaspoon hot sauce

CREAMY SLAW

4 cups (300 g) finely shredded napa cabbage

½ cup (65 g) julienned carrots

½ cup (115 g) mayonnaise

2 tablespoons (30 g) sour cream

2 tablespoons (28 ml) sugarcane vinegar or white vinegar

1 teaspoon celery salt

Kosher salt and freshly ground black pepper

BREAD BOATS

4 loaves French bread (10 inches, or 25 cm each)

8 tablespoons (1 stick, or 112 g) unsalted butter, softened

4 teaspoons (12 g) minced garlic

½ cup (50 g) freshly grated Parmesan cheese

Kosher salt

POTATO STRINGS

4 large baking potatoes, peeled and cut into spiral "strings" or regular fries

Canola oil, for frying

Cajun Seasoning Blend (page 13)

SHRIMP

24 colossal (8/10 count) shrimp, peeled, tail-on, and deveined

3 bags (1 pound, or 455 g each) spicy, kettle-type potato chips, such as Zapp's Cajun Crawtators

2 cups (250 g) unbleached all-purpose flour

1 tablespoon (10 g) Cajun Seasoning Blend (page 13)

2 large eggs, beaten

3 cups (700 ml) buttermilk

Canola oil, for frying

Salt

4 lemon wedges

TABLE TIPS

★ If you can't find Zapp's, use a crunchy, kettle-type potato chip with a spice profile that you enjoy.

★ The frying time is fast, so butterfly the shrimp to ensure they cook quickly before the potato chip crust becomes too brown.

SHRIMP

With a sharp paring knife, slice halfway through the back of each shrimp and butterfly them for even cooking.

Pulse the chips in a food processor until crushed, but stop short of a bread crumb texture. Spread the potato chip breading out on a large baking sheet. Put the flour in a shallow bowl and stir in the Cajun Seasoning Blend. Put the eggs in another shallow bowl and whisk in the buttermilk to combine.

In a large pot, add enough oil to come halfway up the side of the pot (you may reuse the potato frying oil, if you wish). Bring the oil to a temperature of 350°F (180°C).

Working in batches, add the shrimp to the flour and coat evenly, shaking off any excess. Move the floured shrimp to the egg wash and coat evenly. Add the shrimp to the potato chip breading and coat generously. Place the battered shrimp on a plate.

Holding each shrimp by the tail, gently lower into the hot oil. Fry in batches to prevent overcrowding. The shrimp will brown quickly because the potato chips are already brown, so watch carefully and remove when golden, about 3 minutes. Drain on a wire rack (not paper towels) to retain a crisp texture. Season with salt immediately.

For serving, place a mound of potato strings inside each toasted bread loaf. Add 6 shrimp on top of each. Lay the toasted bread top along the side of the loaf. Garnish with a lemon wedge and serve with the cocktail sauce and creamy slaw.

ZAPP YOUR TASTE BUDS

I first crossed paths with the late Ron Zappe in the 1980s, when he was a struggling local business owner trying to gain entry into the competitive snack foods market. He was the epitome of the Cajun entrepreneur—full of spicy ideas and a taste for adventure. He succeeded in turning that small chip-making outfit in Gonzales, Louisiana, into Zapp's Potato Chips, a national brand.

As the story goes, his wife came home from the grocery store with a bag of kettle-fried chips and sparked the idea for a new career. True to his Louisiana roots, it was the spice that created a differentiation for his products, and it was a creative branding approach that separated him from the national competition. Crawtator potato chips—with the spiciness of a Cajun crawfish boil—were born and were an instant success.

CORN MAQUE CHOUX WITH SHRIMP

Long before the French Acadians landed, Indian tribes dotted the Louisiana coast and plains. They shaped the food culture with a variety of ingredients and methods that are mainstays of every Acadiana table. Corn maque choux is at the top of that list. Most all Cajun and Creole cooks have their version, and they are all good.

Over the years, basic corn maque choux has been infused with all sorts of added ingredients—shrimp, crab, and crawfish being the most common. In some pots, tasso and other sausages are used to punch up the spice level, and some versions feature the smooth texture that sweet cream can bring. The one key is to use quality ingredients, the fresher the better.

Using a sharp knife, slice the corn kernels off the cobs, shaving as close to the cob as possible. Once the corn is off, pull the back of the knife and across the cob, releasing the corn "milk." Place the corn and any liquid into a bowl.

Melt the butter in a large cast-iron skillet over medium-high heat. Add the onions, celery, and bell peppers, sautéing until the onions turn translucent, about 5 minutes. Add the garlic, tomatoes, and corn kernels with any liquid and cook for another 5 minutes.

Add the cream and clam juice and lower the heat to medium. Add the paprika, cayenne, Cajun Seasoning Blend, and white pepper and stir. Add the shrimp and continue to stir as the cream reduces, the mixture thickens to a sauce consistency, and the shrimp turn pink and become cooked through, about 10 minutes. Season to taste with salt and pepper, along with a dash of hot sauce. Sprinkle with the chopped chives right before serving.

TABLE TIPS

★ When in season, I always use fresh corn on the cob, but I have also used frozen yellow corn kernels with good results.

★ Don't be afraid of the seasoning levels here; it is supposed to be a spicy Cajun dish.

★ Crabmeat works well in this dish if shrimp are not available.

SERVES 4

6 ears of yellow corn, husks and silk removed, or 5 cups (820 g) frozen yellow corn kernels

4 tablespoons (½ stick, or 55 g) unsalted butter

1 cup (160 g) diced yellow onion

½ cup (60 g) diced celery

½ cup (75 g) diced green bell pepper

½ cup (75 g) diced red bell pepper

1 teaspoon minced garlic

1 can (10 ounces, or 280 g) mild diced tomatoes with green chiles, drained

½ cup (120 ml) heavy cream

2 tablespoons (28 ml) clam juice

1 tablespoon (7 g) paprika

1 teaspoon cayenne pepper

1 teaspoon Cajun Seasoning Blend (page 13)

1 teaspoon freshly ground white pepper

1 pound (455 g) small (61/70 count) shrimp, peeled and deveined

Kosher salt and freshly ground black pepper

Dash of hot sauce

½ cup (24 g) chopped fresh chives

CRAB GUMBO

In my lineup of soups, this crab gumbo ranks up there with peppery crawfish bisque and sherry-infused turtle soup as being in a league of its own. It is a brilliant dish of Creole origin that in the subtle hands of a cook with respect for its fresh, natural ingredients is otherworldly. This gumbo explodes with the intense flavor of the sea and gently thickens with a flavor-filled roux. I like to make the base of this gumbo a few hours ahead (or overnight) and let the pot rest to bring the flavors together. Just before serving, jumbo lumps are added for a final flourish.

Heat the oil in a large cast-iron pot with a heavy lid over medium-high heat. Add the onions, celery, and bell pepper and while stirring, cook until the onions are browned, about 10 minutes. Add the garlic. Stir the vegetables and add the crab stock, along with the roux and bay leaves. Add the blue crabs and submerge into the stock. Bring the liquid to a low boil. Lower the heat to a simmer, cover, and cook for 1 hour, stirring every 15 minutes; skim off any fat or foam from the surface.

Uncover the pot and season with Cajun Seasoning Blend, hot sauce, salt, and pepper. You can prepare the base gumbo to this point and hold it there indefinitely. It gets even better the longer it sits. When you are ready to serve it, add the crabmeat (remember that it is already cooked) and let it heat up, about 5 minutes.

Taste the gumbo once again and season with a light hand; your guests can always add their own hot sauce and filé powder at the table.

Remove the bay leaves.

Ladle the gumbo around a mound of white rice and sprinkle with the diced green onions.

SERVES 4 TO 6

2 tablespoons (28 ml) vegetable oil

2 cups (320 g) diced yellow onion

1 cup (120 g) diced celery

1 cup (150 g) diced green bell pepper

2 tablespoons (20 g) minced garlic

12 cups (2.8 L) crab stock or seafood stock (page 55)

½ cup (120 ml) dark roux (page 14)

2 bay leaves

4 blue crabs (1 pound, or 455 g total), cleaned, cracked, and quartered

Cajun Seasoning Blend (page 13)

Dash of hot sauce

Kosher salt and freshly ground black pepper

1 pound (455 g) white lump crabmeat, picked over for shells and cartilage

Filé powder as needed

6 cups (948 g) cooked long-grain white rice

1 cup (100 g) diced green onion tops

WHOLE FRIED SPECKLED TROUT WITH ROSEMARY FRIES AND TABASCO TARTAR

No doubt, fried speckled trout is as good as it gets, and I've spent half my life fishing the shallow coastal waters for them. Their reputation in Louisiana is at the top of the culinary seafood chain. But over the years, I've stumbled on a technique that takes fried trout to a whole new level. When you cook speckled trout (or most any flaky fish) whole on the bone, it is instantly transformed into an otherworldly dining experience. Not only is the presentation dramatic, but the crispy crust also contrasts with the close-to-the-bone sweetness of the flesh. And the blanched and twice-fried potatoes are like no other you've had. Generously sprinkled with rosemary-infused sea salt, these crunchy fries have a creamy center—a texturally complex combination.

TABASCO TARTAR SAUCE

Combine all of the ingredients in a bowl. Cover and refrigerate.

ROSEMARY FRIES

Preheat the oven to 200°F (93°C). Fill a large pot halfway with water and bring to a boil.

Cut the potatoes into long, thick slices and discard any shorter, end pieces. Add the potatoes to the boiling water and let it come back to a boil. Cook for 2 minutes and then transfer to an ice water bath to stop the cooking. Remove the potatoes and dry on paper towels. Place the slices on a baking sheet and place in the freezer until frozen.

Meanwhile, make the rosemary salt by adding the chopped fresh rosemary to the sea salt on a large metal baking sheet. Spread it out and combine. Place it in the oven until the rosemary dries out, about 30 minutes. Set aside.

Fill a large pot with a wire basket set in it with oil until it reaches about 5 inches (13 cm) deep. Bring the oil to 250°F (120°C) and add the potatoes. Cook for 5 minutes and transfer to paper towels.

For the second cooking, bring the temperature of the oil to 350°F (180°C) and add the potatoes again. Fry until the potatoes become crispy golden brown. Remove with a slotted spoon and drain on a wire rack set over paper towels. While hot, generously sprinkle the rosemary salt over the potatoes. Keep warm for serving.

TROUT

Bring the oil up to a temperature of 375°F (190°C). Pat the trout dry with paper towels.

Whisk the eggs and milk in a bowl. Add 1 tablespoon (10 g) of the Cajun Seasoning Blend and whisk to combine. Pour the mixture onto a large rimmed baking sheet and place beside the pot with the hot oil.

SERVES 4

TABASCO TARTAR SAUCE

6 tablespoons (84 g) mayonnaise

2 tablespoons (18 g) chopped dill pickle

1 teaspoon Creole mustard or other coarse-grained mustard

1 teaspoon chopped capers

1 teaspoon Worcestershire sauce

1 teaspoon Tabasco sauce

Pinch of salt

ROSEMARY FRIES

1 tablespoon (18 g) salt

2 large russet potatoes, peeled

1 cup (272 g) sea salt

2 tablespoons (4 g) chopped fresh rosemary

Canola oil, for frying

TROUT

2 whole speckled trout (2 to 3 pounds, or 900 g to 1.4 kg), scaled and gutted with head and tail on

2 large eggs

1 cup (235 ml) whole milk

2 tablespoons (20 g) Cajun Seasoning Blend (page 13), divided

1 cup (125 g) unbleached all-purpose flour

1 cup (140 g) yellow cornmeal

1 tablespoon (6 g) freshly ground white pepper

1 teaspoon kosher salt

TABLE TIPS

★ Take the trout out of the refrigerator when you start the recipe to take the chill off the fish.

★ Serving fish on the bone is impressive, and it only takes a simple technique to eat it: To avoid the bones, use the back of a spoon to gently push the fillet away from the dorsal fin and use a fork or knife to slide the fillet off the vertebrae.

Whisk the flour and cornmeal together in a bowl. Add the remaining 1 tablespoon (10 g) Cajun Seasoning Blend and the white pepper and combine. Pour the dry mixture onto another large rimmed baking sheet and spread out. Place closest to the pot, alongside the baking sheet holding the wet mixture.

Add the whole trout to the wet mixture and evenly coat all sides. Move the trout to the dry mixture and evenly coat all sides. Place the trout in the basket and immerse in the hot oil.

Cook the fish until it is crispy golden brown, about 15 minutes. Lift the basket and set over a wire rack lined with paper towels to drain. Carefully, lift the fish out of the basket and place on the wire rack to drain. Sprinkle with salt.

Serve the fish and fries on a platter family-style with the Tabasco Tartar Sauce on the side. Be sure to demonstrate to your guests how to use a fork and spoon to carefully slide the flaky fish off the bone on each side.

SEAFOOD SKILLET LASAGNA

Let's construct the perfect Cajun casserole: Sheets of lasagne noodles are the foundation for this one-dish recipe featuring Louisiana seafood. With a cheese-enriched béchamel, the creamy white sauce is the mortar that brings together the shrimp, crawfish, and crabmeat into a bubbling rich dish that builds flavor. This is an easy project that is sure to cement your kitchen reputation.

Preheat the oven to 375°F (190°C, or gas mark 5).

Melt the butter in a large nonstick saucepan over medium heat. Whisk in the flour and cook for about 5 minutes. Add the clam juice and milk, whisking until the sauce comes to a boil and thickens, about 10 minutes. Turn off the heat and let it cool to room temperature.

Whisk in the sherry, eggs, 1 cup (120 g) of the white Cheddar, the fontina, and mozzarella until the cheeses melt and the sauce is smooth. Season the sauce with salt, white pepper, and a dash of hot sauce. Move to the side and keep warm.

Heat 1 tablespoon (15 ml) of the oil in a 12-inch (30 cm) cast-iron skillet over medium-high heat. Add the spinach and cook until wilted, about 8 minutes. Pour into a cheesecloth-lined bowl and drain all the moisture from the spinach by twisting the cheesecloth and squeezing out the liquid. Place the spinach in a bowl.

In the same skillet, wiped clean and set over medium-high heat, heat 1 tablespoon (15 ml) of the olive oil and add the mushrooms. Cook until browned on both sides, about 10 minutes. Add the onions and celery and cook until the onions turn translucent, about 5 minutes. Add the garlic, parsley, green onions, and shrimp and cook for 5 minutes longer or until the shrimp begin to turn pink. Drain the mixture in a colander and keep warm.

In the same skillet or a large casserole dish sprayed with nonstick spray, spoon in a layer of the white sauce and top it with an even placing of lasagne noodles. Spread the spinach on top, followed by the mushroom-vegetable-shrimp mixture, and the crabmeat and crawfish tails. Top with more white sauce. Add more lasagne noodle sheets on top and a final layer of the remaining white sauce. Sprinkle with the remaining 1 cup (120 g) white Cheddar cheese.

Place the skillet on a baking sheet, cover with foil, and place in the hot oven. Bake for 45 minutes or until the cheese is melted and the sauce is bubbling. Remove the foil and turn the heat to broil as you watch it brown on top, about 3 to 5 minutes. Serve immediately.

TABLE TIPS

★ I find that the no-boil flat lasagne noodles work perfectly in this dish.

★ Be sure to drain excess moisture from both the spinach and the shrimp-vegetable mixture. Otherwise, you'll have a soggy lasagna.

SERVES 4 TO 6

8 tablespoons (1 stick, or 112 g) unsalted butter

1 cup (125 g) unbleached all-purpose flour

1 bottle (8 ounces, or 235 ml) clam juice

2 cups (475 ml) whole milk

¼ cup (60 ml) dry sherry

2 large eggs, beaten

2 cups (240 g) freshly grated white Cheddar cheese, divided

1 cup (110 g) freshly grated fontina cheese

½ cup (150 g) freshly grated mozzarella cheese

Kosher salt and freshly ground white pepper

Hot sauce

2 tablespoons (28 ml) olive oil, divided

3 cups (90 g) firmly packed fresh spinach leaves, stem ends removed

3 cups (210 g) sliced button mushrooms

1 cup (160 g) diced yellow onion

1 cup (120 g) diced celery

1 tablespoon (10 g) minced garlic

2 tablespoons (8 g) chopped flat-leaf parsley

2 tablespoons (12 g) diced green onion tops

1 pound (455 g) medium (41/50 count) shrimp, peeled and deveined

12 lasagne pasta sheets (fresh, no-boil, or precooked)

1 pound (455 g) Louisiana crawfish tail meat

1 pound (455 g) white lump crabmeat, picked over for shells and cartilage

SHRIMP ÉTOUFFÉE OVER SOFTSHELL CRABS

It doesn't get more coastal Cajun than this: An expertly fried softshell crab topped with a rich shrimp étouffée, all over a mound of white rice. It's the perfect balance of taste and texture. Crispy crab gives way to creamy smothered shrimp in a spicy hurricane of flavor.

SHRIMP ÉTOUFFÉE

In a large cast-iron pot or skillet over medium-high heat, melt the 2 sticks of butter and add the onions, bell pepper, and celery. Sauté until the onions turn translucent, about 5 minutes. Add the garlic, lower the heat to simmer, and stir to combine.

Sprinkle the flour over the mixture, stir to incorporate, and begin cooking the flour until it turns light brown, about 10 minutes. Add the seafood stock, tomato paste, and lemon juice. Cook and stir until you reach a stew-like thickness, about 5 to 8 minutes.

Add the shrimp and stir the mixture to combine. Simmer the shrimp in the pot for another 15 minutes.

Season to taste with cayenne, salt, and pepper. As a final touch, stir in the remaining 1 tablespoon (14 g) butter and the chopped parsley.

SOFTSHELL CRABS

In a deep pot over medium-high heat, bring the oil to a temperature of 375°F (190°C).

Rinse the crabs and pat dry with paper towels to remove any moisture.

In a shallow container, blend the flour and Cajun Seasoning Blend. In another shallow container, whisk together the half-and-half, buttermilk, and hot sauce. Sprinkle the crabs with salt and pepper, place in the liquid, and then dredge in the seasoned flour, coating both sides.

Shake off any excess flour from each crab and place in the hot oil, being careful not to crowd the pot. Fry the crabs until golden brown on both sides, about 5 minutes. Transfer to a paper towel–lined platter and keep warm. Repeat until all the crabs are cooked.

For serving, scoop a mound of rice onto each plate and top with a softshell crab. Bring the Shrimp Étouffée back to a simmer and spoon a portion over the crab, making sure to evenly distribute the shrimp. Sprinkle with the green onions and serve.

SERVES 4

SHRIMP ÉTOUFFÉE

1 cup (2 sticks, or 225 g) unsalted butter, plus 1 tablespoon

1 cup (160 g) diced yellow onion

1 cup (150 g) diced bell pepper

1 cup (120 g) diced celery

1 tablespoon (10 g) minced garlic

¼ cup (31 g) unbleached all-purpose flour

2½ cups (570 ml) seafood stock (page 55)

2 tablespoons (32 g) tomato paste

1 tablespoon (15 ml) lemon juice

2 pounds (900 g) small (61/70 count) shrimp, peeled and deveined

1 teaspoon cayenne pepper

Kosher salt and freshly ground black pepper

¼ cup (15 g) chopped flat-leaf parsley

SOFTSHELL CRABS

1 gallon (3.8 L) canola oil

4 large softshell blue crabs (1 pound, or 455 g total), cleaned

2 cups (250 g) unbleached all-purpose flour

2 tablespoons (20 g) Cajun Seasoning Blend (page 13)

1 cup (235 ml) half-and-half

1 cup (235 ml) buttermilk

1 tablespoon (15 ml) hot sauce

Kosher salt and black pepper

6 cups (948 g) cooked long-grain white rice

1 cup (100 g) diced green onion tops

CHILLED CRAB DIP WITH SWEET PEPPERS

Even in Louisiana, crabmeat isn't cheap, and the jumbo lump can go for more than $20 a pound (455 g), which is why you see families lining the waterfront docks with their nets and crab traps. A morning of crabbing fun can yield enough crabs for an afternoon boil, as well as a few mounds of hand-picked crabmeat for some great Cajun and Creole recipes.

One of my favorites is a dip that showcases the sweetness of delicate blue crabmeat. If followed carefully, the simplicity of this recipe and a light hand on ingredients will result in a dip unlike any you've ever tried before. This is not a heavily spiced, beer-drinkin' dip, but rather one that can be enjoyed with a nice glass of chilled white wine on a lazy summer evening.

Whisk the cream cheese and mayonnaise in a bowl until blended. Add the onions, celery, green onions, parsley, thyme, lemon juice, hot sauce, and Cajun Seasoning Blend, and stir. Add the crabmeat and stir to incorporate evenly. Season to taste with salt and pepper. Taste again and adjust with more hot sauce if you like it spicy. Cover the bowl and chill to allow the flavors to meld together.

Serve with fresh sweet mini peppers for dipping.

TABLE TIPS

★ For the best flavor, splurge on fresh lump white crabmeat, not canned, for this recipe.

★ I like the crunch and freshness of sweet (not hot) mini peppers for dipping, but crackers or crostini will work just fine.

SERVES 4 TO 6

6 ounces (170 g) cream cheese

2 tablespoons (28 g) mayonnaise

½ cup (80 g) finely diced white onion

1 cup (120 g) finely diced celery

1 tablespoon (6 g) diced green onion

2 tablespoons (8 g) chopped flat-leaf parsley

2 fresh thyme sprigs, stemmed and chopped

Juice of ½ of a lemon

1 tablespoon (15 ml) hot sauce

1 tablespoon (10 g) Cajun Seasoning Blend (page 13)

Kosher salt and freshly ground black pepper

8 ounces (225 g) white lump crabmeat, picked over for shells and cartilage

12 red and yellow sweet mini peppers, sliced vertically with seeds and membrane removed

IF IT FLIES, IT FRIES

CHAPTER

SEVEN

POULTRY OF ALL KINDS SHOWS UP ON THE TABLES OF SOUTH LOUISIANA: DUCK, QUAIL, TURKEY, CORNISH GAME HEN, AND OF COURSE, CHICKEN. THEY ARE NOT ONLY FRIED, BUT ALSO GRILLED, STEWED, ROASTED, PANÉED, AND FRICASSÉED, AND THEY ALL FLY INTO THE GUMBO POT OF CAJUN AND CREOLE COOKING.

Frying chicken is a Southern art form, and family recipes are protected and passed down through generations. Techniques, ingredients, and methods vary, but the end result is most always good. Fried chicken is best cooked in the home kitchen, and while there is good restaurant fried chicken out there, I have never tasted one that came close to my momma's recipe.

Peggy Graham—my momma—passed away some time ago, but not before I learned the secret to her prized fried chicken. She was a wiz in the kitchen and taught me the basics of cooking. She was a patient cook and knew that time was the most important element of cooking. Rush a recipe and you are sure to come up short.

Those in the know understand that properly fried chicken can only be achieved through the heat-conducting magic of cast iron. Keeping a consistently high temperature throughout the cooking process ensures that the chicken cooks evenly. Listen carefully: If the temperature falls, you are sure to fail. That said, always use a thermometer and start out with extra-hot oil. Once your chicken hits the pan, the hot oil will cool and you will reach your ideal frying temp.

"Take your time and brine" is a cardinal rule of chicken cooking in the Graham kitchen. A good soaking in spiced-up buttermilk with a healthy dash of hot sauce adds flavor to the chicken and gives the flour something to stick to. And that's that.

It's all very simple, but it is an adherence to those few traditional rules that is the difference between making chicken and making memories. Fried chicken—more than any other dish of the Deep South—is an emotional tie to memories of childhood. Most every good Southern cook has a treasured recipe, and I'm proud to share my momma's.

FRIED CHICKEN AND WAFFLES WITH PEPPER JELLY SYRUP

This is a basic Southern fried chicken recipe with a Cajun addition of bacon waffles and a spicy glaze. Rest assured, this chicken would be just as good with mashed potatoes and white gravy.

SERVES 4

CHICKEN

1 chicken (4 pounds, or 1.8 kg), cut into individual pieces

4 cups (946 ml) buttermilk

2 tablespoons (36 g) salt

2 tablespoons (12 g) freshly ground black pepper

2 tablespoons (18 g) garlic powder

2 tablespoons (14 g) onion powder

½ cup (75 g) Cajun Seasoning Blend (page 13)

2 tablespoons (28 ml) hot sauce

1 gallon (3.8 L) peanut oil

3 cups (375 g) unbleached all-purpose flour

¼ cup (28 g) smoked paprika

2 tablespoons (12 g) freshly ground white pepper

Kosher salt

PEPPER JELLY SYRUP

½ cup (120 g) spicy pepper jelly

½ cup (120 ml) sugarcane syrup

CHICKEN

Place the chicken pieces in a large container and cover with the buttermilk. Add the salt, pepper, garlic powder, onion powder, ¼ cup (38 g) of the Cajun Seasoning Blend, and the hot sauce. Stir to combine the ingredients and cover. Refrigerate for at least 3 hours or, preferably, overnight.

Two hours before cooking, remove the chicken from the brine and place on a wire rack to drain and come to room temperature.

Pour enough oil into a large cast-iron skillet or pot to reach a 3-inch (7.5 cm) depth (no more than halfway up the side). Heat the oil to 400°F (200°C).

In a shallow pan, combine the flour, the remaining ¼ cup (38 g) Cajun Seasoning Blend, the paprika, and white pepper. Add several of the chicken pieces to the flour mixture and turn to coat. Add the chicken to the hot oil, being careful not to crowd the pan. As the temperature of the oil drops, adjust the heat to maintain a consistent 375°F (190°C) level.

Let the chicken cook uncovered until it begins to brown on one side and then turn. Cook the other side until golden brown and crispy, about 15 minutes total. Check for doneness by inserting a meat thermometer into the thickest piece, without touching bone, and look for an internal temperature of 160°F (71°C). Remove the chicken and let drain on a wire rack. Sprinkle with kosher salt. Keep warm until all the chicken is fried.

PEPPER JELLY SYRUP

In a saucepan over medium heat, stir together the pepper jelly and syrup until the pepper jelly begins to melt, about 5 minutes. Turn off the heat and continue stirring until fully combined. Pour the mixture into a serving container and keep warm.

WAFFLES

Whisk the eggs, milk, and oil in a large bowl until thoroughly combined. In another large bowl, stir together the flour, baking powder, baking soda, salt, Cajun Seasoning Blend, garlic, green onions, and crumbled bacon. Add the dry ingredients to the wet ingredients and stir to combine.

Following the waffle iron instructions, preheat and coat it with nonstick spray. Add enough batter to make one waffle. Continue until all the waffles are made. Keep warm until serving.

For serving, place a warm waffle on each plate and top with 2 pieces of fried chicken. Drizzle the Pepper Jelly Syrup over all and serve with more syrup on the side.

WAFFLES

2 large eggs

2 cups (475 ml) whole milk

2 tablespoons (28 ml) canola oil

2 cups (250 g) unbleached all-purpose flour

2 teaspoons (9 g) baking powder

1 teaspoon baking soda

1 teaspoon salt

1 tablespoon (10 g) Cajun Seasoning Blend (page 13)

2 tablespoons (20 g) minced garlic

2 tablespoons (12 g) diced green onion tops

4 strips of crispy cooked bacon, crumbled

TABLE TIP

For even frying, cut the larger chicken breasts in half to about the same size as the other pieces. White Lily brand all-purpose flour is the go-to coating for most Southern cooks, and my momma was no different. She used Crisco for frying as most cooks of the time did, but these days I like to fry my chicken in peanut oil. In South Louisiana, we like to season our flour with an extra dose of Cajun spice along with a punch of paprika and black pepper. Fry enough chicken to not only feed your hungry guests but also to have enough for a late-night snack for yourself. You deserve it.

CHICKEN SKINS WITH SPICY SEA SALT

Crunchy fried chicken skins (let's call them chicken cracklin's) are an indulgence that I take with a grain of salt—spicy sea salt, to be exact. These crispy-skinned diet destroyers make you hate yourself for indulging; I'll just have one, okay, maybe ten. They're just that good—gone-in-sixty-seconds good.

★ ★ ★ ★ ★

Place the salt, chili powder, paprika, and black pepper in a jar with a lid. Cover and shake.

Add enough oil to a large cast-iron pot to come halfway up the side of the pot. Bring the oil to 375°F (190°C).

Spread the chicken skins out on paper towels and pat dry. Drop them into the hot oil one at a time, being careful not to crowd the pot. Fry until the fat is rendered out and the skin becomes ultra crispy and golden brown, about 8 minutes. Transfer them to a wire rack and immediately season with the spicy salt. Repeat until all the skins are cooked. Serve in the center of the table with ice-cold beer.

SERVES 6 TO 8

1 cup (272 g) coarse sea salt

½ tablespoon (4 g) chili powder

½ tablespoon (4 g) smoked paprika

½ tablespoon (3 g) freshly ground black pepper

Peanut oil, for frying

36 chicken thigh skins

TABLE TIP

I buy skin-on chicken for most every use and remove the skin and freeze it for just this recipe. The skins from the thighs are best, but any chicken skin will work. I like the chili powder–infused sea salt, but feel free to use Cajun seasoning instead.

SMOKED WILD DUCK CASSOULET

While duck confit is the cornerstone of a traditional cassoulet of southern France, simmering duck legs in a cauldron of duck fat for 12 hours is a bit excessive. And besides, I have no idea where to get my hands on enough duck fat for the job. Smoked wild ducks are an obvious stand-in and more in keeping with the simplicity of rural Louisiana cooking.

This South Louisiana version of cassoulet is more like a stew than the traditional French version. Duck camp cooks use smoked wild ducks because confit duck legs are hard to find along the bayou. It gets its thickness from both the stewed-down beans releasing their starch and a rich duck stock—a flavorful combination for introducing the smoked duck and sausage. Accented with a cheesy bread crumb and parsley gratin, this cassoulet is down-to-earth comfort food.

Remove the duck meat from the bones and reserve the meat for later. Put the duck bones in a large stockpot, along with the onions, celery, and carrots. Add enough water to cover the ingredients and simmer for 4 hours over low heat. Remove from the heat, let cool, strain the stock, and refrigerate overnight. The next morning, skim the fat from the top of the stock.

Drain the soaked beans and put in a large cast-iron pot, along with the tasso, andouille, onions, carrots, celery, bell pepper, green onions, tomatoes, and herbs. Cover with the white wine and 4 cups (946 ml) of the duck stock, reserving the rest. Bring to a boil over medium heat and, then lower to a simmer and cover the pot. Simmer for about 1 hour, watching carefully as the beans absorb the liquid and adding more stock if needed to prevent burning. Add the smoked duck meat and cook with the beans for another 30 minutes. The beans should be creamy, but not watery. Drain some of the liquid if too loose. Season to taste with salt, black pepper, and hot sauce.

Combine the bread crumbs, parsley, and Pecorino Romano cheese with the olive oil in a large bowl. Stir to incorporate and let the bread crumbs soak up the oil. Add more oil if needed until the mixture is moist.

For serving, ladle a portion of the cassoulet into a warm plate or bowl. Top with a couple of spoonfuls of the bread crumbs. Serve with crusty French bread.

SERVES 6 TO 8

4 smoked wild ducks (2½ pounds, or 1.1 kg each) or 8 store-bought duck confit legs

1 whole yellow onion

2 celery stalks

2 large carrots

2 pounds (900 g) dried large white beans, rinsed and picked over, soaked overnight in water to cover

1½ cups (225 g) diced tasso (preferably) or smoked ham

1½ cups (12 ounces, or 340 g) chopped andouille sausage (preferably) or smoked pork sausage

2 cups (320 g) diced yellow onion

1 cup (130 g) diced carrot

2 cups (240 g) diced celery

2 cups (300 g) diced green bell pepper

2 cups (200 g) diced green onion

1 cup (180 g) chopped tomatoes

1 cup (60 g) chopped flat-leaf parsley

¼ cup (40 g) minced garlic

¼ cup (8 g) chopped fresh rosemary

1 tablespoon (3 g) dried thyme

½ cup (120 ml) dry white wine

8 cups (1.9 L) duck stock or chicken stock

Kosher salt and freshly ground black pepper

Dash of hot sauce

2 cups (230 g) coarse bread crumbs or panko

1 cup (60 g) chopped flat-leaf parsley

½ cup (50 g) freshly grated Pecorino Romano cheese

2 tablespoons (28 ml) extra-virgin olive oil, plus more if needed

TABLE TIP

If you own a smoker, feel free to buy domestic ducks and smoke them for this recipe. Even using the whole roasted rotisserie chickens from the supermarket will give you a tasty version of this French classic.

DUCK HUNTING ON PECAN ISLAND

As I drove the bayou backroads through the coastal marsh of Vermilion Parish heading to Pecan Island for the first time, I realized that I had just left civilization. Crossing over the Intracoastal Bridge, I was indeed on an island with the Gulf of Mexico headwaters on my left and the wetlands of White Lake on my right. I had driven through remote bayou country before, but even I had never seen a landscape as third-world foreign as this, flat land lined with swamp grass and cattail shrubs.

But the drive was therapeutic. With each mile marker, the solitude and desolation separated me from life's complications and removed me from my stress-filled grind. As I was discovering, the isolation is what makes this place so magical and mysterious.

To begin to describe Pecan Island, you must first understand that it is at Louisiana's epicenter for both duck hunting and Hurricane Rita. The aftermath of the destruction caused by Rita, the 2005 category 4 storm, turned this quaint Cajun community into a war zone. It was swamped by complete devastation and has just now begun to rebound. Every house—those that survived and those rebuilt—is now raised. With a storm surge of 15 feet (4.6 m), caution now dictates that pilings are driven deep and raised enough to drive a pickup underneath.

Duck hunters are the main reason this 12-gauge community even exists. From the mom-and-pop grocery to the feed-and-seed store selling decoys, shotgun shells, and beer, lots of beer, Pecan Island has little else going for it. Even the local community school was sold off and is now a duck-hunting lodge. But the hundred or so carefree and colorful residents are resilient and among the finest Cajun folks I've met.

Folks in South Louisiana make no distinction between which gender is allowed in the kitchen. Men are just as likely to wield a wooden spoon as a shotgun. The tradition of hunting, especially duck hunting, is a likely reason this area of America boasts more men who cook per capita than most anywhere else. "Kill it and grill it"—that's the mantra of most men in Acadiana.

Many men I know are much more adept at the culinary arts than just the barbecue. They are students of the heritage of the culturally significant foodways of the region. They know and appreciate the art of the boucherie: how to butcher a pig and use every part, from tail to snout. They understand the patience needed for simmering a sauce piquante for six hours and the arduous prep that it takes to brine and season a pork shoulder destined for the smoker.

My friend Don Bacque is a world-class duck hunter, as well as a rustic camp cook of extraordinary talent. When he designed his Pecan Island duck camp on stilts, he built kitchens upstairs, cleaning stations downstairs, smokers, and grills lining the first-floor slab. Sharpened knives and rustic wooden cutting board in hand, Donnie brought out a sack of smoked wild ducks—pintail, mallard, teal, and even a specklebelly goose—all cleaned and smoked over hickory. Time for a Cajun cassoulet, with those smoked ducks taking center stage surrounded by spiced white beans cooked down with smoky andouille and a gnarled piece of tasso.

CORNISH GAME HENS STUFFED WITH APPLE-SAUSAGE CORNBREAD DRESSING

Get out the fine china; dust off the crystal goblets. This noble entrée is reminiscent of Louisiana plantation–era dining. It channels the grand Creole-inspired dinner tables with a combination of flavors: the wild taste of Cornish game hen, the floral notes of apple, the smoky depth of sausage, and the comfort of Southern cornbread. This stuffed game hen is destined to be a classic on your Sunday dinner table.

Preheat the oven to 400°F (200°C, or gas mark 6). Line a baking sheet with parchment paper.

Rinse and dry the game hens. Rub them with oil, sprinkle with salt and pepper, and place them on the baking sheet.

Put the sausage, cornbread, apple, vinegar, and chicken stock in a large bowl. With your hands, mix well to combine. Add the onions, celery, rosemary, parsley, garlic, Cajun Seasoning Blend, and just a dash of hot sauce. Crack the egg into the mixture and mix until well combined. It should be a thick, wet consistency.

Stuff the mixture into each of the game hens until filled. Pull the flap of the skin together and place the birds back on the prepared baking sheet. Cover with aluminum foil and bake for 1 hour. Test with a thermometer to make sure both the hens and the stuffing are cooked to a minimum internal temperature of 165°F (74°C).

Turn the oven to broil. Remove the foil and place the baking sheet back into the oven. Watch carefully as the skin crisps on the birds, about 5 minutes. Remove and let rest for 10 minutes before serving.

TABLE TIP

These stuffed game hens can be made ahead the day before and slipped into the oven for an easy preparation. Any leftover stuffing can be saved for another use or baked in a pan and served alongside the game hens. You can use most any fresh bulk sausage, but I particularly like the taste of sage in the Jimmy Dean breakfast sausage.

SERVES 4

4 Cornish game hens (1½ pounds, or 680 g each)

Olive oil as needed

Kosher salt and freshly ground black pepper

1 package (1 pound, or 455 g) pork sausage with sage, such as Jimmy Dean

2 cups (230 g) crumbled day-old cornbread

1 tart apple, cored, peeled, and chopped, such as Granny Smith

1 teaspoon apple cider vinegar

½ cup (120 ml) chicken stock

½ cup (80 g) diced yellow onion

2 tablespoons (20 g) diced red onion

2 tablespoons (15 g) diced celery

1 tablespoon (2 g) chopped fresh rosemary

1 tablespoon (4 g) chopped flat-leaf parsley

1 tablespoon (10 g) minced garlic

1 teaspoon Cajun Seasoning Blend (page 13)

Dash of hot sauce

1 large egg

FIRECRACKER BARBECUE CHICKEN WITH GRILLED CHERRY BOMB SALAD

Fire up the burners and light a fuse under an explosive new interpretation of a Deep South backyard barbecue standard. The chicken is set afire with a chipotle-infused sugarcane glaze, and the grilled romaine and cherry tomatoes ignite with a brushing of pepper jelly. This is the proverbial taste-bud explosion that will wake up your senses.

BARBECUE SAUCE

Heat the olive oil in a saucepan over medium heat. Add the onions, celery, cilantro, and garlic. Cook until the onions are translucent, about 5 minutes. Add the chili sauce, vinegar, molasses, Worcestershire, and brown sugar and stir until the mixture is heated through. Add the chipotle peppers and adobo sauce, paprika, mustard powder, and Cajun Seasoning Blend. Stir until the sauce reaches a simmer and then turn down the burner to its lowest setting. Cook on low heat, stirring every 5 minutes, for about 30 minutes. The sauce should be thickened enough to coat the back of a spoon.

Blend the sauce with an immersion blender or pour into a food processor and blend until smooth. Refrigerate until ready to cook the chicken.

CHICKEN

Put the chicken in a large container and make a saltwater brining solution by mixing the salt with enough water to cover the chicken. Cover and place in the refrigerator for at least 4 hours or up to overnight.

Remove the chicken from the brine and wipe away any excess moisture from the chicken with paper towels; brush the skin of the chicken with a light coating of olive oil on all sides.

Make a rub by mixing the Cajun Seasoning Blend, lemon pepper, and garlic powder. Sprinkle the rub on all sides of the chicken halves; place on a tray and let rest at room temperature.

Turn on only one of the burners on a gas grill to medium-high heat; once the grill reaches a temperature of 250°F (120°C), add the chicken, skin-side down, to the part of the grill that is not above the lit burner. Indirect heat is the key. Once the chicken is on the grill, close the hood and cook for 30 minutes. Turn the chicken over and grill for another 20 minutes.

Brush the inside (non-skin) part of the chicken with some of the sauce and let the chicken cook with the hood up for another 15 minutes. Watch carefully for any flare-ups. Turn the chicken and brush the skin side with sauce and place on the hottest part of the grill for a final few minutes of cooking. Watch carefully and adjust the burners to prevent flare-ups. The sauce will burn if left unattended, so when you first begin to see blackened edges, transfer the chicken to a platter.

(CONTINUED)

SERVES 12 TO 16

BARBECUE SAUCE

3 tablespoons (45 ml) olive oil

2 cups (320 g) finely diced yellow onion

1 cup (120 g) finely diced celery

½ cup (8 g) chopped fresh cilantro leaves

¼ cup (40 g) minced garlic

2½ cups (550 g) chili sauce

⅓ cup (80 ml) sugarcane vinegar

½ cup (170 g) sugarcane molasses

2 tablespoons (30 g) Worcestershire sauce

1 cup (225 g) light brown sugar

4 chipotle peppers in adobo sauce, chopped, with 1 tablespoon (15 ml) of the sauce

1 tablespoon (7 g) smoked paprika

1 tablespoon (9 g) mustard powder

2 tablespoons (20 g) Cajun Seasoning Blend (page 13)

CHICKEN

4 chickens (3 to 4 pounds, or 1.4 to 1.8 kg each), halved lengthwise

2 cups (576 g) salt

¼ cup (60 ml) olive oil

1 cup (150 g) Cajun Seasoning Blend (page 13)

½ cup (96 g) lemon pepper seasoning

¼ cup (36 g) garlic powder

(CONTINUED)

Check the internal temperature with a meat thermometer placed in the center of the thigh without touching bone. The internal temperature should be in the range of 175° to 180°F (79° to 82°C). If it isn't, wrap the chicken in foil (to prevent the sauce from burning) and return the chicken to the grill, cooking it until done.

Cut into portioned pieces and move to a platter. Cover with aluminum foil and keep warm until serving.

GRILLED CHERRY BOMB SALAD

Make sure your grill grates are cleaned and wiped with a light coating of oil. Turn the burners on low to medium heat.

Pour the red pepper jelly into a small pan and place on the grill away from direct heat.

Make a simple dressing by whisking the vinegar, lemon juice, and Creole mustard in a small bowl; while whisking, slowly drizzle enough olive oil into the bowl to form an emulsion. Season with a pinch of salt and black pepper. Set the dressing aside.

Slice the tomatoes in half and place the halves in a wire grilling basket (or on a wire rack), skin-side down. Leave the spring onions whole, with stalks attached. Sprinkle all the vegetables lightly with salt and black pepper.

Place the romaine leaves on a large plate. Lightly coat the leaves with the dressing and sprinkle lightly with salt and pepper. Place the onions on the grill with the bulbs over direct heat and the green stalks away from the flame. Cook until softened and charry, about 10 minutes, and then remove from the grill.

While the onions are cooking, place the grill basket of tomatoes, skin-side down, on the grill over direct heat. Cook just until the tomatoes warmed through, about 5 minutes. Remove the basket from the grill and brush the open side of the tomato halves with a light coating of the red pepper jelly. Turn the basket over and grill over direct heat. Watch carefully, as the sugars in the red pepper jelly will burn quickly. Once you have char marks on the tomatoes, remove them from the grill.

Clean the grates with a wire brush and oil them again. Set the burners on different heat levels, with one side hot and the other side just warm. With long-handled tongs, add the romaine leaves and spread them out evenly across the grill. You want a very quick charring, as the dressing will drip and cause flare-ups in the hotter section of the grill. With the tongs, flip the romaine leaves around the grill to control the amount of char. This is a very quick process, and you should never leave the grill. It should take no more than 5 minutes to grill all the romaine leaves.

For serving, arrange the grilled lettuce leaves on a large platter, with the tomatoes and onions placed evenly throughout. Arrange the chicken on the platter. Drizzle all lightly with extra-virgin olive oil and sprinkle lightly with salt and black pepper.

GRILLED CHERRY BOMB SALAD

1 jar (10 ounces, or 280 g) spicy red pepper jelly

2 tablespoons (28 ml) sugarcane vinegar

1 tablespoon (15 ml) freshly squeezed lemon juice

1 tablespoon (21 g) Creole mustard or other coarse-grained mustard

½ cup (120 ml) extra-virgin olive oil, plus more for finishing

Kosher salt and freshly ground black pepper

24 large cherry tomatoes or small Roma tomatoes

2 heads of romaine lettuce, leaves separated

12 large spring onions, green stalks attached, or green onions

TABLE TIPS

★ My recipe is written for a gas grill. If you have a charcoal pit, the same techniques apply, but you will need to monitor your temperature and flare-ups more closely.

★ I buy the whole chickens and cut them into halves for cooking, which prevents moisture loss that smaller individual pieces suffer from. (You can cut them into smaller pieces for serving later.) To protect the meat from drying or burning, always leave the skin on when barbecuing chicken.

SOULFUL CHICKEN SOUP

Food evokes emotion to me: A hot bowl of chicken soup on a cold, wintry day warms my soul. It's been said that the secret to understanding cooking lies in the bottom of a bowl of chicken soup. Well, after tasting this soup, you will clearly understand why. This dish reveals more about basic flavors than any I can name, and it takes a lot of thought and time. The patience involved in making an ultra-concentrated stock from long-simmered roasted chicken bones and carefully caramelized vegetables is rewarded here.

DARK CHICKEN STOCK

Preheat the oven to 400°F (200°C, or gas mark 6).

Pat all the chicken pieces dry with paper towels. Place the pieces on large baking sheets and rub the pieces lightly with ¼ cup (60 ml) of the oil. Roast until browned (not burnt), about 1½ hours.

Place the onions, carrots, and celery on another baking sheet and rub with the remaining ½ cup (60 ml) oil. Roast until browned (not burnt), about 30 to 40 minutes.

In a large stockpot over medium-high heat, combine the chicken bones and vegetables. Deglaze each of the baking sheets with a little water and scrape up the bits and pieces with a spatula. Add to the pot, along with the thyme, garlic, parsley, peppercorns, bay leaves, and chicken feet. An important note: I do not season my stock with salt or any dry seasoning because the spice level should be defined by the finished dish.

Add enough cold water to cover. Bring to a simmer and then lower the heat to low before it begins to boil. Simmer the stock for 8 hours, periodically skimming the surface of fat and scum. Turn off the heat and let the stock cool down.

With a fine-mesh strainer set over a large container, strain the stock. Make sure to strain off all bones and solids and discard them. Refrigerate the stock overnight.

Remove the stock from the refrigerator and using a large metal spoon, remove and discard the thick fat cap that formed on top. The stock will be congealed and almost like Jell-O in texture. This is a sign that the collagen has released from the chicken bones and feet. Spoon the stock into a stockpot and bring to a simmer on the stovetop. Continue cooking, uncovered, to reduce the stock to approximately 1 gallon (16 cups, or 3.8 L). Let the stock cool down.

With a fine-mesh strainer set over a large container, strain the stock a final time, removing any scum or particles. Use the stock immediately or divide into containers with tight-fitting lids (I use 1-quart [946 ml] mason jars, with 1 inch [2.5 cm] of headspace between the stock and the lid) and freeze until ready to use. Another option, if you think you will be storing the stock for many months, is to leave a layer of fat on top by reserving some of the fat from the first cooking stage and layering it on top of the finished stock. Like paraffin in a jam jar, when frozen, this layer of chicken fat will preserve the stock for safekeeping. Additionally, I like to freeze a portion of the stock in ice cube trays and once frozen, pop them into freezer storage bags. Then you can take them out one at a time for sauce making, adding to vegetables, and so forth.

(CONTINUED)

SERVES 6

DARK CHICKEN STOCK

6 pounds (2.7 kg) chicken bones (backs, necks, wings, thighs, and legs are best) or leftover chicken carcasses you have stored up

½ cup (120 ml) vegetable oil, divided

4 large yellow onions, quartered

4 large carrots, coarsely chopped

6 celery stalks, coarsely chopped

2 fresh thyme sprigs

4 cloves of garlic

1 cup (60 g) firmly packed fresh flat-leaf parsley (leaves and stems)

1 tablespoon (5 g) black peppercorns

4 bay leaves

3 pounds (1.4 kg) chicken feet, cleaned

(CONTINUED)

SOUP

Pour the Dark Chicken Stock into a large pot over medium heat and add the chicken legs. Simmer for 20 minutes. Add all of the vegetables and herbs, along with the chicken breast and thigh meat, and simmer for 15 minutes longer or until the chicken is fully cooked. Season to taste with salt. Serve in large bowls, making sure that the chicken is evenly dispersed with a whole chicken leg in each bowl.

TABLE TIP

For a heartier soup, feel free to add cooked egg noodles or even cooked rice.

SOUP

12 cups (2.8 L) Dark Chicken Stock (page 215)

6 chicken legs, skin removed

1 large yellow onion, diced

2 celery stalks, diced

2 large carrots, peeled and shaved into ribbons

½ cup (15 g) tender green leafy vegetable, such as celery leaves or spinach

1 tablespoon (10 g) minced garlic

¼ cup (15 g) chopped flat-leaf parsley

1 tablespoon (2 g) chopped fresh rosemary

1 tablespoon (2 g) chopped fresh thyme

2 pounds (900 g) boneless, skinless chicken breasts, cut into bite-size chunks

2 pounds (900 g) boneless, skinless chicken thighs, cut into bite-size chunks

Kosher salt

DUOS
CAJUN CORNER
SWEET POTATOES
GREEN SAUSAGE
Duos cajun coner
HOMEMADE
BEEF JERKY
HOG CHEESE
BOILED
SHRIMP
&
DUO'S
CAJUN CORNER
1ST
PLACE

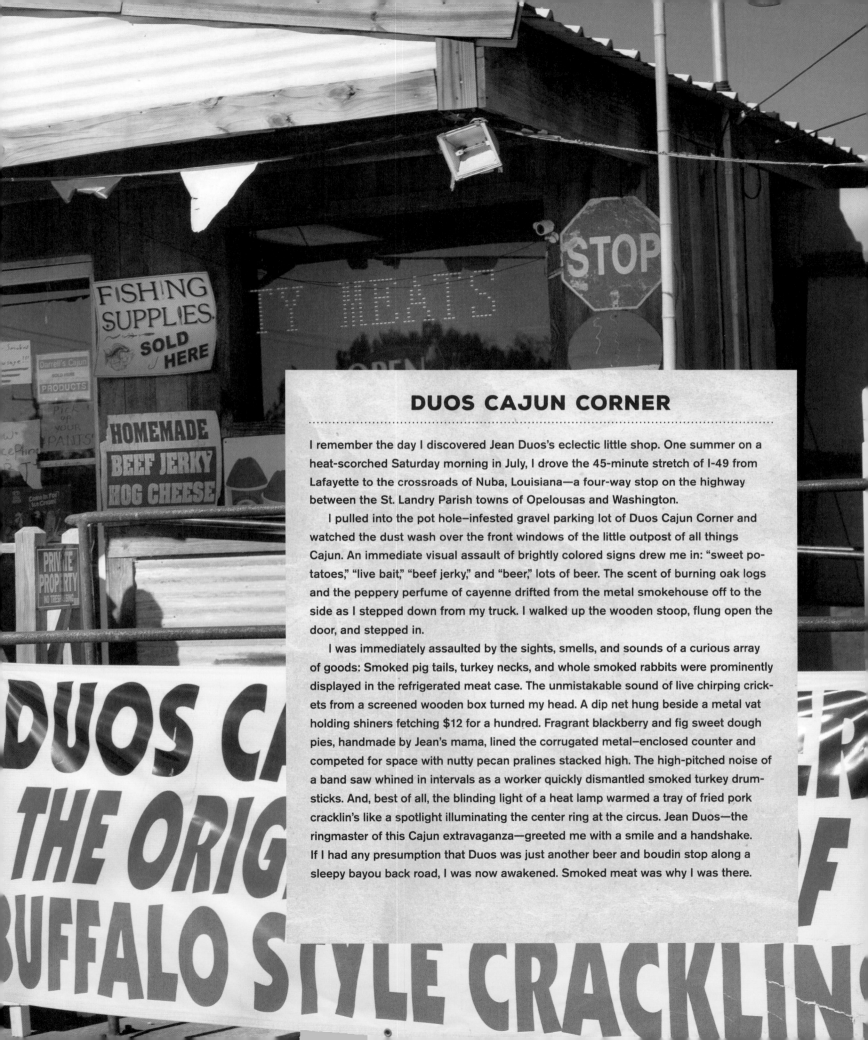

DUOS CAJUN CORNER

I remember the day I discovered Jean Duos's eclectic little shop. One summer on a heat-scorched Saturday morning in July, I drove the 45-minute stretch of I-49 from Lafayette to the crossroads of Nuba, Louisiana—a four-way stop on the highway between the St. Landry Parish towns of Opelousas and Washington.

I pulled into the pot hole–infested gravel parking lot of Duos Cajun Corner and watched the dust wash over the front windows of the little outpost of all things Cajun. An immediate visual assault of brightly colored signs drew me in: "sweet potatoes," "live bait," "beef jerky," and "beer," lots of beer. The scent of burning oak logs and the peppery perfume of cayenne drifted from the metal smokehouse off to the side as I stepped down from my truck. I walked up the wooden stoop, flung open the door, and stepped in.

I was immediately assaulted by the sights, smells, and sounds of a curious array of goods: Smoked pig tails, turkey necks, and whole smoked rabbits were prominently displayed in the refrigerated meat case. The unmistakable sound of live chirping crickets from a screened wooden box turned my head. A dip net hung beside a metal vat holding shiners fetching $12 for a hundred. Fragrant blackberry and fig sweet dough pies, handmade by Jean's mama, lined the corrugated metal–enclosed counter and competed for space with nutty pecan pralines stacked high. The high-pitched noise of a band saw whined in intervals as a worker quickly dismantled smoked turkey drumsticks. And, best of all, the blinding light of a heat lamp warmed a tray of fried pork cracklin's like a spotlight illuminating the center ring at the circus. Jean Duos—the ringmaster of this Cajun extravaganza—greeted me with a smile and a handshake. If I had any presumption that Duos was just another beer and boudin stop along a sleepy bayou back road, I was now awakened. Smoked meat was why I was there.

COQ AU VIN

Like classic French cooking, the technique behind coq au vin—slowly braising a tough bird in liquid—is basic to every Cajun cook. The ingredients may differ (less emphasis on wine and mushrooms), but much remains the same. Roosters and tough hens are sought for their intense, rustic flavor and their ability to stand up to a long braise.

There are traditional elements that define a French coq au vin from which I will deviate in my Louisiana version—thickening method being one key difference. You see, holding true to French tradition, the blood of the rooster would be reserved to add to the sauce as a thickening agent, but that isn't for everyone. Instead, I will substitute another classic French method, the beurre manié—combining flour and butter.

Discard any neck and giblets from the rooster. Rinse the pieces in cold water. Pat dry and place on a platter. Sprinkle both sides with salt and pepper and let rest at room temperature.

In a large cast-iron pot over medium heat, sauté the bacon pieces until they are lightly browned. Transfer the bacon to a paper towel–lined dish to drain. Save for later.

Pour off all but 2 tablespoons (28 ml) of the bacon grease from the pot, reserving the grease you pour off. Add the small boiler onions to the pot, sauté until browned, about 8 minutes, and then transfer to a platter.

Add 2 tablespoons (28 g) of the butter to the bacon grease remaining in the pot; add the mushrooms and cook until browned, about 8 minutes; transfer the mushrooms to the platter with the onions.

Put the ½ cup (63 g) flour in a large bowl, add the rooster pieces, and toss to coat lightly on all sides. Add more bacon grease to the pot, turn the heat to medium-high heat, add the rooster pieces, and cook until browned on all sides. Transfer the rooster pieces to a platter.

Add 2 tablespoons (16 g) of the breading flour from the bowl to the grease in the pot and stir to make a light roux. Once the roux has turned a light beige color, add the bottle of red wine, chicken stock, tomato paste, onion, celery, garlic, bay leaves, thyme, rosemary, and parsley. Add the rooster pieces and the bacon pieces back to the pot. Cover, lower the heat to simmer, and cook for 2 hours, stirring occasionally.

Once the rooster is done, transfer the pieces to a casserole dish and place in the oven on low heat to keep warm.

Using a colander set over a pot, strain the sauce, removing all vegetables, herbs, and bacon pieces. Place the pot on the stove over medium-high heat. Mix 2 tablespoons (28 g) of the softened butter with the remaining 2 tablespoons (16 g) flour to make a beurre manié (a classic French culinary technique) to thicken the sauce. Cook, stirring, until it is thick enough to coat the back of a spoon.

SERVES 4

1 rooster (4 to 5 pounds, or 1.8 to 2.3 kg), cleaned and butchered into serving pieces

Kosher salt and freshly ground black pepper

1 pound (455 g) smoked bacon, cut into small pieces

12 small boiling onions or pearl onions, stem end removed

5 tablespoons (70 g) unsalted butter, softened

1 pound (455 g) assorted mushrooms, cut into bite-size chunks

½ cup (63 g) unbleached all-purpose flour, plus 2 tablespoons (16 g)

1 bottle (750 ml) red wine

2 cups (475 ml) Dark Chicken Stock (page 215)

2 tablespoons (32 g) tomato paste

1 yellow onion, halved

3 celery stalks, chopped

2 tablespoons (20 g) minced garlic

3 bay leaves

6 fresh thyme sprigs, chopped

2 fresh rosemary sprigs, chopped

¼ cup (15 g) chopped fresh flat-leaf parsley

1 pound (455 g) baby carrots

4 cups (632 g) cooked long-grain white rice

TABLE TIP

While it's not traditional, you could make this dish with chicken thighs. However, the cooking time will be drastically reduced, and I take no responsibility for the outcome. I can assure you it will not come close to the flavor or experience of cooking this true French classic. And please, out of respect for French chefs everywhere, let's not call that coq au vin.

Add the boiler onions, sautéed mushrooms, and baby carrots to the sauce. Cook for 20 minutes over medium heat until the largest onion is tender. Taste the sauce and adjust the seasoning with salt and pepper. Add the remaining 1 tablespoon (14 g) butter to the sauce for a finishing touch. Add the rooster pieces back to the pot.

For serving, place the rooster in the center of a large platter. Arrange the onions to one side and the mushrooms on the other, with the carrots in between. Add a few spoonfuls of sauce over the rooster and serve the rest on the side. Noodles are the traditional French accompaniment for this dish, but a bowl of white rice is more than acceptable in French Louisiana.

HONEY-HERBED POUSSIN

Poussin is French for a young spring chicken (1½ to 2½ pounds [675 g to 1.1 kg] in weight). This dish shows how mind-blowing a roast chicken can be—it is a gustatory revelation. While it looks complicated, it is quite straightforward. The flavor of poussin is already delicate, and when brined in a salty orange juice solution for a couple of hours, it becomes ambrosial. I finish it off devilishly glazed with heavenly honey intensified with coarsely ground black peppercorns, cayenne, and cumin seeds. It's brushed and broiled under searing heat that renders the skin to a crisp amber hue while the meat still oozes its juices. The aroma alone will call your guests to the table.

Place the chickens in a large container with a tight-fitting lid. Add the orange juice and salt. Pour in enough water to cover the chicken. Cover and refrigerate for at least 2 hours and up to 4 hours.

Preheat the oven to 350°F (180°C, or gas mark 4). Line a large baking sheet with parchment paper.

Remove the chickens from the marinade and pat dry. Place on a platter and let come to room temperature.

In a small skillet over medium heat, toast the peppercorns and cumin seeds until you begin to smell them, but remove from the heat before they burn. Using a spice grinder or a mortar and pestle, crack the peppercorns and pulverize the cumin seeds. Pour the spices into a small bowl, add the cayenne and honey, and stir to combine.

Sprinkle the chickens with salt. Brush the honey-spice mixture all over the outside and in the inside cavity. Place the chickens on the prepared baking sheet and add some of the orange slices to the tops of the birds.

With a vegetable peeler, remove the outer skin from the carrots and remove the stem and leaves. Toss the carrots with the olive oil to coat. On a platter, combine the chili powder and brown sugar. Roll the carrots in this spice mixture. Add the carrots to the baking sheet with the chickens and place several of the orange slices on top. Add any remaining orange slices to the inside cavity of the chickens.

Roast until the internal temperature of the thickest part of the chicken thigh reads 160°F (71°C) without touching bone, about 50 minutes. Remove the baking sheet from the oven and transfer the carrots to a serving platter.

Increase the oven temperature to broil and place the chickens back in the oven. Watch carefully as the top of the chickens browns and becomes crispy, about 5 minutes. Be sure to remove the chickens before the skin burns.

For serving, transfer the chickens to a cutting board and cut each in half lengthwise. Arrange the halves on the platter with the carrots.

SERVES 4

2 chickens (1½ to 3 pounds, or 680 g to 1.4 kg each)

4 cups (946 ml) orange juice

¼ cup (72 g) salt

½ cup (40 g) black peppercorns

½ cup (48 g) cumin seeds

1 tablespoon (5 g) cayenne pepper

1 cup (340 g) honey

Kosher salt

2 oranges, thinly sliced

3 pounds (1.4 kg) baby carrots

½ cup (120 ml) extra-virgin olive oil

¼ cup (30 g) chili powder

¼ cup (60 g) firmly packed dark brown sugar

BACON-WRAPPED CHICKEN BREASTS WITH ORANGE BLOSSOM HONEY MUSTARD GLAZE

To me, boneless, skinless chicken breast has no place in the food world. If you think about it, a chicken breast—a natural chicken breast—with skin, bone, and a bit of fat is a thing of beauty—and flavor. But this thing that has been thrust upon us—this stripped-down version—is devoid of flavor and unworthy of any serious table. Or is it? Sliced, pounded, stuffed, wrapped, skewered, brushed, and panéed, these chicken breasts defy culinary logic. They're all rolled up into a sweet package for an easy—and easily impressive—dinner presentation. I suggest serving this with creamy mashed potatoes.

HONEY MUSTARD GLAZE
Place the honey, Grand Marnier (if using), Creole mustard, and rosemary in a saucepan over medium heat. Stir and cook until the honey has melted and the mustard is thoroughly incorporated. Remove from the heat and let stand at room temperature.

Preheat a gas grill to medium heat.

BACON-WRAPPED CHICKEN
Spread a piece of plastic wrap over a cutting board. Place a chicken breast on the plastic and cover with another piece of plastic wrap. With a meat mallet or a heavy saucepan, pound the chicken until flattened. Repeat with all of the chicken breasts.

Place the 4 flattened chicken breasts on a foil-lined baking sheet. Sprinkle with the Cajun Seasoning Blend and generously with salt and pepper. In the center of each breast, place 3 asparagus spears and top with a liberal sprinkling of the Havarti cheese. Roll each breast up and wrap bacon strips around each breast until covered. Secure with toothpicks.

Grill the chicken, rotating periodically until the bacon is crisp on all sides and the chicken is almost completely cooked through, about 15 minutes total. Open the cover and brush on all sides with the honey mustard glaze. (Note: If the asparagus tips start to burn, you should wrap the ends with foil while the chicken continues cooking.) Turn the fire down and continue grilling for another 10 to 15 minutes until the glaze browns and the sugars caramelize. Be careful not to burn the glaze.

Remove from the grill and serve immediately with the remaining Honey Mustard Glaze on the side.

SERVES 4

HONEY MUSTARD GLAZE

1 cup (340 g) orange blossom honey

1 tablespoon (15 ml) Grand Marnier (optional)

½ cup (168 g) Creole mustard or other coarse-grained mustard

2 tablespoons (4 g) chopped fresh rosemary

BACON-WRAPPED CHICKEN

4 large boneless, skinless chicken breasts (8 ounces, or 225 g each)

1 tablespoon (10 g) Cajun Seasoning Blend (page 13)

Kosher salt and freshly ground black pepper

12 asparagus spears, woody ends removed

1 pound (455 g) Havarti cheese, grated

1 pound (455 g) smoked bacon

TABLE TIP

The crispy texture of the bacon contrasts sharply with the creamy stuffing, and it shields the meat from dryness.

SMOKED QUAIL STUFFED WITH SYRUP SAUSAGE AND MUSCADINE SAUCE

Quail shows up on my table regularly. In this dish, I fire up the smoker for these plump, juicy birds that are stuffed whole with a blend of green onion–infused syrup sausage. I love the contrast of smoky heat and spicy sweet when these bacon-wrapped birds are glazed with my sauce made from muscadine grapes.

MUSCADINE SAUCE

Place 2 cups (330 g) of the muscadine grapes in a pot over medium-high heat and add the sugar, cider, and vinegar. Bring to a boil and add the molasses, cinnamon, and red pepper flakes. Lower the heat to a simmer and cook for 30 minutes or until the sauce thickens enough to coat the back of a spoon. Turn off the heat and let cool.

Pour the sauce into the container of a blender. Blend on high speed until smooth and the grape skins are pulverized. Return the sauce to the pot over medium heat, add the remaining 1 cup (165 g) muscadine grape halves, and let cook for another 15 minutes. Turn off the heat and let cool. Refrigerate in a jar with a tight-fitting lid.

SYRUP SAUSAGE

In a bowl, combine the pork, green onions, Cajun Seasoning Blend, garlic powder, salt, pepper, and red pepper flakes. Slowly drizzle in the syrup as you mix the sausage. Cover and refrigerate.

QUAIL

For brining, place the quail in a 1-gallon (3.8 L) freezer bag. Add the buttermilk, salt, and hot sauce. Refrigerate for 3 hours. Remove the quail, pour off the brining liquid, and pat dry.

Prepare a smoker with applewood chips. Place a pan containing the apple cider between the heat source and the quail. Bring the smoker to a temperature of 225°F (107°C).

Stuff the quail with the Syrup Sausage. Wrap each quail with a strip of bacon and secure with a toothpick. Sprinkle all sides with Cajun Seasoning Blend. Place the quail in the smoker and let smoke for 1 hour. Remove and check to see that the quail have reached an internal temperature of 165°F (74°C). If not, place them on a baking sheet and finish them in a 300°F (150°C, or gas mark 2) oven.

Prepare a gas grill with the burners set to high or preheat the oven to broil. Brush the quail with the muscadine sauce. Add the quail to the grill, or place under the broiler, and cook for 1 minute per side to set the sauce.

Slice the quail in half lengthwise. Serve on a platter in the center of the table with extra Muscadine Sauce on the side.

SERVES 4

MUSCADINE SAUCE

3 cups (495 g) muscadine grapes, seeded and halved

½ cup (100 g) granulated sugar

½ cup (120 ml) apple cider

2 tablespoons (28 ml) sugarcane vinegar

2 tablespoons (40 g) sugarcane molasses

1 teaspoon ground cinnamon

1 tablespoon (4 g) red pepper flakes

SYRUP SAUSAGE

2 pounds (900 g) ground pork

2 tablespoons (12 g) finely diced green onion tops

1 tablespoon (10 g) Cajun Seasoning Blend (page 13)

1 teaspoon garlic powder

1 teaspoon kosher salt

1 teaspoon freshly ground black pepper

1 teaspoon red pepper flakes

2 tablespoons (28 ml) sugarcane syrup

QUAIL

8 quail (6 ounces, or 170 g each)

2 cups (475 ml) buttermilk

2 tablespoons (36 g) salt

1 tablespoon (15 ml) hot sauce

2 cups (475 ml) apple cider

8 strips (1 ounce, or 28 g each) of smoked bacon

Cajun Seasoning Blend (page 13)

TABLE TIPS

★ Look for the deep purple muscadine grapes, which tend to be sweeter than green muscadines. If you can't find muscadines, I suggest substituting 3 cups (495 g) pitted and halved ripe purple plums.

★ Some folks like to strain off any muscadine pulp or skin from the sauce, but I like the texture I get from blending it all together on high speed.

SEARED DUCK BREAST WITH RASPBERRY-ROSEMARY SAUCE AND SPICED PECANS

Duck breasts deserve a vibrant herb-laced sauce and also, for my money, a fruity sauce. Marrying fresh, plump raspberries with rosemary in a red wine reduction is a combination that works well here. The delicate balance of microgreens and mint with the bold taste of duck fat–roasted Brussels sprouts and sweet chile-kissed Louisiana pecans add flavor complexity. It is a beautiful thing.

RASPBERRY-ROSEMARY SAUCE

Heat the olive oil in a saucepan over medium-high heat. Add the rosemary and thyme and sauté just until the herbs begin to sizzle and wilt. Add the raspberries and wine, lower to a simmer, cover, and cook until the wine reduces, about 5 to 10 minutes. Add the pecans and stir. Stir in the butter and season with salt and pepper to taste. Move the sauce off the stovetop and keep warm for serving.

SPICED PECANS

In a cast-iron skillet over medium-high heat, toast the pecan halves, turning often. Once you smell the unmistakable aroma of roasted pecans, add the butter. Lower the heat to a simmer and add the salt, chili powder, and brown sugar. Stir the pecans into the melted butter and seasonings to coat. Transfer the spiced pecans to a wire rack to drain any excess butter.

DUCK AND BRUSSELS SPROUTS

Preheat the oven to 400°F (200°C, or gas mark 6). Let the duck breasts come to room temperature.

Score the fat side of the duck breasts by cutting diagonal slices just through the layer of fat. Season the fat side with salt and pepper.

In a heavy cast-iron skillet over very high heat, sear the duck breast, fat-side down, for 5 minutes. Lower the heat to medium and continue cooking another 5 minutes as the fat renders. Pour off most of the fat and turn the breasts over. Transfer to the oven and roast until the breast meat is cooked to medium-rare (an internal temperature of about 125°F [52°C]), about 10 minutes. Transfer the duck to a platter and let rest as the carryover heat brings the breast to a perfect medium-rare pink at 135°F (57°C). Keep warm for serving.

Remove all but 2 tablespoons (28 ml) of duck fat from the skillet. Over high heat, add the Brussels sprouts. Sauté until cooked through and browned with blackened edges, about 10 minutes. Sprinkle with salt and pepper and keep warm.

For serving, place slices of duck breast on each plate and top with a spoonful of Raspberry-Rosemary Sauce. Surround with lettuce, Brussels sprouts, spicy pecan halves, raspberries, and mint leaves. Garnish with a sprig each of rosemary and thyme. Serve extra sauce on the side.

SERVES 4

SAUCE

1 tablespoon (15 ml) olive oil

2 tablespoons (4 g) chopped fresh rosemary

1 tablespoon (2 g) chopped fresh thyme

1 cup (125 g) fresh raspberries

¼ cup (60 ml) dry red wine

¼ cup (28 g) chopped pecans

1 tablespoon (14 g) unsalted butter

SPICED PECANS

2 cups (200 g) pecan halves

2 tablespoons (28 g) unsalted butter

1 teaspoon salt

1 tablespoon (8 g) chili powder

1 tablespoon (15 g) light brown sugar

DUCK AND SPROUTS

4 boneless duck breasts (8 ounces, or 225 g each), such as Muscovy, Moulard, or Pekin

Kosher salt and freshly ground black pepper

2 cups (176 g) Brussels sprouts, halved lengthwise

2 cups (110 g) spring lettuce mix

1 cup (96 g) fresh mint leaves

1 cup (125 g) fresh raspberries

4 fresh rosemary sprigs

4 fresh thyme sprigs

LEMON-ROSEMARY CHICKEN THIGHS

Chicken thighs have a bad reputation, and the majority of folks opt for the white breast meat over the juicier dark meat. "Oily" and "fatty" are how many describe chicken thighs, but with the right preparation, they explode with fresh flavor.

I like to call this dish "thighs and whispers" because it is so easy and effortless that you can steal away for a little quiet time while it cooks. A cold cast-iron skillet is the platform for caramelizing the skin—no seasoning, no oil. I weigh the thighs down with a heavy pot and let low heat against the iron surface do its job. The result is ultra-crisp skin.

Before she tasted these little beauties, my wife refused to eat chicken thighs. Now she's a convert and lovingly calls me the chicken whisperer.

If still attached, trim the rib bone from the end of each chicken thigh. Using a sharp paring knife, slice around the leg bone about an inch (2.5 cm) from the end and peel back the skin and meat. Cut away any tendons. Pull the skin down to the end of the leg bone and using kitchen shears or a heavy knife, slice off the tip end of the bone. Push up on the rest of the leg meat and expose the bone.

Preheat the oven to 400°F (200°C, or gas mark 6).

Place the chicken in a cold (not preheated) cast-iron skillet, skin-side down. Weigh down the meat to make maximum surface contact by placing a pan that is a bit smaller than the diameter of the skillet on top of the chicken. Add weight to the pan (stacked up canned vegetables work well) and push down.

Turn the heat to medium and let cook undisturbed for 20 minutes. You will hear sizzling and see oil leaching from the skin, but do not be tempted to check the chicken.

Remove the pan from the heat and using a metal spatula with a sharp edge, scrape up the chicken pieces along with the crust and fond underneath. Flip them over and inspect that the skin is browned and crispy.

Slice one of the lemons and quarter the other. Place the lemon slices on the bottom of the skillet, under the chicken. Remove the leaves from the rosemary branches and add to the skillet. Place the skillet in the oven. Roast uncovered until the internal temperature of the thickest part of the thigh reaches 165°F (74°C), about 15 minutes. Transfer the chicken pieces to a platter to rest.

Place the skillet with the lemon slices, rosemary, and pan juices over medium-high heat and add the chicken stock. Bring the sauce to a boil and then lower the heat to a simmer. Cook until the stock has reduced by half, about 5 minutes. Season to taste with salt and serve with the chicken and quartered lemons for squeezing at the table.

SERVES 4

4 bone-in, skin-on chicken leg quarters with thighs (about 1½ pounds, or 680 g)

2 large lemons

4 fresh rosemary sprigs

½ cup (120 ml) chicken stock

Kosher salt

TABLE TIP

With no added oil, this is a healthy way to cook chicken thighs, and the herbal flavors are fresh and bright. I tried this technique with chicken breasts, with lackluster results; the lack of added fat resulted in dry meat.

BEER CAN DUCK WITH RAISIN CANE GLAZE

Whole roasted duck is a classic in many cultures, Cajun included. That said, I've taken a clever Southern technique—beer can cooking on the grill—and loaded up a 4-pound (1.8 kg) Muscovy duck rather than the usual chicken. With a hit of applewood smoke and an internal basting from the wheat-infused beer, this duck renders out its fat and produces moist, flavorful meat. With a final blast in a hot oven and brushed with a sugarcane glaze, it's crispy, tender, and ready for your dinner table.

SERVES 4

BRINE

3 bottles (12 ounces, or 355 ml each) of beer

4 cups (946 ml) water

4 chicken bouillon cubes

2 cups (256 g) kosher salt

½ cup (115 g) firmly packed light brown sugar

3 cinnamon sticks

2 tablespoons (10 g) black peppercorns

RAISIN CANE GLAZE

1 cup (145 g) golden raisins or black raisins

1 cinnamon stick

1 cup (235 ml) bourbon

1 cup (340 g) sugarcane molasses

¼ cup (60 ml) apple cider vinegar

1 tablespoon (15 ml) freshly squeezed lemon juice

2 tablespoons (30 g) Worcestershire sauce

2 tablespoons (28 ml) soy sauce

1 tablespoon (10 g) minced garlic

(CONTINUED)

BRINE

Combine all of the ingredients in a pot over high heat. Bring to a boil and then lower the heat to a simmer. Stir the mixture to combine and continue cooking until the salt and sugar dissolve. Turn off the heat and let cool.

Inspect the duck and discard (or save for stock making) any innards that are packed inside. Using pliers, pull out any remaining feather quills that stick out. Put the duck in a container with a tight-fitting lid and pour over the cooled brine. Seal the container and place in the refrigerator overnight.

RAISIN CANE GLAZE

Put the raisins and cinnamon stick in a pint (476 ml) mason jar. Pour over enough bourbon to cover the raisins, about 1 cup (235 ml). Shake the mixture and place in the refrigerator overnight. (Or make it ahead and refrigerate for up to 1 week.)

Combine all of the glaze ingredients in a medium pot over medium-high heat and bring to a boil. Lower the heat and simmer for 15 minutes. Remove from the stove and let cool.

DUCK

On only one side of your gas grill, turn on one burner to high and close the lid. Let the temperature come to 300°F (150°C, or gas mark 2).

Meanwhile, remove the brined duck from the refrigerator and pour off all the liquid. Using paper towels, dry the duck. Sprinkle with 1 tablespoon (10 g) of the Cajun Seasoning Blend, along with salt and pepper. (Note: Most folks like to trim the duck of excess fat and prick and score the skin, but with this twice-cooked, beer can method, it is unnecessary.)

Open the can of beer and pour off a little of the beer. Add the remaining 1 tablespoon (10 g) Cajun Seasoning Blend to the beer can, along with the cinnamon stick and lemon juice. Place the beer can in the cooker apparatus and set the duck on top with its legs down. Place the duck head around the wings and tie with kitchen twine. (Note: If your duck does not have the head attached, then seal the opening at the top of the duck with aluminum foil to prevent loss of internal heat.)

(CONTINUED)

THE BEER CAN COOKER

There's much debate over who invented the beer can "drunken" chicken cooker. There are a variety of beer can cookers on the market, but one of the first—Papa Jeabert's Chicken Up—was invented by a Cajun from Lafayette, Louisiana. Phil Gremillion's polished aluminum version features a metal box at the base that catches any drippings. This ingenious device eliminates flare-ups, and it serves as a cooking tray for vegetables to capture the flavor of the roasted chicken drippings. Brilliant.

DUCK

1 domestic duck (4 to 5 pounds, or 1.8 to 2.3 kg)

2 tablespoons (20 g) Cajun Seasoning Blend (page 13), divided

Kosher salt and freshly ground black pepper

1 can (12 ounces, or 355 ml each) of beer

1 cinnamon stick

1 tablespoon (15 ml) freshly squeezed lemon juice

TABLE TIPS

★ Beer can cookers are widely available and inexpensive. However, you can prepare this without one. Be sure to use a grill skillet or a cast-iron pot underneath the duck to catch the dripping fat.

★ Be careful of flare-ups. Lots of fat that will render from the duck, so always be in full view of the grill. Source your fresh duck locally if you can, but don't be afraid to use a thawed frozen duck.

Place the beer can cooker apparatus containing the duck inside the gas grill away from the burner. Position the duck so that the back is facing the heat source. Close the lid and let cook for 1 hour. Open the grill and rotate the duck so that the belly section is now facing the heat. Cook for 1 hour longer. Remove from the grill and let rest while you preheat the oven to 400°F (200°C, or gas mark 6).

While resting, brush all sides of the duck with a coating of the Raisin Cane Glaze. (Note: You will have lots of precious duck fat in the reservoir of the beer can apparatus. Skim, refrigerate, and save for other recipes, such as duck fat potatoes.)

For the second phase of this twice-cooked duck, place the bird skin-side up on a baking sheet on the middle rack of the oven. Roast for 30 minutes or until the skin is crispy and the duck reaches an internal temperature of about 165°F (74°C). Remove and let rest until cool enough to handle.

Turn the duck breast-side down. Using a pair of kitchen shears or a sharp knife, slice along either side of the backbone and remove. Turn over and cut the duck into 4 quarters and then separate the legs from the thighs. Cut off the wing tips and discard. Brush all sides with more Raisin Cane Glaze and then put the duck pieces back into the hot oven for a final 10-minute bronzing. The skin will appear darkened and should have a crisp snap when tapped with a fork.

Serve the duck pieces on a wooden cutting board along with any remaining glaze.

THE LONG, HOT SIMMER

There is one question I never tire of hearing: "Do you make your own chicken stock?" And my answer is always a question: "Why wouldn't I?" I love stock making because it is an introduction to the heart of cooking; a tutorial on everything that is pure, simple, and oh-so-good about my passion for the highest-quality ingredients. While I understand the convenience factor of having a carton or two of store-bought stock on hand (good quality and low sodium, please), I urge you to use it sparingly. Throw away those little jars of foil-wrapped chicken cubes you bought in 1987. They are the ruination of many so-so soups, watered-down gumbos, flavorless stews, run-of-the-mill casseroles, and, well, you get the message. Forgive me for preaching, but this one short lesson will take your culinary creations from mediocre to magical. And it's low cost—the investment is in time, not money.

Let's back up for a moment. As an amateur cook, I do not have access to a restaurant kitchen pantry. I plan my stock making with careful strategic maneuvers. Every green onion end, woody asparagus stalk, carrot butt, or leftover onion husk is tossed into a freezer bag. Over the course of a month or two, these add up and become the sole reason to buy that reach-in freezer. As well, every chicken carcass or turkey leftover is reserved for the pot. You will be surprised how fast they accumulate. When wings, necks, and bone-in thighs are on sale, I stock up. Remove most of the meat from the thighs and breast pieces and reserve for another use. (It is okay if the bones still have meat clinging to them.) Chicken feet are best (rich in cartilage), so find an Asian or Latin market.

I do not add tomato paste or wine to my chicken stock, but I do to my beef stock. You will notice there is no salt, ground black pepper (peppercorns only), or any spicy Cajun seasonings of any kind in my stock. It is important to protect the integrity and purity of the stock from any overt spice components that compete with the flavor of the chicken. Seasonings (including salt) should be used only in the finished dish.

When the day arrives, my labor of love begins with a cup of morning café au lait while I lay out my chicken treasure trove. While the act of making broth from scratch is simple, I never shortchange the art and beauty of the process. It cleanses my mind, soothes my soul, and in a sense, brings order to the chaos of everyday life, but enough philosophy. Here's the deal: A fresh, full-flavored chicken stock will elevate every dish you make with it. It is my secret weapon, and it can be yours, too.

SMOKED TURKEY DRUMSTICKS WITH STEWED WHITE BEANS

Beans and rice is a staple of every Cajun and Creole household. Much like our gumbo, the tradition of beans is handed down from the African influence of plantation workers in the cane fields of South Louisiana. This is one soulful Creole combination that amps up the taste with a bluesy beat all its own. And what makes this jazzed-up combo blast is the gasp-inducing sight of two smoked turkey drumsticks splayed atop a mound of creamy white beans that provide a flavor-filled backbeat to this dish.

DRUMSTICKS

In a pan deep enough to submerge the turkey legs, stir the water together with the salt, sugar, and Cajun Seasoning Blend. Immerse the drumsticks in the brine. Cover and refrigerate overnight.

In a bowl, combine the garlic powder, white pepper, and salt. Remove the drumsticks from the brine and pat dry with paper towels. Sprinkle generously on all sides with the spice mixture.

Prepare a smoker with hickory chips and bring to a temperature of 275°F (140°C). Place the drumsticks on the center rack of the smoker and let smoke for 2 hours. Remove from the smoker and keep warm until you are ready to add them to the beans.

BEANS

Preheat the oven to 375°F (190°C, or gas mark 5).

Sauté the bacon pieces in a stockpot over medium heat until browned and crisp. Transfer the bacon to a paper towel–lined plate.

Add the onions to the bacon grease and sauté until translucent, about 5 minutes. Add the bell pepper, celery, carrots, white beans, ham shank, and cooked bacon pieces. Pour the chicken stock over it all and add the whole carrots and bay leaves. Lightly season with salt and pepper. Bring to a boil, cover, and turn the heat to low to simmer for 1 hour, stirring occasionally.

Turn off the heat and pour the beans into a large cast-iron pot with a heavy lid. Add the smoked turkey drumsticks on top of the beans and cover. Bake for 1 hour. Uncover the pot and crank up the temperature to broil. While watching closely, cook just until the tops of the turkey legs are browned and the skin is crisp. Remove and let rest for 10 minutes.

Check the beans for doneness. The beans should be soft and creamy; if not, remove the turkey drumsticks and continue cooking in the oven until tender.

Remove the bay leaves.

Either serve it up in the pot or transfer to a platter, with the white beans and drumsticks surrounding a mound of white rice. Once your guests are seated, break apart the tender smoked turkey legs with two forks. Serve with crusty French bread and hot sauce (of course) on the side.

SERVES 4 TO 6

DRUMSTICKS

2 quarts (1.9 L) water

½ cup (144 g) salt

2 tablespoons (26 g) granulated sugar

½ cup (75 g) Cajun Seasoning Blend (page 13)

2 large turkey legs

1 tablespoon (9 g) garlic powder

1 tablespoon (6 g) freshly ground white pepper

1 tablespoon (8 g) kosher salt

BEANS

6 strips (1 ounce, or 28 g each) of bacon, chopped

1 large yellow onion, diced

1 red bell pepper, seeded and chopped

1 cup (100 g) coarsely chopped celery

1 cup (130 g) diced carrot

1 pound (455 g) dried white beans (large limas), rinsed and picked over

1 smoked ham shank (1½ to 2 pounds, or 680 to 900 g)

8 cups (1.9 L) chicken stock

2 carrots

2 bay leaves

Kosher salt and freshly ground black pepper

6 cups (948 g) cooked long-grain white rice

SMOTHERED QUAIL AND CHANTERELLES WITH PICKLED RED ONIONS

Pan-fried and smothered, these birds are fork-tender with a pan gravy that's just begging to cover a mound of white rice. Chanterelles grow wild on my friend Don Bacque's farm, and come late summer we load up. While most any mushroom will work in this recipe (the real star is the quail), I urge you to seek out and pay extra for fresh chanterelles. And promise me you'll give the pickled red onions a whirl; I'm betting they'll become one of your favorite condiments.

PICKLED RED ONIONS

Place the sliced onions, sugar, and enough vinegar to cover (about 1 cup, or 235 ml) in a container. Stir to combine. Cover and refrigerate overnight.

QUAIL

Cut each quail in half down the breastbone. Remove the backbone and any protruding portion of the neck. Put the quail into a container and pour over the buttermilk. Cover and marinate in the refrigerate for 2 to 4 hours.

Heat enough oil in a cast-iron skillet with a lid over medium-high heat to come at least 1 inch (2.5 cm) deep up the side of the skillet. Bring the oil to a temperature of 375°F (190°C).

Remove the quail from the refrigerator and drain on a wire rack. Combine the 2 cups (250 g) flour and the Cajun Seasoning Blend in a shallow bowl. Dredge the wet quail halves in the flour and add to the hot oil, in batches, without crowding the skillet. Fry until golden brown, about 6 minutes each. Remove and drain the quail on a wire rack over a paper towel–lined tray.

Pour off all but 2 tablespoons (28 ml) of the oil from the skillet. Over medium-high heat, add the onions, celery, bell pepper, and mushrooms. While scraping the bottom of the pan with a spatula, sauté the vegetables until browned, about 8 minutes. Add the garlic, rosemary, and the remaining 2 tablespoons (16 g) flour. Lower the heat and stir the mixture for 2 minutes to allow the flour to cook.

Add the quail back to the skillet and pour in the chicken stock, tomatoes with chiles, and chopped tomato; cover and simmer for 40 minutes. Uncover and taste the sauce, adding salt, pepper, and hot sauce to taste.

Garnish with the pickled red onions and serve with white rice on the side.

SERVES 4

PICKLED RED ONIONS

2 large red onions, thinly sliced

1 tablespoon (13 g) granulated sugar

White vinegar, as needed

QUAIL

4 quail (6 ounces, or 170 g each)

2 cups (475 ml) buttermilk

Vegetable oil, for frying

2 cups (250 g) plus 2 tablespoons (16 g) unbleached all-purpose flour

2 tablespoons (20 g) Cajun Seasoning Blend (page 13)

1 cup (160 g) chopped yellow onion

½ cup (60 g) diced celery

½ cup (75 g) diced green bell pepper

2 cups (108 g) chanterelle mushrooms or other fresh mushrooms

1 tablespoon (10 g) minced garlic

1 tablespoon (2 g) chopped fresh rosemary

3 cups (700 ml) Dark Chicken Stock, plus more if needed (page 215)

1 can (10 ounces, or 280 g) mild diced tomatoes with green chiles, drained

1 medium tomato, ends removed and chopped

Kosher salt and freshly ground black pepper

Dash of hot sauce

4 cups (632 g) cooked long-grain white rice

QUAIL ON THE TABLE

Try as I might, I cannot quell my passion for quail. It all began when I was a kid growing up in Washington Parish in the southeastern part of Louisiana. My uncle Jerry—the closest thing I had to a grandfather—was an extraordinary fisherman and hunter who never hesitated in taking me along for an adventure. We fished for specs and reds in the coastal marshes along Lake Borgne, but it was his quail-hunting skills that captured the family's attention every holiday season.

My uncle hosted an annual Christmas Eve dinner that brought all the Grahams together at the dinner table to feast on a magnificent quail dinner with all the trimmings. My aunt Lucy would fry up the quail and then smother them down into a stew infused with celery, peppers, onions (the holy trinity), and wild mushrooms. I recall the ensuing family feeding frenzy interrupted only by the occasional discovery of birdshot against a tooth, which always got a chuckle from my uncle. "No store-bought quail here, this is fresh-killed," he'd proudly shout to everyone within earshot.

My dear uncle lived to see almost ninety holiday seasons, but like most family traditions, our quail dinners finally ended. Oh, we tried to relive the revelry on a couple of occasions, but with no hunter in the family, it never quite lived up to the memory.

Flash-forward a bunch of years and quail is now back on the Graham table. It should be on yours as well, with this smothered quail and chanterelles recipe.

CHAPTER

EIGHT

MEATS AND THE MASTERY OF THE BOUCHERIE

 IME WAS, EVERY CAJUN FAMILY TOOK PART IN THE BOUCHERIE. A RITUAL PASSED DOWN THROUGH GENERATIONS, THE SLAUGHTER AND COOKING OF THE WHOLE HOG EVENTUALLY DIED OUT. BUT THANKFULLY, THESE DAYS IT IS NOW RESURFACING ACROSS ACADIANA AS A MAINSTREAM EVENT TO BE CELEBRATED FOR ITS CULTURAL SIGNIFICANCE.

A boucherie is hard work, and it is a communal effort. As the pig is dismantled, various stations are busy prepping and cooking their specialty. Sausage, boudin, backbone stew, jambalaya, and pork roast are cooking away. And always a big pot of hog lard is heating up for making my favorite—pork cracklin's.

Cracklin's are addictive. I was first grabbed by the demon porcine pleasure at a later stage of life, when I should have known better. What is essentially fat fried in fat should have been an obvious clue, or the little grease-stained brown paper bags should have certainly been a tip-off. But I was hooked fast.

The fact that most every little store around Acadiana sells pork cracklin's (also known as grattons) at the register bodes well for how far this porky addiction has spread. Oh, I tried to quit, but Earl's Cajun Market, my neighborhood pusher, drew me back in every time I opened the front door and breathed in the heady siren call of pig bits frying in

a black iron cauldron of lard. I can't resist the bacony flavor or the contrast of crunch with the smooth ooze of pork tallow.

Be warned. These little taste bombs will decimate your diet, derail your noble sensibility, and send you down the path of sinful consumption. These little bags sold on every street corner in Cajun country are just the start. Soon you'll be smothering a sausage-stuffed pig's stomach, roasting a boudin-stuffed pork loin, and Lord forbid, making a fried pork jowl BLT.

Over the years, I've embarked on a healthier life-style that no longer includes this delicacy, but from time to time, I have been known to come home with grease-stained fingers and a look of guilt on my face. And from the acrid smell of my clothes, my wife knows immediately that I've fallen off the wagon once again.

Curse you, cracklin's! Curse you for being so decadent and deliriously delicious.

CAJUN CRACKLIN'S

Be forewarned, this is not your standard follow-the-recipe formula. In fact, cracklin is more an artisan craft than a kitchen recipe. There are varying methods for cracklin, as with gumbo, and they are all correct, as long as they achieve a quality product. Some like to start the cubes of fat off in water, but I am going with the "fat-in-fat" method. You'll need an enormous pot (I use a deep, 20-quart [19 L] black iron pot), a long-handled paddle for stirring, a clip-on deep-fry thermometer, and an outdoor burner. After that, the only ingredients are rendered hog lard and pork belly. But that's where the simplicity of cracklin comes to a screeching halt. It takes trial and error to get it right, and in South Louisiana there are generations of families that pass down this time-honored tradition.

SERVES A PARTY

4 to 6 pounds (1.8 to 2.7 kg) hog fatback or pork belly, cut into ¾ x 4-inch (2 x 10 cm) strips

Hog lard (amount varies with the pot size)

Cajun Seasoning Blend (page 13)

Salt

★ ★ ★ ★ ★

The first fry: With the pot on a low fire, add all the pieces of pork to the pot. Pour enough lard to come three-quarters the way up to the top of the pork. Be careful in this first phase of cooking, as the moisture trapped in the fat cubes will burst and create little grease bombs.

Here, the long, slow process of the first rendering of fat is crucial as you begin to reduce the raw pieces of pork fat, revealing the meat. The lard should be on a low fry, 225° to 275°F (107° to 140°C), and continual movement of the fat by stirring with a long-handled spoon will keep it from sticking together. Be sure to stir the pot every 3 minutes or so.

There are some important physical principles to remember. The grease will get hotter and will increase in quantity as the fat melts off the pork. It is important to use a thermometer to check the temperature of the lard. The longer it cooks, the hotter it gets. Lower the fire to lower the temperature. Ladle off some lard if it increases to a dangerous overflow level. Continue to cook for what might be close to 1 hour or more.

Once the cubes of pork have rendered and achieve a light brown color, transfer the cracklin's to a metal wire rack set over a tray. Think you're done? Think again.

The second fry: It's just like twice-fried potatoes. The science of heating oil to varying temperatures and returning the product to a higher, flash-fry heat achieves something miraculous in taste and texture. Once-fried cracklin's can become tough and difficult to bite through the exterior skin. This second fry will crisp the skin—some say "pop" the skins—that literally defines cracklin's. (Note: Some folks like to add a handful of ice to the oil at this stage, but I haven't experimented with that technique. It supposedly makes the grease boil rapidly and "blisters" the skin crisp. If you try it, be very careful.)

Make sure the quantity of oil still approximates the original amount and turn the fire on high until your thermometer reads between 375° and 400°F (190° and 200°C). Add the rendered pork back to the pot and turn the fire off.

Continue to cook until the pork pieces begin to achieve a rich, golden brown color. This is a crucial stage because some cracklin's will cook faster than others, so remove in stages based on color. Transfer to a wire rack set over a large tray lined with paper towels to soak up the grease. Season with Cajun Seasoning Blend and salt.

TABLE TIPS

★ Find a butcher who understands pork and the art of the cracklin'. There needs to be just the right amount of skin, fat, and meat. Some prefer the back fat, and some prefer the belly. Have the butcher cut the cracklin' fat into strips. They will shrink to thumb size during the cooking process.

★ If you live in an apartment, forget it. This is an outdoor adventure only. The overwhelming smell of a vat of frying fat, along with the risk of a hog lard inferno, are prime reasons to take it outside. A big black iron pot, a long-handled spoon or paddle, an oven mitt, a variable heat source, and a thermometer are the essential equipment needed. Oh, and you might want to wear a long-sleeved shirt and protective eyewear.

HOG'S HEAD CHEESE

In French culture—Cajun French, too—a terrine featuring pork parts cooked down and finely chopped, laced with a sublime balance of herbs and spices, bound in a gelatinous cloak, and served cold is a thing of beauty. Okay, so it's hog's head cheese. But before you turn the page, please read on, and you just may learn to appreciate this spunky, funky, and just-plain-tasty Cajun delicacy. South Louisiana meat markets have been serving up terrines of pork for generations. A classic terrine combines ground and chopped pieces and parts of the pig, along with a healthy dose of spice and heat, all held together with a binder (this version uses pig's feet, not gelatin).

Here in Acadiana, most butchers can provide you with all the pig parts you need. If you have a Latin or an Asian grocery near you, they are also great sources for pork pieces. And, if adventurous, find the whole pig's head and braise it in a big pot on the stovetop for 2 hours to get the good stuff. I will be most proud of you.

Preheat the oven to 375°F (190°C, or gas mark 5).

Place the cleaned and butchered pork jowls, tail, feet, and leg portions in a bowl under running cold water. Rinse them and inspect to see that they are clean and free of any blood. Dry the pieces on paper towels, place them on a large baking sheet, and cover with aluminum foil. Roast for 1 hour covered. Uncover and roast for 30 minutes longer.

Remove from the oven and let cool. With a paring knife, remove the pieces of pork meat from the bones. Remove and discard any large fatty pieces. You should have at least 2 cups (450 g) of pork meat. Dice the meat into small pieces. Cover and refrigerate.

Put all the pork bones and pig's feet in a large pot. Add enough water to cover. Bring the water to a boil and then lower the heat to a simmer. Cook until the water reduces by half, about 1 hour. Strain the stock through a fine-mesh strainer and discard the bones and any other pieces. Skim any fat from the stock, cover, and keep at room temperature.

Heat the oil in a large skillet over medium-high heat. Add the ground pork and cook until browned and fully cooked, about 8 minutes. Transfer the pork to a bowl, cover, and refrigerate.

Pour off all but 1 tablespoon (15 ml) of grease from the pan and add the butter. Turn the heat to medium-high and when the butter begins to sizzle, add the onions, celery, carrots, and bell peppers. Lower the heat to medium and cook the vegetables until the onions turn translucent, about 5 minutes. Add the garlic and white wine and cook until the alcohol in the wine mostly evaporates, about 5 minutes.

Turn off the heat and add the chopped rosemary, thyme, parsley, and green onions. Season with the hot sauce, cayenne, and white pepper. Stir to incorporate and taste the mixture. Add salt and black pepper to taste. Transfer to a bowl and add the chopped pork pieces, along with the ground pork. Stir the mixture to incorporate, making sure to break up any clumps of meat or vegetables.

(CONTINUED)

SERVES 6 TO 8

2 pig's jowls, butchered and cleaned

1 pig's tail, butchered and cleaned

4 pig's feet, butchered and cleaned

1 pig's leg, butchered and cleaned

1 tablespoon (15 ml) canola oil

1 cup (8 ounces, or 225 g) ground pork

2 tablespoons (28 g) unsalted butter

1 cup (160 g) diced yellow onion

1 cup (120 g) diced celery

1 cup (130 g) diced carrot

1 cup (150 g) diced green bell pepper

½ cup (75 g) diced red bell pepper

½ cup (75 g) diced yellow bell pepper

2 tablespoons (20 g) minced garlic

1 cup (235 ml) dry white wine

2 tablespoons (4 g) chopped fresh rosemary

2 tablespoons (5 g) chopped fresh thyme

1 cup (60 g) chopped flat-leaf parsley

1 cup (100 g) diced green onion tops

1 tablespoon (15 ml) hot sauce

1 tablespoon (5 g) cayenne pepper

1 tablespoon (6 g) freshly ground white pepper

Kosher salt and freshly ground black pepper

1 envelope (¼ ounce, or 7 g) powdered gelatin, if needed

Coat a 5 x 9-inch (13 x 23 cm) loaf pan or terrine with nonstick spray and add enough of the mixture to come to the top of the pan. Press down on the mixture to compact it into the pan and add more mixture if needed to fill the pan. Slowly pour the pork stock into the loaf pan until it comes to the top of the pan. Shake the pan gently to make sure the stock is surrounding all the meat and vegetable mixture. Cover with plastic wrap and refrigerate for at least 2 hours or overnight.

For serving, remove the loaf pan and uncover. Check to see that the gelatinous stock has set firmly. (If the stock did not develop enough gelatin from the pig's feet and did not set properly, you should pour off the stock into a bowl and stir the gelatin into the stock until dissolved. Then add the stock back to the loaf pan and refrigerate again.) Once the stock has set, slide a thin knife around the edges of the pan to loosen the mixture.

Place the platter on the table. Serve with crackers or toasted bread rounds along with grainy Creole mustard. Ice-cold beer is a must.

FRIED PORK CHOPS AND CREOLE RED BEANS WITH PICKLED PIG'S FEET

Mondays make me drool; it's time for red beans. To a born and fed Louisiana boy, a pipin' hot bowl of beans is the key to my heritage. Red beans are more than sustenance, they are my birthright, and I work to preserve the cultural reverence I hold for them. My beans are peppered with precision: the heat of cayenne, bite of red onions, smoke of andouille, spice of tasso, all in a pool of dark hock stock thickened by the velvet touch of pickled pig's feet—a whirling cauldron of Cajun flavors. And a Creole soul food cook once shared her wisdom with me as she whispered the secret of her red beans in my ear: "My baby, you gots to make the bean cream" is all she said. And I clearly understood.

And for me, fried pork chops always come with a bowl of red beans. My chops have a crunchy outer crust that shields a moist interior with just enough brined flavor sealed in. I love the tang of buttermilk and the twang of cayenne that make these pork chops sing like a Bocephus tune. These are bona fide, countrified, and Southern-fried pork chops.

Why can't every day be Monday?

BEANS

Fry the bacon in a cast-iron pot with a heavy lid over medium-high heat until browned and then transfer to a paper towel–lined plate. Reserve for later.

Add the onions, celery, and bell pepper to the bacon drippings. Sauté until the onions turn translucent, about 5 minutes. Add the garlic, tasso, smoked sausage, pig's feet, and reserved bacon pieces; continue cooking for 1 minute.

Drain the soaked beans and add them to the pot, along with enough water to cover them. Turn the heat to high until the water reaches a boil, and then lower the heat to a simmer and cover the pot. Simmer for 20 minutes.

Uncover and stir. Check the water level and add more so that the liquid comes above the top of the beans. Add the Cajun Seasoning Blend and hot sauce, along with a sprinkle of salt and black pepper. Cover the pot and simmer for another 20 minutes.

Uncover and stir again. The beans should be plump as they soak up the liquid. Add more water if needed. Cover and simmer for another 20 minutes.

At this point, the beans have cooked for 1 hour and should be fully cooked. With a measuring cup, scoop out 1 cup (177 g) of beans with their liquid and pour into the container of a blender. Blend on high speed until the beans are pulverized and have achieved a creamy texture. Pour the "bean cream" back into the pot of beans and stir to incorporate. Cover the pot and continue to simmer on very low heat for 1 hour longer. Turn off the heat and keep the beans warm.

SERVES 4

BEANS

1 pound (455 g) smoked bacon, chopped

1 cup (160 g) diced yellow onion

1 cup (120 g) diced celery

1 cup (150 g) diced green bell pepper

2 tablespoons (20 g) minced garlic

1 cup (150 g) diced tasso (preferably) or smoked ham

2 links of smoked andouille sausage, sliced

2 pickled pig's feet or raw pig's feet

1 pound (455 g) dried red kidney beans, rinsed and picked over, soaked overnight in water to cover

1 tablespoon (10 g) Cajun Seasoning Blend (page 13)

Dash of hot sauce

Kosher salt and freshly ground black pepper

4 cups (632 g) cooked long-grain white rice

1 cup (100 g) diced green onion tops

(CONTINUED)

(CONTINUED)

PORK CHOPS

In a large covered container, combine the buttermilk, salt, honey, garlic powder, onion powder, and 1 tablespoon (10 g) of the Cajun Seasoning Blend. Add the pork chops and submerge in the buttermilk. Cover and let marinate in the refrigerator overnight or for at least 4 hours.

Remove the container with the marinated chops from the refrigerator and let come to room temperature.

In a large paper bag, combine the flour, cornstarch, smoked paprika, garlic powder, onion powder, and the remaining 1 tablespoon (10 g) of Cajun Seasoning Blend. Add a generous pinch of salt and black pepper. Shake all of the ingredients in the bag until combined.

Pour the oil into a large cast-iron skillet over medium-high heat. There should be at least ½ inch (1 cm) of oil in the pan. Bring the oil up to 375°F (190°C), checking to make sure with a kitchen thermometer.

Drop 6 chops at a time into the paper bag with the flour mixture and shake vigorously. Make sure to coat all sides and edges. Remove the breaded pork chops and place on a platter. Add the chops to the pan slowly, cooking in batches as needed. Make sure to maintain the 375°F (190°C) temperature of the oil. Fry until browned on one side and then turn over and fry for another 5 minutes or until golden brown. Transfer the pork chops to a wire rack and sprinkle with salt.

For serving, scoop some rice into the bottom of a shallow bowl, ladle a generous portion of red beans on top, and sprinkle with diced green onions. Serve with the fried pork chops nestled next to the beans and plenty of hot sauce on the side.

THE LAST MEAL

What would you eat as your last meal? Have you ever thought about it? I have, and I have a quick answer: Creole red beans with fried pork chops. As a lifelong Southerner raised in Louisiana, I had always eaten each dish separately, but it was later in life during a visit to a real soul food kitchen that I discovered the combination. I remember it like it was yesterday. Buster Holmes ran a Creole lunchroom on the edge of the French Quarter just a block or two off Bourbon on Burgundy at Orleans. I recall popping in for a quick lunchtime bite at the suggestion of a lifelong New Orleans friend. It was a revelation. The chalkboard called out the day's lineup, and it was all served communally. You bellied up to one of the long family-style wooden tables with anyone who shared your hunger for a home-cooked meal—a trucker, a bellhop, a horse and carriage driver, or maybe even an Uptown aristocrat. It didn't matter. Nobody cared. We were all equals in Buster's eyes—at Buster's table.

I was brought a large jar of sweet tea and a huge hunk of Leidenheimer French bread. As I sliced my knife through the 1-pound (455 g) block of butter on the table, I knew I was in for something special. Seconds later, a large Schwegmann's grocery bag was spread out before me, and three pipin' hot fried pork chops were plopped down on top of the sack. The grease immediately started soaking into the brown paper as the steam rose from the chops. A huge bowl of smoking hot red beans with a couple of chunks of smoked sausage on top was seated next to it. A spoon was the only utensil needed. As I nestled a hot pork chop in the edge of that bowl to soak up the bean juice, I took another bite. I was ready to meet my maker. Sweet Jesus, come and take me home.

PORK CHOPS

4 cups (946 ml) buttermilk

1 tablespoon (8 g) kosher salt

1 tablespoon (20 g) honey

2 tablespoons (18 g) garlic powder, divided

2 tablespoons (14 g) onion powder, divided

2 tablespoons (20 g) Cajun Seasoning Blend (page 13)

12 thin-cut, bone-in pork chops

2 cups (250 g) unbleached all-purpose flour

¼ cup (32 g) cornstarch

1 tablespoon (7 g) smoked paprika

1 tablespoon (9 g) garlic powder

1 tablespoon (7 g) onion powder

Kosher salt and freshly ground black pepper

2 cups (475 ml) peanut oil

CRABAPPLE-BRAISED WHOLE PIG'S LEG

This stunning braised pork leg comes with a guarantee: You will gain the utmost respect for the traditions of cooking Cajun and forever cement your kitchen credibility with family and friends. With a long slow braise in a fragrant crabapple-infused bath, the meat renders down into fork-tender pork with a crisp outer skin. Leaving the trotter on the end of the shank adds velvety texture to the cider-based sauce, as the gelatinous bits will release to form a condensed pork gravy.

Make a brine by combining the water, cider, sugar, and salt in a large container with a lid. Stir until the sugar and salt have dissolved. Add the pork and close the container. Refrigerate overnight.

Preheat the oven to 350°F (180°C, or gas mark 4). Line a large baking pan with aluminum foil.

Remove the pork leg pieces from the brine and place in the prepared baking pan. Add the onions, celery, bell pepper, and carrots, along with 6 of the crabapples. Pour the jar of applesauce into the pan and distribute evenly. Add the vinegar and rosemary. Season with salt and pepper. Cover the pan with foil.

Roast for 1½ hours. Remove the pork pieces and transfer everything else (including the pig's foot) to a pot. Place the pork pieces back in the baking pan and roast uncovered for another 30 minutes. Cover with foil to keep warm.

Bring the contents of the pot to a boil over medium-high heat and add the pork stock. Lower the heat to a simmer and cook for 15 minutes. Using a slotted spoon, remove all of the vegetables and the pig's foot from the liquid. Add the remaining 6 crabapples to the pot. Bring back to a simmer and cook for another 20 minutes as the liquid slowly reduces and the crabapples cook down.

To thicken the sauce, make a slurry by combining the cornstarch and cold water in a small bowl. Stir to combine and add one-half of it to the simmering pot of stock. Bring the pot to a boil and watch as it thickens to the desired thickness. If the sauce is not thick enough, add more cornstarch slurry and stir until it is thick enough to coat the back of a spoon. Sample the sauce and season with salt and pepper to taste.

For serving, arrange the pork pieces on a platter. Spoon the sauce over the pork and place the cooked crabapples alongside on the platter.

SERVES 4

2 quarts (1.9 L) water

4 cups (956 ml) apple cider, divided

¼ cup (50 g) granulated sugar

¼ cup (72 g) salt

1 whole leg of pork (4 pounds, or 1.8 kg), butchered, cleaned and cut into pieces with the pig's foot

1 onion, quartered

2 celery stalks, cut into chunks

1 green bell pepper, cut into chunks

2 carrots, cut into chunks

12 crabapples

1 jar (12 ounces, or 340 g) applesauce

2 tablespoons (28 ml) apple cider vinegar

4 fresh rosemary sprigs

Kosher salt and freshly ground black pepper

2 cups (475 ml) pork stock (preferably) or chicken stock

2 tablespoons (16 g) cornstarch

2 tablespoons (28 ml) cold water

TABLE TIPS

★ You might be tempted to trim off the pig's foot. Don't. Pig's feet add flavor and a certain gelatinous texture to the sauce that is indescribable.

★ If crabapples are not available, use small tart apples cut in half.

★ Serve with sautéed carrots and Cajun rice dressing along with a pitcher of sweet tea.

CAJUN BOUDIN

This is a basic starting point for exploring boudin. The key to boudin is the balance of ingredients: meat, liver, rice, and spice. You must experiment with different levels to find the proper ratio for your particular taste.

Preheat the oven to 400°F (200°C, or gas mark 6).

Place the pork roast in a heavy pot with a tight-fitting lid and fill the pot with water to a depth of 4 inches (10 cm). Cover and roast the pork roast for 2 hours or until falling apart. Remove the pork from the pot, reserving the cooking liquid.

Fill a pot with water and bring to a boil over high heat. Add the liver and boil until well-done, about 10 minutes. Remove and drain on a paper towel–lined plate.

Put the pork, liver, yellow onions, and garlic in a food processor. Pulse until it reaches a smooth, yet chunky, consistency. (You will need to do this in batches.) Be careful not to over-process to a pasty, mushy stage.

Incorporate the cooked rice in a ratio of about 80 percent meat mixture to 20 percent rice. Gradually add the reserved cooking liquid until the mixture is moist. Add the Cajun Seasoning Blend, cayenne, and green onions. Add salt, black pepper, and hot sauce to taste. Evenly incorporate the ingredients—using your clean hands is the most effective way.

Stuff the mixture into sausage casings using a sausage stuffer. Optionally, you can form the bulk boudin into patties.

To keep the boudin warm without drying out, I suggest wrapping it tightly in aluminum foil and placing it into the ceramic bowl of a slow cooker set to Warm with ½ inch (1 cm) of water in the bottom. If your boudin is not in a casing, then first wrap it in plastic wrap before wrapping it in foil.

Boudin links should be eaten hot with an ice-cold beer and saltine crackers.

SERVES 4 TO 6

1 pork roast (4 pounds, or 1.8 kg)

1 pound (455 g) pork liver

2 large yellow onions, diced

6 cloves of garlic, chopped

2 cups (316 g) cooked long-grain white rice

¼ cup (40 g) Cajun Seasoning Blend (page 13)

1 tablespoon (5 g) cayenne pepper

1 cup (100 g) diced green onion tops

Kosher salt and freshly ground black pepper

Dash of hot sauce

TABLE TIP

Boudin balls can be rolled in cracker crumbs and fried. And boudin patties—one of my favorites—are perfect as a base for fried eggs at breakfast. Any way you try it, boudin is perfectly delicious.

What's That?

Boudin (*boo-DAN*) is a curious blend of herbs and spices with bits of pork and liver included. Mixed with Louisiana long-grain white rice, it's all combined, put through a grinder, and stuffed into a pig's intestine casing. The good stuff, when you can find it, is boudin noir (pig's blood is added)—but that discussion is for a different time. It's been said that a seven-course Cajun meal is a link of boudin and a six-pack of beer.

Boudin stops short of becoming a true smokehouse sausage because it is steamed rather than smoked. The character of boudin is its moistness—its squeez-ability. Eating boudin is akin to squeezing a tube of toothpaste directly into your waiting mouth. It is the essence of Cajun life and is sold in near about every roadside grocery, convenience store, and gas station around.

ALONG THE BOUDIN TRAIL

If you are fortunate enough to live in Louisiana or are planning a trip to the state, the bayou backroads are a source of delicious discovery. The food culture abounds along these rural highways and byways that offer up a treasure trove of tasty eating. But, one irresistible culinary prize you will find linking all four corners of the state is boudin.

Arguments abound on the source of the best boudin. The Louisiana state legislature almost came to a screeching halt a few years back as the Acadiana towns of Broussard and Scott fought over who should be named the Boudin Capital of the World. Even marriages have been known to break up over such a quandary. There are so many options, so many differing styles, that it is nearly impossible to answer the question.

There is even an official Cajun Boudin Trail pinpointing the location of most every stop along the roads selling the stuff. Dr. Robert Carriker has a Ph.D. in boudin (well, actually, history), and he heads up the project, as well as the history department at the University of Louisiana at Lafayette. Dr. Boudin, as he is most affectionately called, wrote the book on boudin. He not only mapped out the spicy spots on the trail, peppered throughout South Louisiana, but he has also reviewed every single one of them.

Styles differ, and certain well-known specialty houses have become meccas for the boudin aficionado. Comeaux's, Don's, Best Stop, Boudin King, Earl's, Poche's, Bourque's—these are just a few of the five-star rated versions of boudin that provoke endless debate. "Too ricey . . . too spicy . . . too livery . . . too bland"—the dispute rages on.

I have a clear winning solution that, if adopted (and it won't be), will end this babbling battle over boudin: They're all good. Each has a taste profile all its own. But that's too easy. To broker an end to the discussion would be a diplomatic impossibility and, well, clearly wrong. So the debate rages on, and as you travel the boudin trail in search of the missing link, it's not hard to see who the real winner is.

BACON-WRAPPED STUFFED PORK LOIN WITH CHARRED PEACH GLAZE

As if the bacon-encased pork loin pumped full of cream cheese and jalapeño weren't enough, it is then burnished and bronzed with a fruit-singed glaze and served with sizzling onions and charred peaches. Fragrant ripe peaches are good enough on their own, but with a spike of chile and a blast of searing heat on a hot griddle, they release their sugars and perfume your world. This pork dish ramps up the heat and pours on the sweet.

PORK

Preheat the oven to 350°F (180°C, or gas mark 4). Line a deep baking pan large enough to hold both tenderloins with aluminum foil.

Slice each pork tenderloin lengthwise along the middle, but stop short of going all the way through. Form a pocket ½ inch (1 cm) from each end and open it up. Spread the cream cheese liberally along the full length of the bottom of the pocket. Line the jalapeño peppers over the cheese along the inside of the pocket. Close the pork loin, encasing the stuffing. Lay strips of bacon on the top, side by side, along the length of the tenderloin, wrapping the ends of the bacon underneath to close it up. Sprinkle the tenderloins with the Cajun Seasoning Blend and rosemary.

Place the tenderloins in the prepared baking pan and add the chopped onions and garlic. Pour in the peach nectar. Cover the top of the pan with foil and bake for 1 hour.

Remove and pour off the pan drippings into a medium pot. Increase the oven temperature to 400°F (200°C, or gas mark 6). Move the pan back to the oven, uncovered, to begin finishing the meat. After 15 minutes, check to see that the tops of the tenderloins are starting to brown and the bacon is just beginning to crisp. The bacon should not be totally crispy, but still hold its shape along the length of the tenderloin. Watch closely and remove once the pork reaches an internal temperature of 150°F (66°C). Cover with foil and let rest in a warm place.

CHARRED PEACH GLAZE

Preheat a large cast-iron skillet over medium-high heat. Sprinkle the peach halves with chili powder and coat the onion slices with the Cajun Seasoning Blend. Once hot, add the peach halves to the skillet, cut-side down, along with the sliced onion. Cook until the bottoms begin to caramelize and with a metal spatula, flip to the other side. Continue cooking until all the bottoms char. Remove from the heat.

Turn the burner under the pot with the peach nectar drippings to high. As it begins to reach a simmer, add the peach liqueur and molasses. Turn the heat down to a simmer and let the mixture reduce by one-half, about 15 minutes. With an immersion blender, blend the

SERVES 4 TO 6

PORK

2 pork tenderloins (1½ pounds, or 680 g each)

1 package (8 ounces, or 225 g) cream cheese

4 fresh jalapeño peppers, stems, seeds and ribs removed

1 pound (455 g) thick-cut smoked bacon

2 tablespoons (20 g) Cajun Seasoning Blend (page 13)

2 tablespoons (4 g) chopped fresh rosemary

1 cup (160 g) diced yellow onion

2 tablespoons (20 g) minced garlic

2 cups (475 ml) peach nectar

CHARRED PEACH GLAZE

4 ripe but firm freestone peaches, halved and pitted

1 tablespoon (8 g) chili powder

2 large yellow onions, cut into 1-inch (2.5 cm) slices

1 tablespoon (10 g) Cajun Seasoning Blend (page 13)

¼ cup (60 ml) peach liqueur

1 tablespoon (20 g) sugarcane molasses

1 tablespoon (8 g) cornstarch

1 tablespoon (15 ml) cold water

1 tablespoon (14 g) unsalted butter

Kosher salt and freshly ground black pepper

Fresh rosemary sprigs

onions and garlic to a purée. To thicken, make a slurry by stirring the cornstarch and cold water together. Stir it into the glaze and let it come to a boil to reach the desired thickness. Add richness to the glaze with the knob of butter. Stir and add salt and pepper to taste. The glaze should be just thick enough to coat the back of a spoon, but not like gravy. Pour the glaze into a serving bowl and keep warm.

For serving, move the tenderloins to a cutting board and brush with Charred Peach Glaze. The bacon will serve as a mark for portioning as you slice in between each strip. Position the pork pieces on a large platter, retaining the shape of the tenderloin. Place the charred peaches and onion slabs around the platter. Spoon more peach glaze over the pork and peaches and garnish with sprigs of rosemary. Serve the remaining glaze on the side.

SMOKED PONCE WITH PORK JUS AND CRISPY PIG'S EAR

This dish transports me to a long-ago time and place when French cooks took food seriously and approached cooking skillfully. Long before the heyday of Julia Child hawking the mastery of French cuisine in America, before Bocuse and the culinary renaissance of nouvelle cuisine, before Escoffier and the five mother sauces, even before Brillat-Savarin, French Acadian cooks in South Louisiana kitchens prepared ponce. And even now, almost 300 years later, it is a classic that provokes delicious curiosity.

Prepare a smoker with hickory wood and bring to 175°F (79°C) by following the equipment directions.

Place the pig's stomach in a colander and rinse thoroughly under cold water. In a large bowl, mix the salt with enough cold water to fully submerge the stomach and place the stomach in the water. Place the bowl in the refrigerator for 30 minutes. Remove and inspect the stomach to make sure that it is clean, being careful not to tear the delicate tissue. Place on paper towels and let dry. Refrigerate until ready to stuff.

Heat 2 tablespoons (28 ml) of the oil in a large skillet over medium-high heat. Add the onions, celery, and bell pepper and cook until the onions become translucent, about 5 minutes. Add the garlic and thyme and cook for 1 minute more. Remove the skillet from the heat and pour the contents into a large bowl. Add the ground pork, Cajun Seasoning Blend, and black pepper. Combine and make sure that the ingredients are evenly distributed.

Move the pig's stomach to a large cutting board and open it up. Using your hands, gently stuff the meat mixture inside the stomach. Add just enough filling so that the lining of the stomach can come together and seal. Using butcher's twine, sew the stomach closed. (Note: Alternatively, some use toothpicks to close the stomach.)

Place the stuffed ponce on a rack in the smoker. Smoke for 4 hours at 175°F (79°C).

Preheat the oven to 350°F (180°C, or gas mark 4).

Place the smoked ponce in a heavy cast-iron pot with a tight-fitting lid. Add the carrots, onions, and celery to the pot, along with enough chicken stock to come halfway up the side of the stuffed ponce. Cover the pot and bake for 2 hours.

Once the ponce has finished roasting, transfer it to a platter and keep warm. Pour the jus and vegetables through a strainer to remove the vegetables. Add another cup (235 ml) of chicken stock to the jus if you have it left over. Over high heat, bring the stock to a simmer and skim off any fat or particles from the jus. Lower the heat and simmer for 5 minutes. Turn off the heat and keep warm.

Wash the pig's ear thoroughly and dry with paper towels. Heat 2 tablespoons (28 ml) of the oil in a cast-iron skillet with a heavy lid over medium heat. Add the pig's ear and brown on both sides. Add the water and cover. Lower the heat to low and simmer for 30 minutes. Remove the pig's ear and let cool. Thinly slice the pig's ear into strips.

(CONTINUED)

SERVES 4

- 1 pig's stomach, cleaned and prepped
- 1 cup (288 g) salt
- 6 tablespoons (90 ml) canola oil, divided
- 1 cup (160 g) diced yellow onion
- 1 cup (120 g) diced celery
- 1 cup (150 g) diced green bell pepper
- 1 tablespoon (10 g) minced garlic
- 1 tablespoon (2 g) chopped fresh thyme
- 2 pounds (900 g) ground pork
- 2 tablespoons (20 g) Cajun Seasoning Blend (page xx)
- 1 teaspoon freshly ground black pepper
- 2 carrots, chopped
- 2 yellow onions, quartered
- 1 celery stalk, chopped
- 4 cups (946 ml) Dark Chicken Stock (page 215)
- 1 pig's ear, cleaned
- 1 cup (235 ml) water
- Fresh thyme sprigs
- Diced green onion tops
- Creole mustard or other coarse-grained mustard

TABLE TIPS

★ Rather than buying from a supermarket, source your pig's stomach and pig's ear from a butcher (many Latin grocers specialize in pork) with a good reputation for fresh pork products.

★ Instead of a thinner pork jus, some Cajun cooks like to add several big spoonfuls of dark roux in the roasting stage to make a thicker gravy.

★ Ponce is also delicious roasted in the oven without smoking. Just follow the recipe as directed, eliminating the smoking step.

Wipe out the cast-iron skillet, add the remaining 2 tablespoons (28 ml) oil, and set over high heat. Cook the pig's ear strips until they blister and turn crunchy, about 8 to 10 minutes. (The flesh will crackle and pop, so be careful with grease splattering. Use a pot screen if you have one.) Once the pig's ear portions are cooked to golden brown and crunchy, transfer to a paper towel–lined plate to drain. Before serving, cut the strips into smaller pieces for garnish.

For serving, move the stuffed ponce to a cutting board and remove the stomach casing. Slice the stuffing into ½-inch-thick (1 cm) portions. Ladle some pork jus into each serving bowl and add 2 slices of ponce. Garnish with crispy pig's ear, sprigs of thyme, and diced green onions. Serve with grainy Creole mustard, if desired.

What's That?

Ponce (*pawnce*) or chaudin (*show-DAN*) is essentially a sausage-stuffed pig's stomach. It is a preparation that is seen in most every culinary culture. In Scotland, you'd be dining on haggis (sheep's stomach); in Latin America, hog maw; and in Germany, *saumagen*, but it is the French that always seem to up the ante. Ponce is called chaudin in parts of South Louisiana; some refer to ponce specifically as the smoked version, but the two names are interchangeable. Whatever it's called, it is a dish that in the expert hands of an artisan is a seductive entrée into the inner world of Cajun cooking.

SMOKED BEEF RIBS WITH COCA-COLA GLAZE AND BEER-BAKED BEANS

Let's cut to the meat of this story—bone-in beef ribs are irresistible to me. They harken back to pioneer days and more rustic farm-style butchering techniques. An hour of hickory smoke on the bone imparts enormous flavor and a long three-hour braise in dark beer breaks down the collagen inside to fork-tenderness. Finished with a glaze made with sugarcane-based Mexican Coke and you've got sticky, sweet, melt-in-your-mouth beef ribs. Paired with my beer-baked beans cooked with smoked meats (andouille, hog jowl bacon, and tasso) and peppered with chipotle chiles, this is what my daddy always called a nap-taking meal.

BEANS

Cook the bacon in a heavy cast-iron pot with a lid over medium-high heat until crisp. Remove and set aside. Pour off all but 2 tablespoons (28 ml) of the bacon grease and add the onions, celery, and bell pepper. Cook until the onions turn translucent, about 5 minutes. Add the tasso and andouille and cook until browned, about 5 minutes. Add the garlic and stir to combine.

Add the beer and deglaze, while scraping the bottom of the pot with a spatula to loosen all the bits. Add the chicken stock. Drain the beans and add to the pot. Bring to a boil and then lower the heat to a simmer. Season with the Cajun Seasoning Blend, salt, pepper, and hot sauce. Cover and cook on the stovetop, stirring every 20 minutes, until the beans are tender, about 1½ hours.

Preheat the oven to 400°F (200°C, or gas mark 6). Using a strainer or large spoon, tilt the pot over a bowl and drain off any excess liquid from the beans. Add the crisp bacon pieces, chipotle chiles along with the adobo sauce, Creole mustard, and molasses. Stir to combine. Bake uncovered for 45 minutes. Keep warm until serving.

RIBS

Prepare a smoker with hickory chips and bring to 200°F (93°C).

Slice the ribs along the bones into individual ribs. Rub the ribs with the Cajun Seasoning Blend, salt, and pepper. Place in the smoker and cook for 2 hours. Remove and cover with foil.

Pour 4 bottles of the Coke and the water into a large pot with a heavy lid over medium-high heat. Add the onions. Stack the ribs in the liquid and bring to a boil. Cover and lower the heat to a simmer and cook on the stovetop (check periodically to see if more water is needed) until the ribs are tender and easily pull away from the bone, about 1 hour. Remove the ribs from the pot, cover, and keep warm.

(CONTINUED)

SERVES 4 TO 6

BEANS

6 strips (1 ounce, or 28 g each) of smoked pork jowl bacon or smoked regular bacon, chopped

1 cup (160 g) diced yellow onion

½ cup (60 g) diced celery

½ cup (75 g) diced green bell pepper

½ cup (75 g) chopped tasso (preferably) or smoked ham

1 cup (8 ounces, or 225 g) chopped andouille (preferably) or smoked pork sausage

1 tablespoon (10 g) minced garlic

2 bottles (12 ounces, or 355 ml each) beer, preferably dark ale

4 cups (946 ml) chicken stock

1 pound (455 g) dried red kidney beans, rinsed and picked over, soaked overnight in water to cover

1 tablespoon (10 g) Cajun Seasoning Blend (page 13)

Kosher salt and freshly ground black pepper

Dash of hot sauce

1 tablespoon (8 g) chopped chipotle chiles in adobo sauce, plus 1 tablespoon (15 ml) sauce

1 teaspoon Creole mustard or other coarse-grained mustard

2 tablespoons (40 g) sugarcane molasses

(CONTINUED)

Bring the pot with the remaining braising liquid to a boil over medium-high heat and add the final bottle of Coke. Add the molasses and ketchup. Bring to a boil and then lower the heat to a simmer. Cook until the sauce thickens enough to coat the back of a spoon, about 30 minutes. Pour the sauce into a bowl and let cool. Leave the onions in the sauce if you like your sauce chunky. If you prefer a smooth sauce, strain out the onions or purée the sauce (with an immersion blender or standard blender). Keep warm for serving.

To finish the ribs on an outdoor grill, prepare a medium fire. Place the ribs over the fire and brush on the sauce. Cook for about 5 minutes, just until the glaze sets and the ribs are warmed through.

Or, to finish the ribs in the oven, preheat the oven to 400°F (200°C, or gas mark 6). Place the ribs on a foil-lined baking sheet and brush with the sauce. Bake just until the glaze sets and the ribs are warmed through, about 8 to10 minutes. Watch carefully to prevent the sauce from burning.

Serve the ribs on a large platter along with the pot of beer-baked beans and extra sauce on the side. Hot French bread and ice-cold Mexican Cokes are all that is needed—oh, and plenty of napkins.

TABLE TIPS
★ Pinto beans are the choice for most Southwestern baked beans, but here in southwest Louisiana, it's red beans all the way.

★ Seek out Mexican Coke for this dish, as it is sweetened with cane sugar rather than corn syrup. It's readily available at Latin markets or online.

RIBS

6 pounds (2.7 kg, or 3 slabs) bone-in beef ribs

2 tablespoons (20 g) Cajun Seasoning Blend (page 13)

Kosher salt and freshly ground black pepper

5 bottles (12 ounces, or 355 ml each) of Mexican Coca-Cola

1 cup (235 ml) water

2 cups (320 g) chopped yellow onion

2 tablespoons (40 g) sugarcane molasses

2 tablespoons (30 g) ketchup

DOUBLE-CUT PORK CHOPS STUFFED WITH APPLE SAUSAGE

Slicing open a bone-in double-cut pork chop to expose a deep pocket and filling it with a tangy sausage-based stuffing is pure genius. Stuffed pork chops are a mainstay of Cajun butcher shops and show up frequently on both home and restaurant tables. This hearty combination—sweet apple and fresh herbs infuse the spicy sausage—brings together all that I love about Cajun food: smoky, sugary, spicy, savory, with the heady scent of beer. Stuff this double-cut dish into your recipe box and be sure to file it under "D" for down-right delicious.

Rinse the pork chops and trim any excess fat. Stir the cider, beer, and salt in a lidded container. Add the pork chops, seal the container, and refrigerate for at least 2 hours or up to overnight.

Preheat the oven to 350°F (180°C, or gas mark 4). Line 2 baking sheets with aluminum foil.

Melt the bacon grease in a large skillet over medium-high heat. Add the onions, celery, and bell pepper. Sauté until the onions turn translucent, about 5 minutes. Add the rosemary and chopped apple and continue cooking until the apple softens. Add the ground pork and sauté just until the meat begins to brown. Season with the cayenne, white pepper, Cajun Seasoning Blend, salt, and black pepper. Add the chicken stock and cider, along with the diced green onions, and stir. Gradually, add the bread crumbs as needed until the mixture begins to firm up into a moist sausage consistency.

Remove the pork chops from the brining liquid and pat dry. Heat the oil in a heavy cast-iron skillet over medium-high heat. Once the oil is smoking, add the pork chop and quickly brown on both sides. Remove and let cool.

With a sharp knife, cut a pocket in the center of each pork chop, slicing all the way to the bone. Stand a chop bone side down and open the pocket with your fingers. Sprinkle the pork chop lightly with salt and pepper. Spoon in the apple-sausage stuffing to fill the pocket and place on a prepared baking sheet. Repeat with all chops and place any remaining stuffing on the tray with the chops. Bake until the sausage cooks through and the pork chops reach an internal temperature of 145°F (63°C), about 30 minutes. Remove and let rest for 5 minutes before serving.

Meanwhile, make the baked apple garnish by cutting the apples in half lengthwise and removing any visible seeds. Using a paring knife, slice into each apple half, cutting fan-like slices. Position the apples onto the other prepared baking sheet. Coat the top of each with melted butter and sprinkle lightly with cinnamon and sugar. Place in the hot oven and watch carefully as the apple fans begin to soften and brown, about 10 minutes.

For serving, place each pork chop on a serving plate along with any excess stuffing mixture. Adorn with a baked apple fan.

SERVES 4

4 bone-in pork chops (1¾ inch, or 4.5 cm thick)

2 cups each (475 ml) apple cider and beer

1 cup (288 g) salt

1 tablespoon (13 g) bacon grease

1 cup (160 g) diced yellow onion

1 cup (120 g) diced celery

1 cup (150 g) diced green bell pepper

2 tablespoons (4 g) chopped fresh rosemary

2 tart apples, cored, peeled, and chopped, such as Granny Smith

2 pounds (900 g) ground pork

½ teaspoon cayenne pepper

1 teaspoon ground white pepper

1 teaspoon Cajun Seasoning Blend (page 13)

Kosher salt and freshly ground black pepper

1 cup (235 ml) chicken stock

1 cup (235 ml) apple cider

½ cup (50 g) green onion tops

2 cups (230 g) dry bread crumbs, or as needed

1 tablespoon (15 ml) canola oil

2 apples

4 tablespoons (½ stick, or 55 g) unsalted butter, melted

1 tablespoon (7 g) ground cinnamon

1 tablespoon (13 g) granulated sugar

COFFEE-RUBBED PORTERHOUSE WITH BOURBON BROWN BUTTER

When it comes to meat, my feeling is, the bigger, the better; it is a primal urge. And whenever I see huge hunks of beef stacked up, ravenous hunger kicks in. Steaks portioned in large slabs are not all about the quantity of the meat, but more about the quality of the outcome. I look for bone-in cuts with just enough thickness to char the outside and leave the inside rosy pink.

Here's the dilemma: My wife swears by filet mignon; I insist that a New York strip sirloin is the "king of steaks." Over the years, I've found the solution: porterhouse—tender filet on one side of the bone and strip sirloin on the other. With my coffee rub, I create a crust that seals in the juices, adds enormous flavor, and provides textural contrast. And with a finish in bourbon brown butter, this is char-grilled diplomacy at its best.

BOURBON BROWN BUTTER

Melt the butter in a cast-iron skillet over medium heat. Add the shallots and cook until the butter just begins to brown, then add the garlic, and turn the heat to low. Add the bourbon, being careful to contain any flame. Let the sauce cook for another minute or two as the alcohol evaporates. Season with pepper to taste.

COFFEE RUB

Mix the ground coffee, brown sugar, salt, garlic powder, and pepper in a bowl.

STEAK

Remove the steaks 1 hour before cooking and let them come to room temperature. Coat both sides lightly with vegetable oil and rub with a generous coating of the coffee rub.

Bring a charcoal or gas grill to maximum temperature with the grates set to their lowest level. Have a spray bottle of water at the ready to control flare-ups.

Add the steaks to the grill and let cook. Spray down any excessive flaming. Depending on the thickness and the heat of your grill, it should take about 3 minutes per side for perfect medium-rare or 4 minutes for medium. Cook to your desired level of doneness.

Transfer the steaks to a cutting board and let rest for at least 10 minutes. Either serve the steaks whole or slice them. Using a sharp knife, slice along the inside bone on both the strip side and the filet side. Then cut into bite-size portions, leaving the pieces inside the bone. Brush lightly with the Bourbon Brown Butter and serve with more of the sauce on the side.

SERVES 4

BOURBON BROWN BUTTER

1 cup (2 sticks, or 225 g) unsalted butter

¼ cup (40 g) finely chopped shallot

3 cloves of garlic, minced

2 tablespoons (28 ml) bourbon

Freshly ground black pepper

COFFEE RUB (MAKES 2½ CUPS [325 G])

½ cup (40 g) dark-roast coffee beans, finely ground

½ cup (115 g) firmly packed dark brown sugar

½ cup (48 g) kosher salt

½ cup (72 g) garlic powder

½ cup (48 g) coarsely ground black pepper

STEAK

4 porterhouse steaks (1 pound, or 455 g each)

2 tablespoons (28 ml) vegetable oil

OXTAIL STEW

Plain and simple: It's oxtail stew—literally the tail end of a cow. Oh, you can call it something sophisticated; I even tried out "oxxo buco," to the groans of my wife. Regardless of what you call it, I can tell you that it is one of the great pleasures of eating. As you'll see when you try this dish, it is easy to prep and the long, slow braise is effortless. But, as it turns out, this inexpensive, uncomplicated ingredient produces a result that is surprisingly rich in taste and flavor. From now on, I think you'll look at the tail end of the cow with more respect.

Remove the meat from the refrigerator, sprinkle lightly with salt and pepper, and let come to room temperature.

Heat 2 tablespoons (28 ml) of the oil in a heavy skillet or pot with a tight-fitting lid over medium-high heat. Coat the oxtails lightly in flour and add to the hot oil. Brown on all sides, in batches as necessary, removing the pieces as they are browned. Repeat until all the meat is browned.

Add the remaining 2 tablespoons (28 ml) oil to the pot. Add the onions, celery, bell pepper, and mushrooms. Sauté until the mushrooms begin to brown, about 5 minutes. Add the oxtails and the port and bring to a boil. Lower the heat to a simmer and let the port reduce by one-half, about 20 minutes.

Add the carrots, parsley, thyme, garlic, paprika, bay leaves, and Beef Stock. Cover and lower the temperature to a simmer. Continue braising the meat until tender, about 1 hour.

Uncover and check to see that the meat is tender and the sauce has thickened. Add the butter and stir to incorporate. Season to taste with salt and pepper. Remove the bay leaves. Serve family-style with mashed potatoes or rice along with hot French bread.

SERVES 4

4 pounds (1.8 kg) oxtails

Kosher salt and freshly ground black pepper

4 tablespoons (60 ml) vegetable oil, divided

1 cup (125 g) unbleached all-purpose flour

2 cups (320 g) diced yellow onion

1 cup (120 g) chopped celery

1 cup (150 g) diced green bell pepper

2 cups (140 g) sliced button mushrooms

1 cup (235 ml) port

2 cups (260 g) sliced carrots

½ cup (30 g) chopped fresh flat-leaf parsley

1 tablespoon (2 g) chopped fresh thyme

1 tablespoon (10 g) minced garlic

1 teaspoon smoked paprika

2 bay leaves

2 cups (475 ml) Beef Stock (page 48)

1 tablespoon (14 g) unsalted butter

Mashed potatoes or cooked white rice

TABLE TIP

I use button mushrooms, but most any kind will work fine. I guess you could make this dish without the wine, but the rich tawny port adds a hauntingly dark depth of flavor to this hearty dish. Where I live, oxtails are readily available, but if you have difficulty finding this cut of beef, try a Latin or Asian market. And be sure to buy the meaty oxtails rather than the narrow end pieces, which are more suited for making stock.

CREOLE MEATBALLS IN RED GRAVY

The Creole lunch houses that dot the rural landscape of Acadiana always feature folksy fare that reflects traditional interpretations of South Louisiana cooking. It is true comfort food: stick-to-the-ribs hearty and artery-hardening rich. Make the rounds at any number of steam-table eateries and you're sure to come across a rustic, roux-based meatball stew served over a mound of white rice featuring the holy trinity of onions, peppers, and celery. My philosophy on meatballs is simple: Bigger is better.

MEATBALLS

Preheat the oven to 400°F (200°C, or gas mark 6). Line a large baking sheet with aluminum foil.

Place the bread, milk, eggs, Parmesan cheese, and Worcestershire in a large bowl. With your hands, combine and break up the bread and leave to soak.

Heat 1 tablespoon (15 ml) of the olive oil in a large skillet over medium-high heat. Sauté the holy trinity—onions, bell pepper, and celery—until the onions turn translucent, about 5 minutes. Add the garlic, parsley, and rosemary and continue to cook for 1 minute longer. Remove from the heat and let cool.

Put both meats in a large bowl and combine them evenly. Add the egg-bread mixture and combine. Add the vegetable-herb mixture and combine. Add the cayenne, salt, and pepper, and a good dash of hot sauce to taste. Combine thoroughly and form into golf ball–size meatballs.

Heat the remaining 1 tablespoon (15 ml) olive oil in a large cast-iron pot with a heavy lid over medium-high heat. When the oil reaches the smoking point, add the meatballs in batches and cook them until browned on all sides. As they are browned, transfer them to the prepared baking sheet. Bake for 45 minutes. Do not clean out the pot.

RED GRAVY

While the meatballs bake, make the gravy. In the same cast-iron pot over medium-high heat, sauté the onions, bell pepper, and celery for 5 minutes. Deglaze the pot with the wine and cook for 3 minutes or until reduced. Add the tomatoes with chiles, chopped tomatoes, and tomato paste and stir. Add the roux to the pot and pour in the chicken stock, along with the bay leaf and rosemary. Stir until the roux is completely melted into the stock.

Lower the heat to a simmer and add the meatballs to the gravy. Cover and cook for 1 hour. Remove the bay laf.

Ladle the meatballs and Red Gravy over a mound of white rice. Serve with hot French bread for soaking up the gravy and a bottle of hot sauce on the side.

SERVES 4 TO 6

MEATBALLS

4 slices of white sandwich bread, crusts removed

½ cup (120 ml) whole milk

4 large eggs

½ cup (50 g) freshly grated Parmesan cheese

2 tablespoons (30 g) Worcestershire sauce

2 tablespoons (28 ml) olive oil

1 large yellow onion, diced

1 green bell pepper, diced

½ cup (60 g) diced celery

1 tablespoon (10 g) minced garlic

¼ cup (15 g) chopped flat-leaf parsley

1 tablespoon (2 g) chopped fresh rosemary

1½ pounds (680 g) ground beef chuck (80% lean)

1½ pounds (680 g) ground pork

1 teaspoon cayenne pepper

1 tablespoon (8 g) kosher salt

2 tablespoons (12 g) freshly ground black pepper, or to taste

Dash of hot sauce

RED GRAVY

2 large yellow onions, diced

1 red bell pepper, diced

1 cup (120 g) diced celery

¼ cup (60 ml) dry red wine

1 can (10 ounces, or 280 g) mild diced tomatoes with green chiles, drained

4 medium tomatoes, chopped

2 tablespoons (32 g) tomato paste

¼ cup (60 ml) dark roux (page 14)

3 cups (700 ml) chicken stock

1 bay leaf

Fresh rosemary sprigs

8 cups (1.3 kg) cooked long-grain white rice

COFFEE-LACQUERED PORK BELLY

Pork belly confounds me. I am puzzled by how this fatty piece of the pig wound up as a stellar entrée listing on white-tablecloth menus across the globe. Here in South Louisiana, we've used this slab of pig for years—smoked for bacon, diced for cracklin's, and as seasoning for soup. But in recent years, the culinary world has discovered pork belly and elevated it to center stage of every Michelin three-star chef's repertoire. Why?

One theory is the Asian connection. Pork belly has been a mainstay of Chinese and Korean menus for years, and the fusion of East and West would lead traditional chefs into embracing this ingredient. Another theory is profit margins (or, to put it another way, nose-to-tail eating). As with beef short ribs, the trend of using inexpensive cuts of meat with upscale interpretations is a smart value strategy for reducing food costs on restaurant menus. Operators expect their chefs to mix these dishes into menu rotation.

Whatever the reason, pork belly appeals to the culinary sleuth in me, and I applaud the creativity of cooks everywhere in bellying up to these shortchanged pork cuts. Follow these easy steps and take this cut on a low-and-slow rendering of fat with a flash-finished lacquering of dark Louisiana coffee. Brined, braised, and bronzed, my pork belly unravels the mystery of why this underused cut of meat is a star that shines on any dinner table.

SERVES 4

2 cups (475 ml) apple cider

2 cups (475 ml) water

¼ cup (60 g) Worcestershire sauce

2 tablespoons (11 g) ground ginger

2 tablespoons (30 g) dark brown sugar

2 tablespoons (16 g) kosher salt

1 tablespoon (6 g) freshly ground white pepper

1 pork belly (2½ to 3 pounds, or 1.1 to 1.4 kg)

2 cups (475 ml) brewed dark-roast coffee

½ cup (170 g) honey

½ cup (120 ml) soy sauce

1 teaspoon cayenne pepper

2 tablespoons (16 g) cornstarch

2 tablespoons (28 ml) cold water

Combine the cider, water, and Worcestershire in a baking dish. While stirring, add the ginger, brown sugar, salt, and pepper. Submerge the belly fat-side up in the brine, cover with aluminum foil, and marinate overnight in the refrigerator.

Preheat the oven to 375°F (190°C, or gas mark 5).

Remove the dish with the pork belly from the refrigerator and let come to room temperature. Pour off most of the marinade into a bowl, leaving only enough in the dish to immerse the belly about 1 inch (2.5 cm) deep. Cover the dish tightly with aluminum foil and bake for 3 hours, checking regularly to make sure there is still enough cooking liquid to prevent burning. Remove from the oven, let cool slightly, and pour off any remaining cooking liquid into the bowl with the marinade, stirring to combine.

To make the glaze, pour 1 cup (235 ml) of the marinating/cooking liquid into a saucepan and bring to a boil over medium-high heat; discard the remaining liquid. Stir in the coffee, honey, and soy sauce. Bring back to a boil and lower the heat to a simmer. Add the cayenne and whisk.

Combine the cornstarch and cold water in a small bowl, stirring until the cornstarch dissolves to make a slurry. Pour it into the pot and turn the heat to high. Once the mixture comes to a boil, lower the heat and stir as it thickens enough to coat the back of a spoon. Turn off the heat and keep at room temperature until ready to use.

Turn the oven temperature to 450°F (230°C, or gas mark 8).

With a sharp knife, score the top fat layer of the pork belly in a crisscross pattern, making sure to stop before penetrating the meat. Add the belly back to the baking dish and brush with the glaze, making sure to penetrate between the layers of fat. Place in the oven fat-side up. Keep a close eye on the meat and watch as the top fat layer begins to bronze and lacquer with the coffee glaze, about 10 minutes. Be careful not to let it burn. Remove and brush once again with the glaze. Present the belly on a cutting board and slice into 4 portions for an entrée (or bite-size portions for a starter).

RABBIT POT PIE

My pot pie is a far cry from those little frozen pies of your childhood. This pie features farm-raised rabbit, pan-seared in hog jowl drippings and deglazed with vermouth. Rosemary and thyme from my herb garden, along with carrots, green peas, and a trinity of vegetables, join in the pot. After a long simmer in Dark Chicken Stock (page 215), I bone the rabbit, and this thick and hearty filling is covered with pie pastry and baked to a golden brown. The saucy meat is fork-tender and falling apart, nestled inside the flaky crust. This dish will redefine the pot pie experience for you.

Cut the rabbit into quarters and then cut the back in half. Season with salt and pepper. Unpackage the organ meats (if using). Rinse them in cold water and reserve.

In a large cast-iron pot over medium-high heat, cook the hog jowl until it is crispy and the fat is rendered, about 10 minutes. Remove the meat and all but 2 tablespoons (28 ml) of the rendered fat, reserving the fat that you remove. Once the fat left in the pot is smoking, add the rabbit pieces, skin-side down. Brown the rabbit on all sides. Add the onion and celery, along with the chicken stock. Lower the heat to a simmer and cook on the stovetop for 1 hour.

Uncover to check to see that the rabbit is fork-tender. If so, transfer the pieces to a platter, let cool, and bone the rabbit into bite-size pieces.

Add the organ meats (if using) to the pot with the chicken stock and cook for 10 minutes. Transfer to a cutting board, chop into small pieces, and reserve.

Put 2 tablespoons (28 ml) of the reserved grease in a large cast-iron skillet over medium-high heat. Add the onions, celery, bell pepper, and carrots. Cook until the onions turn translucent, about 5 minutes. Add the garlic, parsley, rosemary, and thyme. Lower the heat and continue cooking for another 3 minutes.

Add the flour, sprinkling it evenly around the skillet. Using a spatula, stir the flour into the fat and vegetables and cook for 5 minutes or until the raw flour taste is gone.

Add the vermouth and deglaze the pan, cooking until the alcohol reduces by half. Add 1 cup (235 ml) of the chicken stock from the pot to the skillet.

Add the rabbit pieces, crispy hog jowl pieces, chopped organ meats, and the green peas.

Stir the mixture until the stock begins to thicken, about 5 minutes. You want a moist yet firmly packed pie-like texture for the filling, not soupy. Turn off the heat and let the pan cool.

Preheat the oven to 400°F (200°C, or gas mark 6).

Roll out the piecrust and cut a hole in the middle to vent steam. Place the piecrust over the skillet containing the rabbit mixture. Fold and crimp the edges to seal. Add a bit of water to the beaten egg and mix. Using a pastry brush, lightly brush the top and edges of the crust with the egg wash. Sprinkle with salt.

Transfer the skillet to the oven and bake until the crust is golden brown, about 30 minutes. Remove the pot pie from the oven and let rest for 5 minutes before serving.

SERVES 4

1 whole rabbit (2½ pounds, or 1.1 kg) with organ meats (organ meats are optional)

Kosher salt and freshly ground black pepper

4 strips (1 ounce, or 28 g each) of hog jowl bacon or smoked bacon

1 whole yellow onion, quartered

2 celery stalks, chopped

2 cups (475 ml) Dark Chicken Stock, plus more if needed (page 215)

2 cups (320 g) diced yellow onion

1 cup (120 g) diced celery

1 cup (150 g) diced green bell pepper

1 cup (130 g) sliced carrots

1 tablespoon (10 g) minced garlic

2 tablespoons (8 g) chopped flat-leaf parsley

1 fresh rosemary sprig

1 teaspoon chopped fresh thyme

2 tablespoons (16 g) unbleached all-purpose flour

¼ cup (60 ml) dry vermouth

1 cup (130 g) frozen green peas

1 frozen ready-made, deep-dish piecrust (10 inches, or 25 cm), thawed

1 large egg, beaten

1 tablespoon (17 g) sea salt

SWEET SURRENDER

CHAPTER

NINE

IT GOES WITHOUT SAYING: ACADIANA—THE HEART OF THE SUGARCANE INDUSTRY IN AMERICA—HAS A SWEET TOOTH. CAJUN COOKS WORK WONDERS WITH INDIGENOUS INGREDIENTS AND IMPROVISE IN THE MOST CREATIVE WAYS. THE EUROPEAN HERITAGE OF MOST FRENCH ACADIANS IS THE SOURCE FOR MANY PASTRY SPECIALTIES SUCH AS THE SWEET DOUGH PIES AND GÂTEAUS OF THE RURAL AREAS. THE ABUNDANCE OF FRESH FRUIT IS A CORNERSTONE FOR PIES AND TARTS. AMONG MY FONDEST MEMORIES OF GROWING UP IN SOUTH LOUISIANA ARE PICKING PAILS OF FRESH BLACKBERRIES IN THE SUMMER. I STILL RECALL THE SWELTERING HOT DAYS NAVIGATING THE LONG FENCE LINE OF BRAMBLE BUSHES, PLUCKING ONE PLUMP MORSEL AFTER ANOTHER. SOUTHERN SUNSHINE RIPENS THE FRUITS UNTIL THEY PRACTICALLY BURST WITH SUGARY JUICE. IT SEEMED LIKE A SMALL-TOWN RITE OF PASSAGE FOR A BAREFOOT BOY DOING HIS PART TO BRING A TASTY TREASURE TO THE DESSERT TABLE.

For Cajun desserts, simplicity rules, and high-concept, eye-popping dessert creations regularly seen in more urban areas are not commonplace here. Layering flavors and contrasts in textures can be just as tasty in a mason jar as on polished china.

Every Cajun cook has a sweet specialty or two that has been handed down from generations before. Whether enjoying a prized pecan pie or a blue ribbon–winning gâteau sirop made with Cajun sugarcane syrup, South Louisiana folks love the sweet life.

SPIKED PEACH BUTTERMILK PIE

Two great Southern ingredients combine in this sweet, tart, and boozy pie. First, these peaches—macerated and spiced in a honey bourbon marinade—are versatile on their own, as a grand garnish for a holiday ham or dished up warm with a scoop of vanilla bean ice cream for a quick dessert. But when incorporated with buttermilk into a classic Southern pie, it's as if I've died and gone to hillbilly heaven. Oh, I love it so.

SPIKED PEACHES

Combine all of the ingredients in a quart-size (946 ml) jar with a screw-top lid. The bourbon should cover the peaches, so add more if needed. Screw on the lid and refrigerate for a minimum of 1 week.

CRUST ·

Combine the flour, pecans, sugar, and salt in a large bowl. Using a pastry cutter, cut the cold butter into the dry ingredients until fully incorporated and the mixture feels similar to cornmeal. Add ice-cold water, 1 teaspoon at a time, just until the dough comes together into a ball. Cut in half and shape into 2 balls.

On a cutting board sprinkled lightly with flour, pat one dough ball down into a disk and with a rolling pin, begin rolling it out into a circle. Rotate the dough and continue rolling until it is about 12 inches (30 cm) in diameter. Line a 10-inch (25 cm) pie plate with the dough, trimming and crimping the edges, and refrigerate until ready to use.

FILLING

Preheat the oven to 400°F (200°C, or gas mark 6). Remove several peach halves (enough to line the bottom of the crust) from the spiced bourbon and drain on paper towels.

Place the melted butter in a bowl. Whisk in the sugar, flour, eggs, buttermilk, and vanilla until combined and smooth.

Arrange the peach halves in the bottom of the crust, cut-side down. Carefully pour the buttermilk mixture over the peach halves. Bake until the filling is set and the edges of the crust are golden brown, about 30 to 40 minutes. Let cool to room temperature before slicing.

SERVES 6 TO 8

SPIKED PEACHES

4 firm ripe freestone peaches, peeled, pitted and halved

2 cups (475 ml) honey bourbon, such as Jim Beam, plus more if needed

2 tablespoons (18 g) juniper berries

2 tablespoons (8 g) cloves

3 cinnamon sticks

1 tablespoon (15 ml) vanilla extract

CRUST

2½ cups (313 g) unbleached all-purpose flour, plus more

½ cup (48 g) ground toasted pecans

1 tablespoon (13 g) sugar

1 teaspoon salt

1 cup (2 sticks, or 225 g) cold unsalted butter, cut into ¼-inch (6 mm) cubes

Ice-cold water, as needed

FILLING

8 tablespoons (1 stick, or 112 g) unsalted butter, melted

1 cup (200 g) sugar

3 tablespoons (24 g) unbleached all-purpose flour

3 large eggs

1 cup (235 ml) buttermilk

1 teaspoon vanilla extract

POIRIER CANE SYRUP

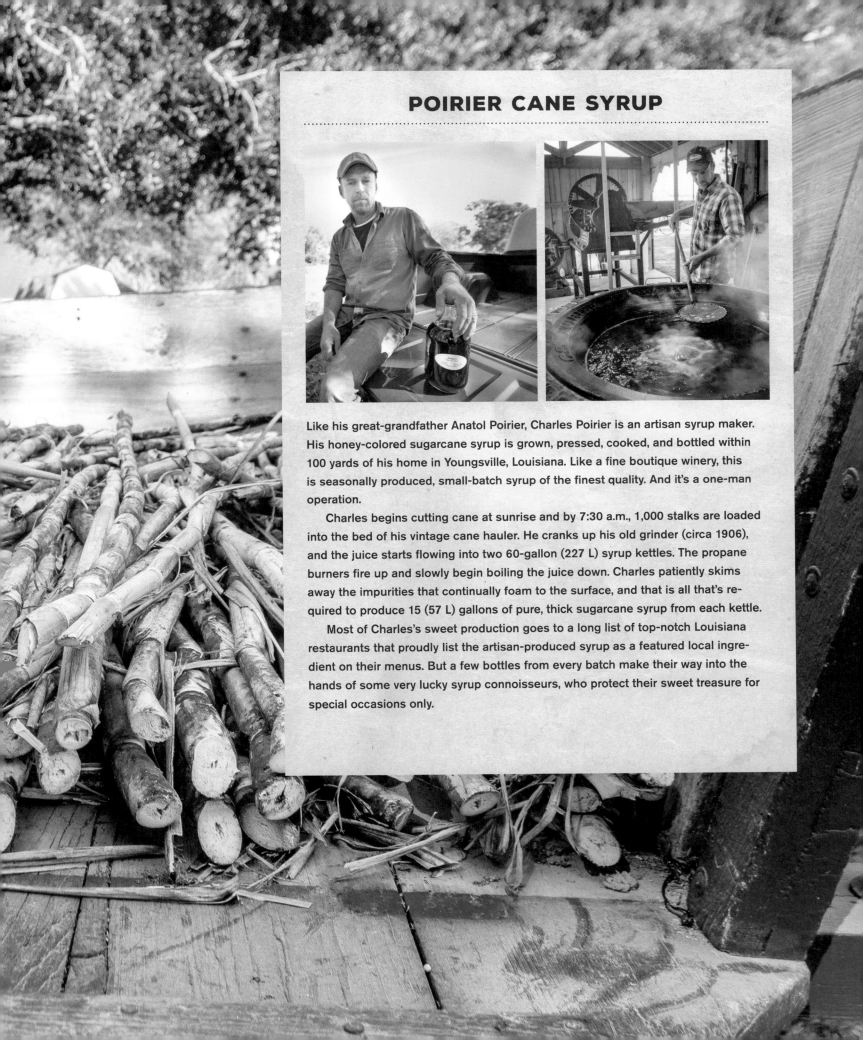

Like his great-grandfather Anatol Poirier, Charles Poirier is an artisan syrup maker. His honey-colored sugarcane syrup is grown, pressed, cooked, and bottled within 100 yards of his home in Youngsville, Louisiana. Like a fine boutique winery, this is seasonally produced, small-batch syrup of the finest quality. And it's a one-man operation.

Charles begins cutting cane at sunrise and by 7:30 a.m., 1,000 stalks are loaded into the bed of his vintage cane hauler. He cranks up his old grinder (circa 1906), and the juice starts flowing into two 60-gallon (227 L) syrup kettles. The propane burners fire up and slowly begin boiling the juice down. Charles patiently skims away the impurities that continually foam to the surface, and that is all that's required to produce 15 (57 L) gallons of pure, thick sugarcane syrup from each kettle.

Most of Charles's sweet production goes to a long list of top-notch Louisiana restaurants that proudly list the artisan-produced syrup as a featured local ingredient on their menus. But a few bottles from every batch make their way into the hands of some very lucky syrup connoisseurs, who protect their sweet treasure for special occasions only.

BERRIES AND BISCUIT JARS

Growing up in Louisiana, we bought berries by the flat (8 quarts, or 7.6 L) rather than the pound (455 g). What we didn't eat in the first couple of days was cut up, blended with sugar, and left to macerate until the fruit broke down into its sweet surrender. In this delightful dessert, I add an orange-infused Grand Marnier liqueur to the fruit and create the residual juice of the gods with which to infuse my cream. A crusty biscuit and some smooth buttermilk cream finish an elegant Southern dessert.

BERRIES

Combine the strawberries, blueberries, and pecans in a large bowl. Add the sugar and liqueur (if using). With a potato masher, mash some of the berries to release their juices. Stir the mixture. Cover it and refrigerate for 2 hours or up to overnight.

Fill 4 shallow mason jars almost the top with the berry mixture. Place in the refrigerator until serving.

CRÈME FRAÎCHE

In a large quart-size (946 ml) mason jar (or upright glass container), combine the milk and buttermilk. Seal and let sit at room temperature for 4 hours. Stir the mixture once again, seal, and refrigerate overnight.

Remove the crème fraîche from the refrigerator and add 2 tablespoons (28 ml) of Grand Marnier–infused juice from the berries. Stir, reseal, and refrigerate until serving.

BISCUITS

Preheat the oven to 450°F (230°C, or gas mark 8). Line a baking sheet with parchment paper.

Sift the flour into a large bowl. In a separate container, whisk together the buttermilk, mayonnaise, and 1 tablespoon (14 g) of the softened butter. Make a well in the center of the flour and add the liquid. Using a spoon, slowly incorporate the flour into the wet ingredients by folding it over. Continue until it has all come together.

Pour the contents of the bowl onto a work surface sprinkled with more flour. If the dough is too wet, add a little more flour. Using your hands, gently bring the mixture together and pat it down to a ½-inch-thick (1 cm) rectangle. Fold the dough over onto itself and pat down once again. Repeat this one more time and pat it down once more to ½ inch (1 cm) thick.

Using the lid of the quart (946 ml) mason jar, cut out 4 biscuit rounds and move them to the prepared baking sheet. Bake until golden brown, about 15 to 20 minutes. Brush on the remaining 1 tablespoon (14 g) softened butter. Keep warm until serving.

For serving, remove the jars of berries from the refrigerator and place on a serving platter. Using a sharp knife, shave off shards of chocolate into 4 even piles of about 1 tablespoon (15 g) each. Add a small spoonful of crème fraîche over the top of the berries to serve as an adhesive anchor for the biscuit. Place the biscuit on top; spoon the crème fraîche over the biscuit; sprinkle the top liberally with the chocolate shards; garnish with mint; and serve with more crème fraîche on the side.

SERVES 4

BERRIES

2 cups (340 g) fresh strawberries, stemmed and sliced

2 cups (290 g) fresh blueberries

1 cup (110 g) chopped pecans

1 cup (200 g) granulated sugar

½ cup (120 ml) Grand Marnier (optional)

CRÈME FRAÎCHE

2 cups (475 ml) whole milk

½ cup (120 ml) buttermilk

BISCUITS

2 cups (240 g) self-rising flour, plus more as needed

½ cup (120 ml) buttermilk

½ cup (115 g) mayonnaise

2 tablespoons (28 g) unsalted butter, softened

FOR SERVING

4 ounces (115 g) unsweetened dark chocolate

4 fresh mint sprigs

TABLE TIPS

★ I know what you're thinking: I'll just buy a can of biscuits and a tub of Cool Whip. Stop it. Follow this recipe and learn how easy it is to cook from scratch. You might never buy store-bought again.

★ Try this with blackberries, raspberries, cherries, or any number of fruit variations. As for the chocolate, find an unsweetened dark chocolate for depth and contrast.

★ For serving, the shallow mason jars add a down-home touch. They're inexpensive, and you can buy them at craft, hardware, or grocery stores.

CHOCOLATE TART WITH CHAMBORD CREAM

I have an infatuation with chocolate and raspberry. Actually, it's a full-blown love affair. I just can't get this sweet combination out of my mind. And it's all because of this decadent dessert: a divinely dark and dense chocolate cake baked in a small tartlet tin served warm with raspberries and drizzled with a Chambord sauce for a spectacular finishing touch. This flourless tart resonates on all levels with its pungent, chocolaty moistness. And when it also includes the robust flavors of South Louisiana coffee and sugarcane molasses, falling in love is easy.

Preheat the oven to 400°F (200°C, or gas mark 6). Spray six individual tart pans with nonstick spray and place the pans on a large baking sheet.

Place the grated chocolate in a large stainless-steel bowl. Scrape the vanilla bean and add the seeds to the bowl. Add the cocoa powder, cinnamon, nutmeg, salt, and molasses. Stir to combine. Add the butter and eggs and using a handheld mixer, beat until all is smooth. Add the coffee and continue mixing until combined. The mixture should be thick, with no lumps.

Pour the mixture evenly into the tart pans and place on the center rack of the oven. Bake until done, about 30 minutes. Use a toothpick to test the center for doneness. Remove and keep warm.

Meanwhile, in a small pot over medium heat, stir the cream until it begins to simmer. Lower the heat and add the liqueur and 2 cups (250 g) of the raspberries. Whisk while the sauce simmers and begins to thicken, about 5 minutes. Remove from the heat and using an immersion blender, purée the sauce until the fruit breaks down and the mixture becomes smooth. Return the pot to the stovetop and return to a simmer. Turn off the heat and keep the sauce warm for serving.

To serve, remove the cakes from the tart pans and plate them individually. Drizzle a small portion of sauce over the top and garnish with the remaining 1 cup fresh raspberries (125 g), a sprinkling of confectioners' sugar, and fresh mint leaves. Serve the remaining sauce on the side.

SERVES 6

12 ounces (340 g) grated dark chocolate, such as Callebaut

1 vanilla bean or 1 tablespoon (15 ml) vanilla extract

½ cup (43 g) unsweetened dark cocoa powder

1 tablespoon (7 g) ground cinnamon

1 teaspoon ground nutmeg

1 teaspoon salt

½ cup (170 g) sugarcane molasses

1 cup (2 sticks, or 225 g) unsalted butter, softened

6 large eggs

1 cup (235 ml) brewed dark-roast coffee

½ cup (120 ml) heavy cream

¼ cup (60 ml) Chambord

3 cups (375 g) fresh raspberries, divided

½ cup (60 g) confectioners' sugar

Fresh mint leaves

TABLE TIPS

★ Day-old coffee is better in this recipe, as it becomes even stronger.

★ The Chambord can be substituted with either a French framboise or a good dark rum. A fine imported dark chocolate, such as the Callebaut or Valrhona, is imperative in this recipe.

★ If you do not have the individual tart pans, then feel free to use a standard 8- or 9-inch cake (20 or 23 cm) pan. The baking time will be about 45 minutes.

STUFFED CREOLE PUMPKIN BREAD PUDDING WITH BOURBON SAUCE

I am not skilled at Halloween creations. I just can't get excited about spider cookies or eyeball cupcakes, so I defer to my wife's creative hand in the kitchen for those ghostly treats. But, when I saw the stack of pumpkins at the farmers' market, I decided to come out of my Halloween hiding place and turn my beautiful gourd into a vessel of sweetness with a classic Creole bread pudding. The pulp of a pumpkin is a natural enhancement to the cream, eggs, and spices that go into the typical custard.

BOURBON SAUCE

Bring the bourbon to a simmer in a medium saucepan over medium heat. Add the molasses and stir to combine. In a small mixing bowl, combine the butter, sugar, and cornstarch and add to the pan.

With a wire whisk, begin stirring in the milk. Increase the heat to high and whisk while the sauce thickens. Once it comes to a boil, turn off the heat and continue to whisk until it is thick enough to coat the back of a spoon. If it is too thick, add a bit more milk. Remove from the stove and keep warm.

BREAD PUDDING

Preheat the oven to 350°F (180°C, or gas mark 4). Coat a 9 x 13-inch (23 x 33 cm) baking pan with nonstick spray and set it inside an even larger roasting pan.

With a sharp knife, plunge into the top of the pumpkin and carve a large round hole to expose the inside of the pumpkin. Reserve the top stemmed portion. Reach inside—use your clean hands, it's fun—and pull out the membrane, seeds, and pulp and discard. Scrape the inside with a spoon, rendering the pumpkin as clean as you can.

Place the eggs in a heatproof bowl. In a large saucepan over medium heat, combine the milk, cream, and vanilla and bring to a simmer. Slowly add some of the hot mixture to the eggs while whisking to temper the eggs. Return the egg-cream mixture to the saucepan and add the butter, sugar, and sugarcane syrup. Cook on low until the mixture begins to thicken, about 10 minutes. Turn off the heat and add the cinnamon, nutmeg, and allspice, along with the canned pumpkin purée. Stir while adding the toasted pecans.

Put the bread in a large bowl and pour over the custard mixture. Make sure that all the bread is soaking in the liquid and let rest for 1 hour until the bread has absorbed all the liquid.

Add the bread mixture to the prepared baking pan. Make a water bath by pouring hot water into the larger roasting pan to one-quarter of the way up the sides of the bread pudding pan. Bake uncovered just until the mixture begins to set, about 45 minutes.

SERVES 12

BOURBON SAUCE

1 cup (235 ml) bourbon

¼ cup (80 g) sugarcane molasses

4 tablespoons (½ stick, or 55 g) unsalted butter, melted

½ cup (100 g) granulated sugar

1 tablespoon (8 g) cornstarch

1 cup (235 ml) whole milk

TABLE TIPS

* Pick up a bag of shelled and roasted pumpkin seeds or find pepitas (roasted pumpkin seeds) at your nearest Latin grocery.

* Brioche, raisin bread, croissants, or any soft, sweet bread works best, but day-old French bread is also acceptable.

BREAD PUDDING

1 large pumpkin (4 to 6 pounds, or 1.8 to 2.7 kg)

8 large eggs

3 cups (700 ml) whole milk

3 cups (700 ml) heavy cream

1 tablespoon (15 ml) vanilla extract

8 tablespoons (1 stick, or 112 g) unsalted butter, melted

½ cup (100 g) granulated sugar

¼ cup (60 ml) sugarcane syrup

1 tablespoon (7 g) ground cinnamon

1 teaspoon ground nutmeg

1 teaspoon ground allspice

1 can (29 ounces, or 810 g) pure pumpkin purée (not pumpkin pie filling)

½ cup (55 g) pecans, toasted and chopped

12 cups (360 g) cubed day-old bread, such as brioche or French

1 cup (140 g) shelled and roasted pumpkin seeds

Rolled wafer cookies

Remove the pan from the oven and spoon the mixture into the hollowed-out pumpkin. Place the top back onto the pumpkin and transfer to a large baking sheet. Put the pumpkin into the hot oven and bake the pudding for 30 minutes longer.

Present the bread pudding inside the pumpkin vessel and serve by scooping it into coffee cups or small bowls. Spoon out a generous portion of pudding and garnish with a sprinkle of toasted pumpkin seeds and a cookie to scoop up the creamy pudding. Pour the warm Bourbon Sauce over top.

CAST-IRON CUSTARD

Flan, clafoutis, crème brûlée, or custard: Whatever you call these egg-based desserts, they are popular on South Louisiana home dinner tables and restaurant menus alike. I like the rustic black iron presentation of this elegant dish, and the blackberry-raspberry combination adds a light freshness to the sugary rich base. For an over-the-top presentation, add a scoop of vanilla bean ice cream and a sugary tuile cookie.

Preheat the oven to 350°F (180°C, or gas mark 4).

Whisk the sugar and eggs vigorously in a large bowl until fully incorporated. Whisk in the milk, cream, and yogurt, as well as the zest and juice of the orange. Add the orange liqueur, vanilla, and cinnamon. Add the flour and whisk to incorporate all. Set aside and let the ingredients rest for 10 minutes.

In a 10-inch (25 cm) black iron skillet, arrange the raspberries and blackberries, alternating the colors in an attractive pattern. Slowly and gently pour the custard mixture into the skillet, being careful not to dislodge or cover the fruit. Place the skillet on a shallow sheet pan and fill the bottom of the sheet pan with water. Place on the middle rack of the oven and bake just until the custard mixture is set, about 30 to 40 minutes. Watch carefully and remove before the top begins to brown or else the berries will begin to burn. Let cool to room temperature.

For serving, sprinkle with confectioners' sugar and let guests serve themselves on individual dessert plates.

SERVES 4

⅔ cup (133 g) granulated sugar

3 large eggs

¾ cup (175 ml) whole milk

¾ cup (175 ml) heavy cream

2 tablespoons (25 g) Greek yogurt

Zest and juice of 1 orange

1 tablespoon (15 ml) orange liqueur, such as Citrónge or Grand Marnier

1 teaspoon vanilla extract

1 tablespoon (7 g) ground cinnamon

½ cup (63 g) unbleached all-purpose flour

1 cup (125 g) fresh raspberries

1 cup (145 g) fresh blackberries

½ cup (60 g) confectioners' sugar

TABLE TIP
You can prepare this custard in individual ramekins instead of the skillet; adjust the baking time to 20 to 30 minutes. Also, you can make this dish a day ahead, cover and refrigerate, and serve cold.

TABASCO CHOCOLATE AND RED CURRANT BROWNIES

Listen up: I have a secret weapon that will redefine the brownie experience and forever make you a rock star in the kitchen. These brownies will ignite your taste buds on all levels—sweet, tangy, and tart—and send you into a darkly delectable place you never knew existed.

Preheat the oven to 350°F (180°C, or gas mark 4). Coat a 9 x 13-inch (23 x 33 cm) baking pan with nonstick spray.

Place the butter, sugar, molasses, and almond extract in a large bowl. With a wire whisk, beat the mixture to incorporate all. Add the eggs and continue whisking until combined.

Sift the flour and cocoa powder, add the salt, and stir to combine. Add the dry ingredients to the wet ingredients.

Melt the Tabasco chocolate by filling a saucepan halfway with water and bringing to a boil. In a metal bowl that will fit into the pan with the water without touching the water, place the chocolate pieces. Lower the heat to a simmer and place the metal bowl over the water. Stir until the chocolate is melted. Remove from the heat. Add the Tabasco chocolate to the batter mixture and stir to combine.

Heat a cast-iron skillet over medium heat and toast the pecans while constantly stirring. Once you smell their nutty aroma, turn off the heat and add the butter. As the butter melts, stir the pecans to coat evenly. On a platter, combine the brown sugar and chili powder. Add the pecan halves and toss to coat each side lightly with the seasonings.

Pour the batter mixture into the prepared baking pan and arrange the red currants and pecan halves evenly on top throughout the mixture. Bake until the brownies are cooked and a skewer comes out clean, about 40 minutes. Let cool on a wire rack before slicing.

SERVES 4 TO 6

1 cup (2 sticks, or 225 g) unsalted butter, melted

1 cup (200 g) granulated sugar

1 cup (340 g) sugarcane molasses

1 tablespoon (15 ml) almond extract

4 large eggs

1½ cups (188 g) unbleached all-purpose flour

1 cup (86 g) unsweetened cocoa powder

1 teaspoon salt

1 tin (1¾ ounces, or 50 g) Tabasco brand chocolates

1 cup (100 g) pecan halves

4 tablespoons (½ stick, or 55 g) unsalted butter

½ cup (115 g) firmly packed light brown sugar

1 teaspoon chili powder

1 cup (112 g) fresh red currants

TABLE TIPS

★ Red currants—their taste is tart, yet fruity—are seasonal, so be on the lookout for them. If you can't find them, substitute cranberries (fresh or dried); pomegranate seeds will work, too.

★ Tabasco brand chocolates show up on some specialty retail shelves or can be bought online (see Sources, page 314).

ROASTED PLUMS WITH BLACKBERRY ICE CREAM

I dream about this dish. Slow-roasted sugarplums dance in my head, oozing their dark, syrupy juices; it hits me right in the sweet spot. I love the transformation of taste and texture that takes place when their golden flesh hits a hot oven. Topped with smooth blackberry ice cream, the plums are a harmonious duet singing an oh-so-sweet Cajun lullaby. This dessert is a splendid send-off to the sweetest of dreams.

BLACKBERRY ICE CREAM

Place the blackberries and superfine sugar in a pot over medium heat. Bring the berries to a simmer; stir just until the sugar dissolves and the juice of the berries oozes out. Pour the mixture into a bowl and refrigerate until cold.

In a large stainless-steel bowl, beat the egg yolks and granulated sugar until creamy. Set aside.

In a pot over medium heat, bring the milk and cream just to a boil and then lower the heat; add the yogurt and stir until incorporated.

Add a large spoonful of the hot cream mixture to the egg yolks and stir. Continue adding a spoonful at a time while stirring to bring the yolks to a warm temperature. Combine all the yolk mixture into the pot of hot cream. Whisking rapidly, heat the custard mixture on the stovetop. Continue whisking until the custard thickens enough to coat the back of a spoon, about 5 to 8 minutes, and then remove from the burner. Pour the hot custard into the stainless-steel bowl and place in the refrigerator to chill thoroughly, several hours or up to overnight.

Pour the custard mixture into the container of your ice cream maker and follow the instructions for making ice cream. Once the ice cream reaches peak consistency, swirl in the blackberry mixture.

Remove the ice cream from the ice cream maker and place in a lidded container. Place the container into the freezer for a minimum of 1 hour before serving, if not longer.

PLUMS

Preheat the oven to 400°F (200°C, or gas mark 6).

Slice the plums in half and remove the pits. Make a cavity by scooping out any membrane from the center of the plum halves. Place the plum halves cut-side up on a rimmed baking sheet. Spoon ½ teaspoon of brandy (if using) into each cavity and top each plum half with a pat of butter. Sprinkle each with 1 teaspoon of the brown sugar. Roast uncovered for 20 minutes then check to see if the plums are beginning to sear around the edges. If not, return to the oven for 10 minutes longer or until the tops begin to brown. Let come to room temperature on a wire rack.

For serving, place 2 plum halves on a dessert plate and top with a scoop of Blackberry Ice Cream. Sprinkle with the confectioners' sugar and top with the fresh blackberries.

SERVES 6

**BLACKBERRY ICE CREAM
(MAKES 2 PINTS [570 G])**

2 cups (290 g) fresh blackberries

½ cup (96 g) superfine sugar

8 large egg yolks

6 tablespoons (78 g) granulated sugar

2 cups (475 ml) whole milk

1 cup (235 ml) heavy cream

¼ cup (50 g) Greek yogurt

PLUMS

6 ripe plums

2 tablespoons (28 ml) brandy (optional)

8 tablespoons (1 stick, or 112 g) unsalted butter

¼ cup (60 g) light brown sugar

½ cup (60 g) confectioners' sugar

1 cup (145 g) fresh blackberries

TABLE TIPS

★ Of course, the brandy is optional, but I like the elegance of flavor it adds to the natural juices of the plums.

★ Certainly you can use store-bought ice cream, but I urge you to buy an ice cream maker and return to the art of making your own.

COMFORT COBBLER

To cobble a comforting dessert casserole using ripe fruit and a quick-and-easy biscuit is brilliant enough, but adding booze-infused rocket fuel to blast the flavors on an upward trajectory sends this one into orbit. Ripe peach, pear, apple, and orange cooked down with a crusty biscuit dough and jacked up with a Southern Comfort sauce is like reaching for the stars.

BISCUITS

Preheat the oven to 450°F (230°C, or gas mark 8). Line a baking sheet with parchment paper.

Sift the flour into a large bowl. In a separate container, whisk together the buttermilk, mayonnaise, and 1 tablespoon (14 g) of the softened butter. Make a well in the center of the flour and add the liquid. Using a spoon, slowly incorporate the flour into the wet ingredients by folding it over. Continue until it has all come together.

Pour the contents of the bowl onto a work surface sprinkled with more flour. If the dough is too wet, add a little more flour. Using your hands, gently bring the mixture together and pat it down into a ½-inch-thick (1 cm) rectangle. Fold the dough over onto itself and pat down once again. Repeat this one more time and pat it to ½ inch (1 cm) thick.

Using a 3-inch (7.5 cm) biscuit cutter, cut out 2 biscuit rounds; reserve the remaining uncooked biscuit dough for later. Place the 2 biscuit rounds on the prepared baking sheet and bake until golden brown, about 15 to 20 minutes. Remove from the oven, split open, and brush with the remaining 1 tablespoon (14 g) softened butter.

COBBLER

Lower the oven temperature to 375°F (190°C, or gas mark 5). Grease a 9 x 13-inch (23 x 33 cm) baking dish with butter.

Slice the peaches, apples, and pears into ¼-inch-thick (6 mm) slices. Place in a pot over medium-high heat, add the water and sugar, and bring to a simmer. Add the orange zest, cinnamon, vanilla, and salt and stir to combine. Add the sugarcane syrup, honey, and butter and bring back to a simmer, stirring to incorporate.

In a small bowl, combine the Southern Comfort and cornstarch, stirring to make a slurry. Add the mixture to the pot and turn the heat up a bit and stir as it continues to cook and thicken for a few minutes. Once it comes back to a low boil, turn the heat off.

Place the 4 biscuit halves, buttered side down, in the bottom of the prepared baking dish. Pour the fruit filling over the top. Use your fingers to break off chunks of the remaining raw dough and place on top of the mixture.

Bake until the cobbler is bubbling and the biscuit topping is golden brown, about 20 minutes. Serve with ice cream of your choice on the side.

SERVES 4 TO 6

BISCUITS

2 cups (240 g) self-rising flour, plus more as needed

½ cup (120 ml) buttermilk

½ cup (115 g) mayonnaise

2 tablespoons (28 g) unsalted butter, softened

COBBLER

2 ripe peaches, pitted

2 tart apples, such as Granny Smith, peeled and cored

2 ripe pears, such as Bosc, peeled and cored

½ cup (120 ml) water

½ cup (100 g) granulated sugar

2 tablespoons (12 g) grated orange zest

1 teaspoon ground cinnamon

1 teaspoon vanilla extract

Pinch of salt

1 tablespoon (15 ml) sugarcane syrup

1 tablespoon (20 g) honey

2 tablespoons (28 g) unsalted butter, softened

2 tablespoons (28 ml) Southern Comfort

2 tablespoons (16 g) cornstarch

BLUEBERRY-BUTTERMILK SHAKES

I have a lifelong obsession: milk shakes. It started at an early age, sitting at the counter of my father's café in downtown Bogalusa, Louisiana. I was barely big enough to climb on the swivel stool at the long Formica-topped counter when I downed the first of a lifetime of creamy ice cream concoctions. Today, I am a bona fide shake master.

But c'mon, admit it: You love 'em, too. And if you have a ready supply of fresh blueberries, you'll love making this, one of my favorite milk shakes of all time. The sweet nectar bursting from these flavor-filled berry bombs is the ideal counterpunch to the tart and tang that buttermilk brings to this combination. And a quality French vanilla ice cream provides a smooth and creamy base. Break out the blender; saddle up to the counter; and let's make shakes.

SERVES 4

8 scoops of French vanilla ice cream

1 cup (235 ml) buttermilk

2 cups (290 g) fresh blueberries, plus more for garnish

Whipped cream

Place the ice cream, buttermilk, and blueberries in a blender container. Blend on high speed until completely blended and the fruit breaks down. Adjust to your desired thickness by adding more ice cream or milk. Pour into glasses, top with whipped cream, and garnish with fresh blueberries.

CHAPTER

TEN

DRINKS AND DRUNKS

★ ★ ★ ★ ★

IN SOUTH LOUISIANA, CELEBRATIONS ABOUND, AND ON MOST WEEKENDS THERE IS A FESTIVAL OF SOME KIND THAT IS REASON TO PARTY. BUT IN ACADIANA, THERE'S ONE WEEKEND PARTY THAT JUST KEEPS ON GOING YEAR-ROUND. FRED'S LOUNGE, LOCATED ON THE MAIN DRAG IN MAMOU, IS AN ORIGINAL, OFFBEAT PIECE OF THE FRENCH ACADIAN TAPESTRY THAT HAS BEEN SIPPED AND SAVORED BY LOCALS AND THE FAMOUS ALIKE. EVERY SATURDAY MORNING, FRED'S LOUNGE OPENS AT 8 O'CLOCK. BUT IT'S NOT UNTIL LATER—9 O'CLOCK SHARP—WHEN THE KVPI-FM RADIO BROADCAST BEGINS, THAT THE FUN CRANKS UP. THE LIVE BAND KICKS INTO HIGH GEAR FOR WHAT IS ANOTHER NO-HOLDS-BARRED, YOU-AIN'T-SEEN-NOTHIN'-YET, CAJUN GOOD TIME.

Characters abound at Fred's, but no one holds a candle to Tante Sue (Fred's eighty-three-year-old widow). She holds court, sippin' her Hot Damn cinnamon schnapps from a holster strapped to her side. Serving up Bloody Marys (the house favorite), barking out the rules (no dancing on the tables), and singing with the live band (in Cajun French, of course) are all part of Tante Sue's Saturday morning routine. The beer-drinking fun goes on until the proverbial last call for alcohol at 2 o'clock in the afternoon, and then the every-Saturday ritual winds down.

Living in Louisiana is special for many reasons, but drinking, dancing, eating, and partying are at the head of the list. While the rest of the country goes about its usual routine, the people of Louisiana celebrate life with passion. South Louisiana is Bloody Mary country, and after one night at a Cajun celebration, it's not hard to figure out why this hangover cure has made its home here. Folks in South Louisiana are quite passionate about their Marys, and I happen to have a crazy-good blend.

A well-made Bloody Mary is cause for celebration, so let's break out the vodka. It's 9 o'clock somewhere. Tante Sue would be proud.

PECAN ISLAND ICED TEA

After a long morning spent in a Pecan Island, Louisiana, duck blind, it is customary to relax with a cocktail or two, and this drink—Pecan Island Iced Tea—is the best way I know to kick back. This duck camp cocktail is a South Louisiana version of the ever-popular Long Island iced tea. But this one combines rum with vodka, and limoncello adds just the right amount of sweetness. I use a splash of praline pecan liqueur for smoothness, and with the addition of freshly brewed iced tea, this drink is a worthy tribute to Acadiana's colorful culture of duck hunting.

★ ★ ★ ★ ★

Fill a cocktail shaker halfway with ice. Add all of the liquors and the iced tea. Shake vigorously and strain the cocktail into a glass filled with ice. Garnish with a lemon wedge.

SERVES 1

Ice cubes

1 jigger (1½ ounces, or 45 ml) rum

1 jigger (1½ ounces, or 45 ml) vodka

½ jigger (¾ ounce, or 25 ml) praline pecan liqueur

½ jigger (¾ ounce, or 25 ml) limoncello

5 ounces (150 ml) brewed iced tea

Lemon wedge

BLACKENED BLOODY MARY

Lots of brilliant culinary masterpieces start out as kitchen mistakes. This is one of them. My journey to discovery began with a pile of ripe tomatoes and peppers and ended with a kitchen timer that never went off. What started out as a roasted tomato soup wound up to be a souped-up version of a Bloody Mary.

On my way to making that soup, I slid the sliced tomatoes and some sweet peppers into a 400-degree (200°C, or gas mark 6) oven for what I thought would be a quick 15-minute roasting to loosen the skins and release the sugars. Forty-five minutes later, I had what I thought was a burnt mess destined for the trash (along with my broken kitchen timer).

But, after removing some of the burnt bits and taking a taste, I discovered the magic of the dark depth of flavor that blackening brings out in tomatoes. It just makes sense. Charring the exterior of a red bell pepper has always been a basic trick for peeling back flavor. But it was the combination of blackened tomatoes and peppers together that woke me up and prompted me to change course.

To remain true to tradition, I adhere to three Bloody Mary mandatories that must always be followed: Tomato is at the base, spice (and lots of it) is imperative, and garnish is all-important. How you construct your Bloody Mary is where the fun comes in.

BASE

Preheat the oven to 400°F (200°C, or gas mark 6). Line a baking sheet with parchment paper

Slice the tomatoes in half and place cut-side up on the prepared baking sheet. Place the whole peppers on the baking sheet. Roast until the skins blacken, about 45 minutes.

Remove the stems from the peppers and place in the container of a blender along with the tomatoes. To the container, add the lemon juice, Worcestershire, Tabasco, garlic, celery salt, and grated horseradish. Add the water, a pinch of salt, and a grind of black pepper. Pulse the blender until all the contents are blended. The base should be thick but still pourable. If it is too thick, add more water.

COCKTAILS

Put the lemon juice in a small bowl and the salt in a shallow bowl. Invert a large glass into the bowl of lemon juice and moisten the rim. Put the rim into the salt and move it around until the salt coats the rim.

Add ice cubes to the glass and pour in 1½ ounces (45 ml) of vodka. Pour in enough base to fill. Repeat for each cocktail. Garnish each with a celery stalk, a pickled okra pod, and a garlic clove on a toothpick. Add a slice of crispy bacon and serve.

SERVES 4

BASE (MAKES 2 QUARTS OR 1.9 L)

3 pounds (1.4 kg) ripe tomatoes

1 pound (455 g) sweet red mini peppers

3 tablespoons (45 ml) freshly squeezed lemon juice

1 tablespoon (15 g) Worcestershire sauce

1 tablespoon (15 ml) Tabasco sauce

2 tablespoons (20 g) minced garlic

2 tablespoons (24 g) celery salt

3 tablespoons (45 g) freshly grated horseradish

3 cups (700 ml) water, plus more if needed

Kosher salt and freshly ground black pepper

COCKTAILS

¼ cup (60 ml) freshly squeezed lemon juice

¼ cup (32 g) kosher salt

Ice cubes

4 jiggers (1½ ounces, or 45 ml each) good-quality vodka

4 celery stalks with leaves

4 pickled okra pods

4 pickled garlic cloves

4 strips of smoked bacon, cooked crispy

SATSUMA RUM FIZZ

Satsuma has a particular herbal note that your basic orange just doesn't have. They first start showing up in the produce bins in early autumn, and by the end of the year, I still can't get enough of the sweet taste. More so than oranges, tangerines, or mandarins, I'll take a locally grown satsuma anytime. I grew up eating juicy, ripe satsumas grown within 10 miles (16 km) of my home in South Louisiana. And these days, with all of the regional Acadiana orchards cropping up, it's an even shorter trip for the fruit. With this cocktail, combining fresh satsuma juice with a shot of smooth rum, topped with a refreshing spritz of club soda and a floater of citrus liqueur, I bet I'll get your creative juices flowing. Think ahead and buy a bushel basket of satsumas and make a large pitcher of these cocktails for your next party.

Place the whole peeled satsumas into a blender container. Blend on high speed until pulverized and the pulp is completely smooth.

In a cocktail shaker with ice, pour 1 jigger (45 ml) of rum, 2 ounces (60 ml) of satsuma pulp (or juice), and 2 ounces (60 ml) of club soda. Shake vigorously and pour into a cocktail glass filled with ice. Finish by floating 1 jigger (45 ml) of citrus liqueur on top. Repeat for each cocktail.

Serve with a skewered satsuma segment and a mint sprig, along with a straw to stir.

SERVES 4

4 satsumas, peeled and seeded

4 jiggers (1½ ounces, or 45 ml each) light rum

1 bottle (10 ounces, or 285 ml) club soda or sparkling water

Ice cubes

4 jiggers (1½ ounces, or 45 ml each) citrus liqueur, such as triple sec

4 satsuma segments

4 fresh mint sprigs

TABLE TIPS

★ I love the taste and texture of fresh pulp, and because the fruit is mostly seedless, I place the whole peeled satsumas in my Vitamix blender. If you prefer a juice-only version, use a juicer and strain off the pulp.

★ If you cannot find satsumas where you live, then try this recipe with mandarins or tangerines.

SIMON CITRUS FARM

I call him "Satsuma" Simon, but his real name is Lynn. He will be quick to tell you that his Vermilion Parish citrus farm started as a hobby but quickly grew into a full-time orchard.

The satsuma is what I like to call "the official citrus fruit of Louisiana." Introduced in the late 1800s, satsuma trees were planted throughout South Louisiana. While Owari is the most popular variety of satsuma grown, Lynn grows the Brown Select, which ripens a little earlier and is much sweeter than other varieties. And when he brings them to market, folks grab them up in bushel basketfuls.

SUGARTOWN WATERMELON RUM PUNCH

Lining the sides of rural roads, watermelon stands are a Southern thing. Truckloads begin arriving from Sugartown as the temperature soars, and there is no better way to cool down than with a slice of ice-cold watermelon on the back porch steps.

Watermelon pulp rocks. When pulverized in a blender, watermelon flesh turns into sweet nectar that becomes a versatile ingredient for any number of recipes: bread, syrup, jelly, and sauce, to name a few. And as a base for a summer punch spiked with rum and spritzed with soda, it is a sweet way to cool down a backyard barbecue.

Cut the watermelon; remove all the rind and any seeds, being careful not to leave any of the white part. Cut it into cubes. Reserve a few of the cubes for garnish.

Put the cubed watermelon into a blender container and blend on high speed. Once completely pulverized, pour the pulp and juice into a pitcher. Continue processing in batches until you have blended all the watermelon.

In a large mason jar filled with ice, pour the watermelon pulp halfway up. Add 1 jigger of (45 ml) rum and fill with club soda. Stir the mixture. Repeat for each cocktail. Garnish each with a watermelon cube and some fresh mint.

SERVES 6

1 medium-size (about 10 pounds, or 4.5 kg) ripe seedless watermelon

6 jiggers (1½ ounces, or 45 ml each) dark rum (optional)

6 bottles (10 ounces, or 280 ml each) club soda or sparkling water

Fresh mint leaves

WELCOME TO SUGARTOWN

The nondescript intersection of LA 112 and LA 113 in rural Beauregard Parish is the proverbial sweet spot—ground zero for Sugartown watermelons. Some say it's the sandy soil that is responsible for growing the dense Crimson Sweet (Charleston Gray) and Jubilee varieties of melons this sleepy Louisiana town has become famous for. I say it's the pride of the growers who maintain the vine-ripened quality year after year. The deeply red flesh of these melons has double the sugar content (12 percent) of average watermelons, and they can grow up to as big as 25 pounds (11.4 kg).

SPARKLING MUSCADINE SANGRIA

At dinner parties, when I see a bottle of blushing pink wine come out, I head for the nearest bottle of bourbon. I'm not sure if it is my hazy memory recalling those college nights chugging Boone's Farm or my male instinct to stay away from anything pink. But, as I discovered, I am wrong. Made right here in Louisiana, muscadine wines are delightful with a refreshing summertime flavor—complex, fruit-forward wines that speak softly. And when blended with ripe summer fruit and a splash of prosecco, it makes for a sangria that sparkles and shines.

Add the fruit slices and mint sprigs to a large pitcher. Pour the muscadine wine and amaretto into the pitcher. Stir to incorporate and refrigerate for at least 1 hour. Just before serving, add the chilled sparkling wine and return to the refrigerator.

For each serving, place a few wedges of fruit into a wine glass. Pour the sangria over the fruit. Garnish with a sprig of mint, an orange peel, and a peach slice.

SERVES 4 TO 6

1 large ripe but firm peach, pitted and sliced

1 sweet apple, cored and sliced

1 pear, cored and sliced

1 large orange, peeled and sliced

4 fresh mint sprigs

1 bottle (750 ml) muscadine wine

4 jiggers (1½ ounces, or 45 ml each) amaretto

1 bottle (750 ml) sparkling wine, such as prosecco, chilled

Fresh mint sprigs

Orange peel

Peach slices

What's That?

Muscadine grapes are native to Southern soil, and the sweet fruit grows wild throughout Louisiana. Once you pop through the thick skin and scoop out the seeds, the juicy flesh of a ripe muscadine is a prize well worth the effort. Like many bayou cooks, I use muscadines—their scuppernong cousins, too—in a variety of recipes. Jams, pepper jellies, and barbecue sauces are just a few examples. And there's nothing like sweet muscadine wine. Landry Vineyards, located in West Monroe, Louisiana, grows a variety of muscadine grapes to produce a semisweet white wine.

TABLE TIP

Muscadine vines run wild in Louisiana, resulting in an abundance of homemade and commercial wine-making. If you cannot find muscadine wine, feel free to substitute any rosé wine with sweet fruity notes, such as white zinfandel or pink moscato.

BLACKBERRY LEMONADE

Everyone should try growing a lemon tree. Mine is small and to call it a "tree" is a stretch; it's more like a scrubby lemon bush. It does, however, produce subtly tart and herby fruit that continually puts my culinary creativity to the test. By the start of autumn, my lemons are bursting with juice, and I have one last chance to squeeze out a little more summer before frosty gumbo weather arrives. The balance of tart and sweet is what makes this blackberry lemonade so refreshing.

SIMPLE SYRUP

In a small pot over medium heat, stir together the sugar and water. Slowly bring to a boil. Lower the heat to a simmer and continue stirring until the sugar dissolves, about 5 minutes. Turn off the heat and let cool. Cover and refrigerate until ready to use.

LEMONADE

Place the 3 cups (435 g) blackberries in a blender container and blend on high speed until pulverized. Strain the blackberry juice into a container and discard the seeds and pulp.

Pour the blackberry juice into a large pitcher. Add the lemon juice and simple syrup. Pour in the water and stir to combine. Cover and refrigerate for 1 hour to allow the flavors to mingle.

For serving, fill tall glasses with ice and pour in the blackberry lemonade. Garnish with a skewered blackberry and lemon wedge and a mint sprig.

SERVES 10

SIMPLE SYRUP

2 cups (400 g) granulated sugar

1½ cups (355 ml) water

LEMONADE

3 cups (435 g) fresh or (450 g) frozen blackberries, plus 10 for garnish

2 cups (475 ml) freshly squeezed lemon juice, pulp and seeds strained

10 cups (2.4 L) water

Ice cubes

10 lemon wedges

10 small fresh mint sprigs

TABLE TIPS

★ Buy blackberries at the peak of season, when they are cheapest, and freeze them to enjoy year-round in this drink.

★ Feel free to add a jigger (1½ ounces, or 45 ml) of gin for an evening cocktail.

ACKNOWLEDGMENTS

I offer my sincerest thanks to:

The love of my life, my wife Roxanne, for supporting my passions and filling me with her Cajun joie de vivre.

My daughter, Lauren, for bringing joyful inspiration and clarity of purpose to my life.

My Cajun mother-in-law, Rosalie Fontenot Waldrop, for sharing family stories of life around her Acadiana table.

All the Graham family, past and present, for their culinary inspiration and lifelong support, especially my father George, Sr. and mother Peggy, my brother Jackie and sister-in-law Lavonia, and my sister Marie.

To all the readers of the *Acadiana Table* blog for their invaluable insight into recipe testing through an endless stream of comments that make my recipes better. Special thanks to the Spoon, Bacque, Randol, and Vazquez families who closely follow my cooking adventures.

To the many Acadiana region chefs, restaurateurs, growers, fishermen, processors, butchers, and purveyors who spice my world and inspire me to write about their passion for our unique culinary culture.

All my Graham Group team for allowing me the time to write this book and assisting me in creating the Acadiana Table brand. A special thanks to: Kathy Andersen and Michelle Constantin for their leadership and bold insight; Beth Perry for keeping me on track; Julia Marks for her technical expertise; the creative genius of Raymond Credeur; the design talent of Kerry Palmer and Bridget Beniest; the socially engaging Candace Domengeaux; and the eagle eye of grammar guru Cori Webre.

The Harvard Common Press and Quarto Publishing Group USA team: Valerie Cimino, the line editor who first touched my manuscript and brought clarity to my otherwise chaotic recipe world. Jenna Patton, copy editor, for polishing my prose with the utmost professionalism, and making sure I have all the commas I need and none that I don't. Anne Re for her art direction and visual style that breathed life into *Acadiana Table*. And to publicist Lydia Finn and social media manager Jessica Pinault, along with the entire publicity team, for promoting my Cajun culinary world to mainstream America. And to project manager, Renae Haines, for shepherding the book through the process with detailed diligence. And to managing editor John Gettings for seeing it through to the finish line.

Especially to Dan Rosenberg, editorial director, who believed in me from the beginning and remained steadfast throughout in preserving the vision of *Acadiana Table*.

And, most especially to Judy Linden, my literary agent at Stonesong, for guidance in navigating the publishing world and, most of all, for her faith in my talent.

To Cajun and Creole cooks everywhere who have inspired me to tell their stories and share their culture with the world. And, most importantly, thanks to God for blessing me with the talent to tell those stories.

ABOUT THE AUTHOR

While some call him the new voice of Louisiana cooking, George Graham discounts that and humbly offers that he's only stirring the black iron pot that generations of great cooks stirred before him. He's got roux-scarred hands, a Tabasco-tinged tongue, and filé gumbo running through his veins.

Born of southern Louisiana restaurant folks, Graham is a sought-after spokesman for his culinary world. He is an award-winning blogger, newspaper columnist, magazine contributor, and is featured on radio and television. He writes, he photographs, and he consumes Cajun and Creole cooking as if each meal were his last.

George lives in Lafayette, Louisiana with his wife Roxanne and daughter Lauren.

SOURCES

When it comes to authenticity, you want to source your ingredients as close to the bayou as possible. These Louisiana brands are those I trust and use often. I urge you to seek them out or order them online.

ONE-STOP SHOPPING FOR LOUISIANA PRODUCTS

CajunGrocer.com
www.cajungrocer.com

ANDOUILLE, TASSO, BOUDIN, CRACKLIN', AND OTHER SAUSAGE PRODUCTS

The Best Stop Supermarket
www.beststopinscott.com

Don's Specialty Meats
www.donsspecialtymeats.com

Poche's Market, Restaurant & Smokehouse
poches.com

Bourque's Super Store
www.bourquespecialties.com

ROUX AND DRESSING MIX

Kary's Roux
www.karysroux.com

Savoie's
shop.savoiesfoods.com

Richard's Cajun Foods
www.richardscajunfoods.com

CREOLE MUSTARD, MAYONNAISE, CRAB BOIL, SPICES, AND OTHER CONDIMENTS

Zatarain's
www.cajungrocer.com

Blue Plate mayonnaise
www.cajungrocer.com

Tabasco Red Pepper Jelly
countrystore.tabasco.com

POTATO CHIPS AND PECAN PRODUCTS

Zapp's Potato Chips
www.zapps.com

Guidry Organic Farms
www.guidryorganicfarms.com

Cane River Pecan Company
www.caneriverpecan.com

SUGARCANE SYRUP AND MOLASSES

Steen's
www.steensyrup.com

HOT SAUCE PRODUCTS AND CAJUN SEASONINGS

Tabasco
countrystore.tabasco.com

Bruce Foods
www.brucefoods.com

Cajun Power
www.cajunpowersauce.com

Slap Ya Mama
slapyamama.com

STUFFED CHICKEN AND TUR-DUC-HEN

Big Easy Foods
www.bigeasyfoods.com

Hebert's Specialty Meats
www.hebertsmeats.com

RICE

Supreme Rice
www.supremericeusa.com

BEANS

Camellia Brand
www.camelliabrand.com

Blue Runner Foods
www.bluerunnerfoods.com

CRAWFISH, CRABS, OYSTERS, SHRIMP, TURTLE, ALLIGATOR, AND FISH

Louisiana's Best Seafood, LLC.
louisianasbestseafood.com

Louisiana Crawfish Company
www.lacrawfish.com

Randol's Crawfish and Crab
www.cajungrocer.com

Tony's Seafood
www.tonyseafood.com

Fisherman's Cove Seafood
www.fishermanscoveseafood.com

Harlon's LA Fish & Seafood
www.laseafood.com

Riceland Crawfish, Inc.
(Crawfish and Alligator)
www.ricelandcrawfish.com

INDEX